EXODUS,
REVISITED

ALSO BY DEBORAH FELDMAN

Unorthodox
Exodus

EXODUS,
REVISITED

MY UNORTHODOX JOURNEY TO BERLIN

DEBORAH FELDMAN

PORTIONS OF THIS BOOK WERE PREVIOUSLY PUBLISHED IN
EXODUS BY DEBORAH FELDMAN

PLUME

PLUME

An imprint of Penguin Random House LLC
penguinrandomhouse.com

Originally published in the United States of America by Blue Rider Press, an imprint
of Penguin Random House LLC, 2014 and by Plume, an imprint of
Penguin Random House LLC, 2015

First revised edition published by Plume, an imprint of
Penguin Random House LLC, 2021

Grateful acknowledgment is made to reprint the excerpt from "My Tribe Speaks," by
Anna Margolin, in *With Everything We've Got: A Personal Anthology of Yiddish Poetry*,
edited and translated by Richard J. Fein, Host Publications, 2009.

LIBRARY OF CONGRESS CATALOGING-IN-PUBLICATION DATA
has been applied for.

ISBN 9780593185261 (paperback)
ISBN 9780593185278 (ebook)

Printed in the United States of America
1st Printing

Some names and identifying characteristics have been changed
to protect the privacy of the individuals involved.

Dem Andenken meiner unvergesslichen Großmutter gewidmet!

AUTHOR'S NOTE

No one expected the story of leaving a Hasidic enclave to find many readers, least of all myself. The many polite rejections of my book proposal back in 2009 referred to my story as too local, too niche, suited at best for a feature article in a regional newspaper or magazine. Later, when a publisher did take a chance on me, I was gently warned not to get my hopes up. So the overnight success of *Unorthodox: The Scandalous Rejection of My Hasidic Roots* (subtitle added by a shrewd marketing department to up the book's chances) caught all of us completely unawares. Suddenly people around me were surmising that perhaps my story was indeed an American one after all, like the tales of runaway Mormons and Mennonites that populated the memoirs of the age, and the rebellious Amish teenagers on reality TV. Editors, publicists, and agents alike pondered if at the end of the day there wasn't some American bottom line in the act of running away from a religious sect in the pursuit of liberty and happiness.

My publisher naturally wanted to follow up on the success

of *Unorthodox*, which ended on the cliffhanger of my departure not because I wanted to deprive my audience of the satisfaction of knowing what happens next, but because I wrote the book too soon after leaving my community to know the next phase myself. He proposed another memoir and enthusiastically advised me to travel across the country and write about finally becoming an American. Sex, drugs, and rock and roll was the phrase mentioned, as if my becoming an American was predicated on embracing the hedonism my family and community had deemed a grave sin. I longed more than anything to be allowed to keep writing, to have a career as a writer, so although I was filled with anxiety, I was determined to try my best to follow this assignment.

Yet I soon realized becoming American was impossible. I had been raised in a world resembling an eighteenth-century European *shtetl*, where I had spoken a different language, had consumed a different culture, and was subjected to religious law instead of civil law. It may well be an American tradition to run away, but if so, it is only because it is American to nurture and protect worlds that need running away from. Certainly, for me, the United States could never be the country I knew and trusted; it could therefore never be home.

I submitted a manuscript to my publisher that was part exploration of unwelcoming territory and part long-awaited discovery of my own ancestral roots abroad. I felt torn between two personas: the one everyone expected of me, and the one I felt magnetically drawn to. I longed to write about the latter, but I was told that the story was too Eurocentric. Americans want to read about themselves, my editor insisted, you're the American dream, write about that! In the end, I became a European despite all the discouragement, and I relocated to a continent rich in narrative heritage. I felt that since I did not have the "right" story or that "American" persona, I was no longer qualified to write about my journey. I switched to a new language, one much closer to my mother tongue, and I plugged into a new yet old culture with greater ease than I could ever have imagined. I began writing about my European experiences for Europeans.

Now, all these years later, the success around the globe of the Netflix series *Unorthodox*, which inspired translations of my work in countless foreign languages, proves the universality of the journey. Regardless of the geographic specifics of my post-religious exodus, the audiences for stories are no longer local or regional, as many once feared. More and more, our treasure trove of stories is becoming a common resource, transcending all boundaries of culture, identity, and language. It is a result of this transformation that I can offer you the fully realized story, revisited from a later vantage point. Although the trajectory of my life has taken some surprising turns since my departure from the Hasidic community, somehow I have the feeling it will prove its universality as well.

EXODUS,
REVISITED

PREFACE

In urban Williamsburg, in the confines of the Satmar Hasidic community where I grew up, children were taught the ancient biblical laws dating from the era of the temple, a time before the diaspora, when Jewish people had a sense of home and the dignity that is its consequence. These laws had been rendered mostly abstract by the changes in our circumstances, but even though we rarely had the opportunity to apply them, they were part of the great inheritance that was to serve as our solace in what is seen as a temporary period of exile.

An exception to those laws was declared for my grandmother's garden, perhaps one of the last plots of land in Williamsburg that had not been smothered with cement, which my grandfather treated as if it was our personal holy land, applying the complex laws of agriculture to that little island of greenery as if it were a farming initiative and not simply my bubby's personal sanctuary, a rare thing of beauty to which she escaped when she needed peace. My grandfather insisted on imposing a religious order on everything in our lives, not only those aspects that were required, and the garden was certainly not to be overlooked. Perhaps this relentless discipline gave him comfort after the chaos he had experienced during wartime. However, it was the order of nature to which my grandmother, also a Holocaust survivor, was still most loyal. The conflict that sputtered between them all their married life, and probably the conflict that brewed early on in my own spirit as well, can very likely be traced back to these competing allegiances. In their case, however, it was my grandfather who eventually triumphed, and biblical law was applied to the garden my grandmother had so lovingly cultivated over the years. The inflexible application of those ancient edicts proved to be the death of that miniature paradise and, in a way, the loss of the grandmother I knew and loved, which I would realize only many years later, when I was wrestling with her sudden physical absence. I had already experienced losing her emotionally and spiritually, as old age seemed to fragment and diminish her, to carry her further and further away from me and into the world she had always privately inhabited.

In the world I grew up in there was no rest or retreat from the omnipresent intrusion of religious tenets. Even then, I imagined I knew God better than any of the old and wise people around me; I suspected they had grievously misunderstood him. Such is the arrogance of a childhood that has known no abject degradation or suffering. These people had survived the apocalypse, and they had conjured a new, postapocalyptic God, a paroxysm of uncontrolled fury, and therefore my community no longer availed itself of the many leniencies and permissions that had once marked our religion like complex embroidery on a simple cloth. Instead it sought to draw a pristine cloth ever tighter around itself, in the hope that the narrowness of structure and belief would restore the sense of security that had been permanently snatched from them. The more open the world around them became, the more they withdrew.

I too should have been subsumed by the regulations as I came of age in our little *shtetl*, but somehow the forces within me conspired to carve out enough mental space for independent thought to flourish. Later, desperate for the physical space in which to apply my own ideas, I left for the outside world, never to return. Upon doing so, I promptly attempted to shed the obligatory personality I had worn like a shell for all those years, hoping that what would emerge from underneath it would be my true self, like a sapling bursting forth from freshly turned earth.

I soon discovered that both of my personalities, the one I saw as authentic and the one I saw as artificial, had inseparably entangled roots, the entirety of which had been torn from its terrain in the process of fleeing. It took time to realize that hacking away at that tangle of roots in an attempt to separate from the parts of my identity I wanted to be free from was doing more harm than good. Finding myself on the other side of the invisible barriers that had always hemmed me in, I felt sure that my future was out there somewhere, waiting for me, but I had no sense of direction to help me navigate through the void between those two points—of what had been and what was to come—except for the moral compass that had been instilled in me by my grandmother, whose spirit seemed to come alive in me now like a quivering magnetic needle striving toward true north. It was this force that helped me realize that the key to reaching this hazy, veiled shore was not to abandon my past, but rather to reach back and sew the ties from it to the future. To do this, I traced back along the fabric, feeling for a place where the weave was still strong, where it could support ties. I wanted to close the chasm as if stitching a wound; to reconcile the forces that had always seemed like contradictions, yet had in truth been complementary parts of a whole all along.

Now, more than ten years since my departure from the Hasidic community, those two personalities that had developed side by side, yet separate from each other, have finally been allowed to integrate, and with that has come the first real sense of a whole self, here in this old yet new world. Within my consciousness I still have the memory of the past; not only the recent past, but also the deeper, older past that comes before it, and because of this, I have acquired the ability to envision the future as something infinite and unqualifiable, something within our collective hands, as opposed to the hands of a temperamental and individual God.

For the period of time this book chronicles, I was a kind of refugee. Sadly, many people I once knew who also followed this path have taken their own lives in the preceding years. After all, what happens when you open a door but all you find on the other side is emptiness? And I mean not just what happens to us, but what happens to any person who embarks on a journey with no return ticket? I have asked myself this question constantly over the last decade: Is it even possible to arrive? As fresh news of each suicide reached me, it felt like a personal blow to my own reserves of hope. They had each answered the question for themselves by taking a decisive leap into the void.

I asked myself why I had not yet done the same. But later I would realize it was because all that time my feet had already been treading on solid ground. In leaving my community I thought I had also lost the only source of love and beauty in my life: my grandmother. Yet it was her personal journey that had blazed the trail I traveled in reverse, and her love of harmony that taught me how to bring together the disparate parts of myself. I felt the magnetic pull of the European continent, the place that my community had declared to be scorched earth, and now, against all probability, I am no longer one who is fleeing, or one who has fled—I am one who has returned.

Berlin 2020

1
FRAGEN
פראגן
QUESTIONS

Bubby, am I one hundred percent Jewish?

I am eight years old when I first dare to formulate the question I had been turning over in my mind for such a long time. I have been worrying that there might be a sinister reason for the way my thoughts tend toward doubt instead of faith. This way of life we lead, it does not come naturally to me, although I know it should. Because no one else suffers from this affliction, I wonder if genealogical contamination can explain the anomaly. I suspect I am regarded as tainted by my mother's actions, so it follows that she too could have been tainted by someone else, by some mysterious, forgotten ancestor in her past. This would explain why I am the way I am, and not like the others.

Bubby, am I one hundred percent Jewish? I ask. Because I think that whether I am or am not is a matter that defines my destiny. Because I need to know if I have a hope of fitting in.

What a silly question! she exclaims in response. *Of course you are Jewish,* she assures me. *Everybody in our community is.*

1

She dismisses my earnest fear with a laugh. But how can she be so certain?

Look at our world, she says. *Look at how separate we live. How we have always lived. Jews don't mix with others, and others don't mix with us, so how do you think you could be anything less than one hundred percent?*

I didn't think to inquire then why so many people in our community have light eyes, pale skin, and fair hair. My grandmother herself had always spoken proudly of her blond children. Pale, non-stereotypically Jewish features were valuable commodities among us. They meant one would be able to pass. It was the gift of disguise that God granted, seemingly at random, although we were led to believe that he had a precise system in terms of granting privileges, so perhaps lack of blondness denoted a spiritual inferiority, or perhaps it was actually the other way around, depending on how you looked at things. When I met my husband for the first time at the age of seventeen, I focused mostly on his golden hair and what that would mean for my genetic legacy. I wondered if the gene was strong enough to guarantee me golden-haired children, children who would be safe when the world, trapped in its unalterable pattern of orbit, turned against them.

Now I understand that those Eastern European features and fair coloring align perfectly with the genetic studies that have long since confirmed that none of us are one hundred percent of anything. But these findings never made it into our midst, and if they did, they probably wouldn't have mattered. In our community, we believed that as long as we were separate, we were pure by default.

This word, though, "pure"—it doesn't come from our language, from our vocabulary. Our word for "pure" is *tuhor*, and its original meaning applies only to spiritual purity. It means to be pure of intention, to be clean of sin. In the Hasidic tradition, this kind of purity ostensibly outweighs the importance of strong ancestry. The obsession with pure bloodlines would come later, perhaps as a by-product of the ideology and laws that defined us by exclusion. One drop of Jewish blood was all it took, not for the first time in Hitler's Germany, so those who could, fought to hide that drop and deny its existence, but out of instinctive protectiveness, those who could not retreated into a perverse pride. They invented a kind of purity for themselves. They created family trees that went back a thousand years to show their intact stems. They discriminated against Jews who couldn't prove their undiluted status. Just like the Nazis, they too withdrew into the false and treacherous cocoon of consanguineous identity. Since they couldn't be a part of that other world, the next best thing was to create a special club to be a member of instead. We are *tuhor*, they said, and they meant our souls of course, but this time they also meant our blood.

If my blood is Jewish, then my soul is as well. This is why I want to know. I want to understand how exactly Jewishness is imprinted on me. What exactly is it that I have inherited? How can I force the concept of it into something graspable? But really, the question underneath all questions is this: How can I make my Jewishness bearable to me?

Bubby says to me, quite absentmindedly, while sitting at the table running individual cabbage leaves under a fluorescent light bulb to check for worms, which would render them unkosher, that God put the other nations onto the planet for the sole purpose of hating and persecuting the Jewish people. It is this opposing force in the end that defines us, like how God created night and day, darkness and light. We need one to define the other. Our Jewishness exists precisely in the context of the attempts to eradicate it.

This statement from her—which is supposed to explain the world to me, which says that everything out there is terrifying and will always be so, because it is the way things have to be in order to justify our existence—it is so extreme that I feel then that she can't possibly mean it; she's just parroting what the rabbi says, what everyone in the community is always repeating. Because wouldn't it be a grave overestimation of ourselves to imagine that all the evil in the world was created for our suffering? Isn't that kind of arrogance a sin in itself, to regard one's suffering as the holiest of holies, submitting to it like an orchestra to its conductor, sacrificing personal will for the sake of some ultimate directorial vision?

Even though in our community we do not interact with gentiles unless there are exceptional circumstances, in which contact is strictly regulated, I know that Bubby had real relationships with non-Jewish people before she joined the Satmar sect. She's mentioned the neighbors in the small village in which her parents ran a store, how they came to turn their water into seltzer by using the pump in the front yard and brought little gifts in exchange; how they traded eggs and milk and meat for the wares that Bubby's parents sold. She remembers being sent off to live with her wealthy grandmother in the city when she was too old to sleep in the common bedroom with her ten siblings, and those elegant women with the fancy French hats and fur stoles her grandmother invited over for tea, tortes, and cards. She traveled with her grandmother to spa towns in Europe, where they stayed in resort hotels and socialized with people from all over the continent. But all that was before the war, and marrying my grandfather and joining Rabbi Joel Teitelbaum's new community with him meant that the only people she was supposed to come into contact with were ones just like us.

But then I think of how she picked up that cleaning lady a short while ago, as we chanced across that ritual that most house-wives in Williamsburg participate in. Every morning, at the corner of Marcy and Division Avenues, the illegal immigrant women from Poland, or sometimes Lithuania, Slovakia, or Ukraine, line up for a black-market job at the place where the street forms a bridge over the expressway. Over the noise of honking horns and tires thumping over shoddy roads, the hu-miliating negotiations are conducted. A Hasidic housewife ap-proaches, looks each woman over carefully as if to assess their physical condition, and beckons to the one deemed satisfactory with a crooked finger, indicating for her to step forward. An offer is made, usually low: five dollars an hour. If the woman is feeling bold that day, if the group waiting is small and it is still early and she thinks her chances are good, she will counter with eight, but probably concede at six. Then off they go, the two of them, the cleaning lady walking behind the housewife in a show of subservience, following her to the home where she will perform the lowliest of chores so the lady of the house will be spared such indignities.

It does not escape me even now that this theater of selection is a bizarre mirror of a collective memory. I see it as an uncon-sciously inherited vendetta playing itself out in miniature against the backdrop of a wire highway fence. The story of our community founders, of survivors who had once been "selected" by the gentiles for a future among the living, is perversely inverted each time a gentile cleaning woman is beckoned forward. A small satisfaction, but a palpable one nonetheless. And yet, my grandmother had never taken part in the performance until that day.

We had been accidentally walking by that street corner on the way home, carrying the bags of groceries my grandmother had acquired, and suddenly my grandmother stopped in her tracks, staring fixedly at a woman behind the group of others pushing forward and clamoring at the housewives, a woman with dull brown hair streaked with gray who was leaning back against the fence with her hands clasped in front of her and her eyes looking down at the floor, waiting to be selected but perhaps too proud to ask for it. My grandmother seemed frozen as if in some reverie. I set my bags down on the ground, regarding the scene with curiosity. Bubby pointed her finger at the woman.

You, she said. The woman looked up.

Magyar vagy, Bubby said, in a way that sounded like a statement rather than a question.

The woman looked surprised; she nodded and stepped forward. She issued a gushing stream of Hungarian words, as if she had been holding them back for hours and now someone had given her permission to finally let them all out. She grasped Bubby's sleeve, her body arched away from the group of others standing there; she bowed before my grandmother as if performing an obsequious curtsy, as if she was begging us to free her from the dread of waiting, the shame of being the last one standing there, the fear of having to go back home with no prospect of earnings for the day.

I don't know how my grandmother knew that the woman was Hungarian. There were very seldom any Hungarian women on that street corner, which my grandmother cited as the reason she refused to hire a cleaning lady. She didn't like the fact that she couldn't communicate with the Polish women; she didn't trust them in her home. Instead she did the grunt work herself, bent on her knees with a rag, a brush, and a wash bucket. But now there was a Hungarian, and indeed, someone from her very own region, not too much younger than herself. Did she recognize this person from her past? Or perhaps this woman was simply a representation to my grandmother of all those neighbors from her childhood, the ones who had counted as friends before the political temperature changed and they gleefully assumed the homes and lives wrested from others, all loyalties forgotten. Goyim were all like that, she had said. Waiting to benefit from your destruction. That's how God made them. They are helpless to go against their inborn natures.

But still I could not decide if it was pity or the personal desire for vindication that drove Bubby to take that cleaning lady home with us. There seemed to be some kind of human connection between her and that woman, who walked at Bubby's side and babbled in that secret language that I had only ever heard my grandparents speak, vibrating with joy at being chosen by someone who could understand her. Did Bubby actually feel loyal to someone who shared her origins, even though that person wasn't Jewish? Or rather, did she feel a need to prove to her how the circumstances of the past had been upended, to show that woman everything she had achieved for herself here in America, with her four-story brownstone house, her chandeliers and carpets and floor-length lace curtains? To show her on which side of history the real triumph lay?

I watched as she brought the woman into the kitchen, gave her various cleaning tools, and set her up with the tasks she normally did herself or handed off to me, the daily routine of ironing, dusting, and polishing. I was perturbed by the fact that she did not ask the woman to wash the floor. That would have been obvious, I surmised: my grandmother watching as a gentile woman from her home region got down on her knees in this large and comfortable home that she now owned. I didn't necessarily want to see this random woman degraded, but I did think that the experience could give my grandmother a kind of closure. I thought it might temper the bitterness of that old, lingering betrayal that she only ever sparsely referred to in my presence, but which I knew still burned in her deepest store of memories.

After a few hours of moderate to light housework, my grandmother called the woman to the kitchen table for a lunch break. To my surprise she received the woman at her table and sat down across from her like an equal. She even served her on real porcelain plates. I was confused, wondering if this was part of some clever and elaborate scheme or an attestation to the nobility of my grandmother's character. Bubby had defrosted some stuffed cabbage, a traditional dish back home that had been established as a culinary staple in our community, and I watched the woman sit down eagerly to eat it, chatting excitedly in Hungarian the whole while. I caught bits and pieces; they were talking about variations in recipes, the way her mother had cooked those rolls. She complimented Bubby's cooking effusively. I sensed she was trying to ingratiate herself; surely there was an incentive to do so, because of course it was the goal of all those cleaning women to get a regular posting, so they would not have to return to that street corner every day in hopes of being selected. A regular position meant security, perhaps even a raise, and referrals to other families if the work was good. Too many weeks spent waiting at the fence were a sure sign you were not a valuable choice; then your hourly wage went lower and lower until no offers came at all. It was the fear of all cleaning women; you could see it in the eyes of some of them in the late morning as you walked past the last stragglers, that panic as time went by and the crowd thinned, and police cars drove ominously past. I was irritated by what I suspected were this woman's ulterior motives.

My grandmother did not say much as the woman prattled on; her chin rested in her palm, her other hand tracing patterns in the tablecloth. Every so often my grandmother nodded or threw in the equivalent of a "yes" or an "I see" in Hungarian. When the woman was finished eating, Bubby took the plate from her and washed it in the sink. She prepared a coffee and served it in a chipped white mug. Then she put a twenty-dollar bill on the tablecloth.

No more work today, she said firmly. *Finished now.*

The woman looked crestfallen. She eyed the bill on the table. Three hours of work plus tip.

I come back next week, yes? Her hands trembled around the coffee cup.

My grandmother said nothing; she simply shook her head no. Then, perhaps feeling sorry for her, she said, *Don't feel bad. I never hire anyone to help me. I prefer to do the work myself.*

The woman tried to convince my grandmother to change her mind. She offered to get down on her knees and wash the floor right then and there, to prove her usefulness. She grasped my grandmother's hands and kissed them. Her desperation made her previous effusiveness seem baldly false in comparison, and I sensed that my grandmother was embarrassed for her.

Bubby said she was sorry but she didn't have any work for

her. All her children were grown, she explained. There wasn't so much left to do. If the woman left her phone number, perhaps she would pass it on to her daughters, see if they were interested. But she couldn't promise anything.

This gave the cleaning lady something to hold on to. She carefully wrote down her information, using the pencil and paper Bubby gave her. *I do very cheap*, she assured her. *Five dollar.*

I closed the door gently behind her as she left, still tripping over her multiple farewells, looking back longingly at the woman who spoke her language, who remembered the same old country, from whom she might have expected solidarity, had it not been for the failure of her parents' generation to show the same, I thought. For a while after the woman left, Bubby sat at the kitchen table sipping her coffee, a small smile playing at the corner of her mouth. I longed to know what she was thinking, but of course I could not ask.

I wondered then, as I folded dish towels on the counter while Bubby sat in silence on her little stool, who was more vindicated in such a scenario, my grandmother, who was kind to the *goyte* but deprived her of both the work and the abasement that came with it, or the neighboring women who happily oversaw the scrubbing of toilets and washing of staircases, taking perverse pleasure in the way circumstances had been upended by history. As a child I was convinced it was a question of effectiveness; I assumed my grandmother was meting out her own subtle version of justice.

Now I look back on this story very differently. I recognize in my grandmother the conflict between her yearning for grace and the frightening yet human impulses she struggled to suppress. To peg her actions that day as one or the other, as compassionate or vengeful, would be too simplistic. What was wonderful about Bubby was that she was so complex, so mysterious. All these forces were at work in her simultaneously, although some never noticed, because she was good at keeping the surface calm and smooth. But there were quiet dramas I witnessed her take part in as a child. Those annual meetings with Edith, for example, with whom she had survived the brutal war years in slave labor camps but who had chosen a secular life with a non-Jewish husband in Chicago and flew to New York solely for that clandestine encounter, meeting my grandmother in the same hotel lobby with a discretion bordering on espionage. Or her battle to maintain the only garden in Williamsburg by insisting to my grandfather that since it yielded the blooms necessary for the Pentecostal tradition of ornamenting one's home with abundant flora, the plot of carefully tended land was no distraction from the work of spiritual dedication but rather an act of spiritual service in itself. All her struggles and secrets, they stayed with me like the fairy tales that other children grow up with. They are the stories I play over and over in my adult mind, looking for clues that might reveal the inner workings of this woman upon whom I have unconsciously modeled myself.

My teachers said that being Jewish was about having within us a *zelem Elohim*, a particle of God. Yet Bubby insisted it was the presence of the other that confirmed our difference. She made it sound as if we would stop being Jewish as soon as others stopped hating us for it.

It wasn't just about being Jewish in my community, though, but about what kind of Jew you were. Because there were endless variations; even if you were Ashkenazi, you could still be separated into minute and specific categories, and between each one and the next lay an enormous division. You could be a *Galizianer*, a *Litvak*, or a *Yekke*. And then there were the many Jews outside the Ashkenazi circle, the *Sephardim*, the *Mizrachim*, the Bucharians, the Yemenites, the Persians . . . all of them with distinctly more Jewish DNA than any of us possessed, but not to be mixed with nonetheless. We had some refugee families in our community in Williamsburg; they were from places like Kazakhstan, Yemen, Argentina, and Iran. But even the ones whose ancestors had still lived in Europe only two generations ago were not like us, for they had been distanced from tradition for two whole generations. This was a span of time they could never compensate for, because in those two generations the meaning of Jewishness had been redefined. The war had etched our divisions deeper. Now each sect only accepted members of the same pure ancestry, survivors who could trace their lineage back to a specific city or region. This lineage decided where you belonged. You would naturally marry someone from the same stock, so that when you produced children, they had a clearly delineated family tree. These children would keep the *shtetl* alive in their veins. In this way, cities like *Bobov* and *Vizhnitz* and *Klausenburg* and *Sanz* and *Pupa* and *Gur* still existed, because the descendants of the residents of those cities had not forgotten where they came from. They had re-created their genetic pools in segregated Brooklyn neighborhoods, the barriers of which, while not visibly marked, were nevertheless imprinted upon our collective consciousness, informing our orientation in time and space.

The *shtetl* we belonged to was Satmar, named for a village not far away from the childhood homes of my grandparents, a group to which they naturally belonged because of this historical proximity. The Satmars were now also fixated on keeping everything in the family. Uncles married nieces; cousins married cousins. Our gene pool went from small to smaller, the circle around us drawn ever tighter. Our neighbors next door, the Halberstams, were the son and daughter of two brothers, and when they had one child after another with cystic fibrosis, seven out of nine in fact, the powers that be seemed to take notice. Something would have to be done.

So they started the testing program, and when I was fifteen, doctors in white lab coats came to my school classroom and unpacked their boxes of equipment onto our shabby desks, while we lined up to fill their tubes with our blood. We took turns rolling up our sleeves, biting down when the needle punctured skin, trying not to show weakness in front of our peers. Next year our families would start marrying us off, but before they could do that, the doctors had to analyze our genetic profile. *Dor Yeshorim* the program was called: *the Righteous Generation.* To preserve the tradition of constant intermarriage, of always remaining isolated from the others, we needed to make sure we weren't also breeding ill health. So before we were matched up to our future spouses, they would compare our genes, make sure we weren't carriers of the same mutations— that our profiles were similar, but not too similar. We'd never find out, though, whatever it was they had discovered in our blood. It was kept in a bank, fully protected. We just received a number that we could reference against any other number. Then it was a matter of comparison and a simple yes or no.

Two years later I'd call the bank to give them my number and the number of my prospective husband. I'd wait breathlessly for the answer. There was still that old fear in me, that they'd find something there that didn't belong, something that would explain why I was the way I was.

"Mazel tov!" they told me. "You will have many healthy children."

And that was all that mattered. If they saw something in my blood that didn't add up, they didn't breathe a word.

———

There is a Yiddish word that I heard all too often during my childhood, a word that filled me with tension: *yichus*. This was such a loaded word for me, because although *yichus* was valuable in that it established one's place in the hierarchy and its accorded status, it was frightening to me because I was reminded whenever I heard the word that I had only the most tenuous grip on any at all and therefore was doomed to a neverending struggle to avoid sinking to the bottom of my society like sediment.

The word *yichus* stems from a common and harmless Hebrew term for "relations," but in Yiddish, it meant something more like "noble lineage," and it was a word that ascribed value to an individual based on who their ancestors were. In our community, families with *yichus* occupied enviable positions in society. They were our version of aristocrats. These families treasured their unpolluted genetic line and presented it as evidence to matchmakers that their sons and daughters deserved only those proposals befitting their pedigree. My own connection to whatever ancestry I might have claimed had been rent by the scandalous failed union of my parents and the resulting chaos that had spread over my family like a permanent stain, eating away at our communal fabric, the weave of which depended on unbroken unions and uninterrupted lines.

When I was fourteen and attending the ninth grade in my religious all-girls school, the project of the year was composing and presenting your own family tree. When the announcement was made during the first week of school, it unleashed a wave of raw panic in me. I raced home that day struggling to hold back the tears until I finally arrived in my grandmother's kitchen. This project spelled out my doom. I knew I was due for yet another humiliation as the girls in my class presented their illustrious, intact, and well-fleshed family trees. I would be forced to put all the brokenness in my family on display.

Bubby took one look at me and immediately dropped the ball of chopped meat she was shaping into *fasirt*. She washed her hands clean and pulled out a paper bag from its hiding place on top of a kitchen cabinet. There was a stash of chocolate-covered orange peels inside that she kept for emergencies like this one. Wordlessly, she handed me one to munch on and bit into one herself. I watched her chew thoughtfully, waiting for the solution she was surely concocting.

"Well, technically everyone has a little bit of *yichus*," she said. "If you look hard enough into anyone's family tree, how can you not stumble upon a small rabbi, a low-level saint? I bet if we search back far enough we can put together enough rabbis to make even Mime-Gitl Rokeach look small in comparison." She joked to make me feel better. We both knew there was no beating Mime-Gitl, whose popularity should by all laws of logic have suffered for her unusually low hairline but would always represent the prestige that came with her rabbinical "connections."

Bubby observed my panic coolly, able to empathize but at the same time not afflicted by the same fear of non-acceptance. She didn't need acceptance, because her world ended with the walls of our property; as long as she had her kitchen and garden, she didn't need anything or anyone else. I was out there every day desperate to prove myself worthy; I was still young and naïve enough to think that this would bring me the inner peace I so craved.

"I'll write to the uncle who helped arrange your parents' marriage," Bubby said, still chewing on a strand of orange peel. "He'll be able to help you fill out your mother's side of the tree."

I wanted to hug her in that moment, but of course I didn't dare. I had never hugged her, and I never would. It simply wasn't done in our world. If I had broken the unwritten rule and put my arms around her, I can only imagine that it would have made her deeply uncomfortable, almost afraid. Outpourings of affection were so dangerous in our world. If you made a point of showing how important someone was to you, didn't it just make it more likely that the universe would take them from you when it was time for punishment?

But I loved her very much on that day, and I would always remember it, because she had cared enough to want to help me fill the gaping hole in me that begged for roots, as many of them as possible, so that I could feel them burrowing into the ground and know that even a strong wind couldn't come and shake me from my perch.

Months of careful research followed. I took to following my grandfather around with a notebook and pen, asking him questions about a past he had mostly lost, having been too young and naïve to ask the important questions of the right people when they had still been alive. Because when people are alive we take them for granted, I knew. I had learned that lesson vicariously through the losses of that generation, and I was studiously determined not to waste any of the time that I still had with the people who would one day be gone, one day when it would be too late to ask questions. I was impatiently directed to the neglected, yellowing paper archives in my grandfather's ground-floor office, where entire rooms had been dedicated to the storage of a past that no one had any desire to revisit. I combed through boxes of faded letters and brittle documents with water stains; from these I was able to formulate new questions, based upon which I wrote letters in cramped Yiddish script to newly discovered distant relatives and former neighbors, who all seemed to have put an incredible distance between themselves and everything from back then. As the answers trickled politely and reluctantly back, a tree began to take shape. And Bubby was right: every tree bears a perfect fruit at some point. Seven generations back on the side of my grandmother's grandmother's grandfather, I found the *lamed-vav'nik*.

This discovery was perhaps the highlight of my research, although other low-level saints popped up as Bubby had promised, such as the Talmudist sage Amram Chasida, the war hero Michoel Ber Weissmandl on my grandfather's side, and other small-town rabbis who had written brief volumes of liturgical text that could be found only in the libraries of the most avid collectors. Bubby had mentioned to me the possibility of there being a *lamed-vav'nik* in her family before; stories had been told to her as a child that she had oft repeated to me. But she was never sure if he had really existed, and if he had, whether he was really her ancestor. So I set about reconstructing the forgotten linkages in the chain that connected them.

A *lamed-vav'nik* was the greatest discovery I could have possibly made. It was like a joker card; it trounced everything else. The pedigrees of the most esteemed rabbinical families were rendered impotent by the most meager tree if it had at some point produced one of the thirty-six hidden saints in each generation.

My grandmother had remembered him as Reb Leibele Oshvari, unable to recall a genuine surname because he was five generations removed on her great-grandmother's side, and because *lamed-vav'niks* were often remembered in this way after their deaths, having arranged for anonymity prior to the event. He had requested that on his grave it should simply say Leibel from the town of Oshvar. You knew it was his tomb from afar, my grandmother had been told, because they had to put a special fence around it after bad things started happening to people who went too close. You had to be free of sin to touch the grave of a *lamed-vav'nik*, and since it was rare that anyone could be such a thing, they put a fence up to protect people from the danger of the holy energy that hovered above his burial site. That's how they knew, she said, that he was a *zadik nistar*, hidden saint. They found out after he died, when all the widows and orphans he had secretly been supporting suddenly found themselves without recourse, and then it became clear who had been performing all that charity for all those years. Such a development was a classic indicator of *lamed-vav'nik* presence.

"There are *lamed-vav zadikim nistarim*," my grandfather had often told me: there were thirty-six hidden saints born into every generation. This was a great mystical legend central to Hasidic beliefs. These thirty-six holy men were nicknamed "the pillars of the world" because it was believed that they were especially pure souls on whose merit the world remained standing, in spite of the ravages of sin. So long as they existed, God would keep the world turning no matter how deeply mankind disappointed him. If only one should go missing, the world would immediately come to an end, as the tolerance of God was then expected to reach its threshold.

Zeidi said the *lamed-vav* existed to remind God that he was doing something good when he created man. They represented the best that a human being could achieve. They were known for their extreme humility and altruism, performing good deeds all their lives without ever enjoying recognition. They forfeited all the usual comforts of life in order to assist others. No one was too low to be deserving of their benevolence. What distinguished the hidden saints from the regular saints was precisely their self-effacement. Standard Hasidic saints were worshipped like royals, living lifestyles that befitted people with an avid following. But a *lamed-vav'nik* sought to forgo every benefit of his spiritual superiority; he kept his saintliness a secret and often suffered ridicule and rejection because of a deceptive outer appearance of poverty and ignorance, thereby achieving the highest level of holiness. A public *zadik*, when confronted with a *zadik nistar*, had no choice but to bow his head in shame, for the trappings he enjoyed kept him bound to the earthly plane. He could never be as close to God as the hidden saint. However, even the holiest *zadik* was likely to remain unaware of the presence of a *lamed-vav'nik* in his midst. The integrity of the system depended on the hidden saint remaining hidden. It was only after their death that their saintliness could be revealed, that their memory could be worshipped. Only then could they benefit their descendants, even such distant and pitiful descendants like myself. After all, wasn't I the perfect candidate for the *lamed-vav'nik*'s blessing? When the time came to present my family tree in class, pointing to a *lamed-vav'nik* buried deep in the roots of my tree would silence any potential critic.

Whatever else my research might still yield, my problem was essentially solved. Leibel from Oshvar would shine at the very center of my presentation, and every single one of my peers would be compelled into a respectful silence. Perhaps they too would speculate about me, wondering if I had inherited those genetics, and whether my unfortunate circumstances simply served as a clever disguise to keep my saintliness from being discovered.

With a new sense of calm and confidence, I continued my efforts at filling out the extended branches of my family tree, knowing that the bulk of my task had been spectacularly accomplished. When the last letter arrived from Uncle Menachem, the youngest brother of my mother's mother, postmarked Bnei Brak, Israel, I did not rip at it with my fingers. Instead I retrieved my grandfather's silver letter opener and slit the envelope carefully at its side. Inside were carefully labeled photographs and a scrupulously drawn diagram of familial connections, which I regarded with only mild curiosity. Having known nothing about my mother's ancestry prior to that letter, I was surprised to learn of this new complex network of branches, of limbs that reached back into so many distant corners of Europe. But I was most astonished to learn that the branch that had produced my mother had originated in Germany, a piece of information I could not afford to put on display.

Of all things my mother could have been, she had to have been a *Yekke*. That was the disparaging term we used for German Jews, whom we had always perceived as having abandoned their Jewishness and replaced it with an appropriated cultural identity out of shame and self-loathing. *Yekkes* were known for expressing extreme versions of stereotypical German characteristics, for being more annoyingly on time than the Germans themselves, for being obsessed with precise calculations, with regulation and order. It was said that they lacked heart, that their homes were deficient in the warmth other

Ashkenazi Jewish communities were known for. *Yekkes* spoke *Daytshmerish*, a dolled-up, uppity dialect of Yiddish that would never sound quite like the *Hochdeutsch* they tried to imitate. They kept their *payos* short and tucked them behind their ears, trimmed their beards, wore suits, all to avoid making their Jewishness conspicuous. And yet the term for them came from the German word *Jacke*, a term the Germans had invented to evoke the long black *Jacke* the Jews had worn before they secularized and discarded the coat in favor of modern fashion. It was a reminder that their costume was only a disguise, that the Germans would never forget their true origins. *Yekkes* had tried to fit into a society that in the end would never have them; therefore, to be a *Yekke* was shameful; it was the mark of the wannabe who had experienced the ultimate rejection. Such was my ancestry. I would have to account for this gross mark on my history. What story could I invent? Better to gloss over it entirely.

Of course it made sense that my family had sought out a *Yekke* for my father. They had had to make compromises, so desperate were they to marry him off. My mother was the perfect candidate, poor and from a broken home. Aside from her grandparents and a sprinkling of aunts and uncles, the entire family tree had been erased by the war, and with it the memory of anything that might have been deemed unpleasant. When she crossed the Atlantic Ocean to join my father's family, her background was forgotten. She simply assumed the familial and communal identities the way one does a loose-fitting dress. There was enough fabric to cover a host of sins.

I was puzzled by the fact that although Uncle Menachem offered me a host of trivial details about the lives of long-since-passed second cousins, there was surprisingly little information offered about his parents, who had fled Germany in 1939. I had the names of his mother's parents, and some documents supporting their existence, but about the parents of his father, my great-grandfather, there was next to nothing. The line on his birth certificate where his father's name should have stood was empty. No matter, I thought. A bureaucratic failure, and perhaps, in the year 1897, a product of the time.

When I finally presented my project in school months later, I had created a glorious map that at some points went back as far as nine generations, but in the space above my mother's grandparents there was a conspicuous void. At the time I distracted myself and my audience with all the new information I had gleaned about the illustrious history of the paternal side of my family. I would end up using all the information that I painstakingly gathered and saved as a fourteen-year-old many years later, when I traveled to Europe as an adult in search of a new identity and, in some ways, a new history. It was only when I made the decision to become a citizen of Europe that I reached back toward that void, looking for proof that would help me make my case to a German bureaucracy seemingly intent on shutting me out.

I will never forget how the blood thrummed through my veins the day I received that phone call from my immigration lawyer. It brought me straight back to my eight-year-old self, who had asked that question of my grandmother for the first time, as if deep down I already knew the discoveries I would make in my future.

But I have gotten ahead of myself. Let me tell this story from the very beginning.

After five years in an unhappy arranged marriage, made all the more miserable by a radical set of religious proscriptions that had only been revealed to me during my engagement, I knew I needed to flee the world that had always been a prison of varying sizes for me. I was loath to condemn a child to the same fate. I had begun to formulate a concrete escape plan as soon as my son was born. I gave myself three years, the time I had until he was to be drafted into the religious school system. My plan would entail many practical measures, but the ultimate priority was figuring out a way to belong in an outside world I knew very little about. It is therefore the case that quite a few years went by before I felt compelled to revisit those carefully gathered documents about my ancestry, which I had the good sense to take with me on the day of my departure. I would later discover that therein lay my only remaining hope for the reconstruction of my identity, but in those early days after leaving I dismissed the importance of far-flung familial origins, trying instead to find myself in America, which was then so unfamiliar to me as to be a foreign land.

I had taken my first step toward "assimilation" by secretly enrolling in Sarah Lawrence College in 2007, at the age of twenty, two years prior to my departure. This was the most crucial phase of my escape plan. Education was the ticket to the American dream of self-reinvention; this much I had learned in my surreptitious glimpses of that society when my world had existed as if in an air bubble, invisible tensions pushing from both without and within to keep those seemingly insubstantial walls intact. The religious school I had attended as a child naturally failed to meet the government standards for accreditation, but despite having no diploma or transcripts to show for myself, I managed to obtain entrance to the prestigious college on the basis of three essays, which I had written in correct and formal English acquired from years of reading the prewar literature stashed under my mattress like contraband. Soon I was pulling over on suburban roads to change into jeans in the back seat of my car and comb out my hair after removing my burdensome wig, before stepping fleetingly into the outside world, all the while trying hard not to give myself away. And yet my wide-eyed gaze must have betrayed me: a classmate handed me a frayed copy of Anzia Yezierska's *Bread Givers* one day, and as I read about the young Jewish woman from an immigrant family who overcame a seemingly endless series of challenges in order to attend college nearly a century ago, I was comforted by the similarities between us, but also deeply ashamed that these parallels had proved so obvious to my peers.

I read that book in stolen moments in supermarket or drugstore parking lots, since I was too frightened to bring it home with me, lest its contents reveal my own true motives. At that time I was not yet what one would call a writer. Certainly I had never written anything before, except my childhood diaries, which I had been forced to give up so as not to render myself vulnerable in my efforts to free myself. Writing had become a kind of Achilles' heel; it had not yet occurred to me that it could also be my salvation.

My brief and infrequent visits to the campus were all the more enchanting for their transience; I was like a tourist on a new continent, trying to pack as much as I could into each moment of experience. I took note of every casual sentence I heard, every offhand bodily movement I observed. I wanted, primarily, to learn what it would require to blend in.

The likes of me had never before been admitted to such a school, an old American institution with sloping eaves and undulating lawns, preparing to gently shake coddled children out of the strangely rarefied, encapsulated realities they had always inhabited. College was the place in which Americans were made, I knew, churned out as if from factories with pre-packaged beliefs and values, with the language and behavior signature of whichever institution they chose to attend. The experience formed one's position in society, solidified each individual's future like so many clay pots in a kiln. Young Americans flocked to university campuses to find themselves, yet I came to find the world. I could not immediately afford the question of a self. I was still in the in-between place, standing at the gateway to something bigger and also more frightening, hesitating before taking my first small step toward the unknown.

While structured learning would often prove to be a mixed blessing, college would provide me with the inestimable privilege of coming into contact with thoughtful and intuitive mentors. As a result, I began to ask myself questions about my identity, about my true self. It began when a much-revered professor of literature called me into her office on a glorious spring day in 2009, when the first pale green leaves were emerging from the branches of the many carefully tended trees on campus, and pulled a book off her shelf, a collection of personal essays edited by Philip Larkin, which she slammed down in front of me, saying: *Read this. Then write your own.* It was clear that this was no official assignment, that there would be no formal grade, that this woman was not in any way obligated to take the time—or indeed recompensed for it—to offer me this experience, which would turn out to be a life-changing one.

I opened the book under the white-blossomed canopy of a pear tree just outside the building and read the essay entitled "Split at the Root," by Adrienne Rich, and my subconscious stirred to life; memories rumbled forth from their depths like boulders, and I began to write furiously, as if it were the only thing preventing me from being crushed by their oncoming force.

Once I started writing, it was as if I could not stop. I gave vent to the fury and grief of the preceding years; not in a diary, but in an anonymous blog, which I composed via proxy server in the college library, so as to prevent anyone from tracing those entries back to me. What had started as a single essay, that independent assignment from a shrewd professor, had snowballed into a kind of literary reckoning. For years everyone in my life had held the narrative reins and dictated my own story to me; now I was determined to wrench those reins back and assert my own narrative power, with my own arsenal of words. To my surprise the blog did not just serve as a personal therapeutic process but attracted a large audience, a significant part of which seemed to be composed of people in situations similar to mine. So online I communicated and interacted with other undercover dissidents as a secretly discontented Hasidic housewife, but in my real, day-to-day life I was desperately trying to become something more than that.

Two years after my enrollment in Sarah Lawrence I had managed to slowly shed pieces of my old self like scales, first in little ways, such as changing my appearance, improving my language proficiency, working on my accent so that it sounded more American, and learning new social mechanisms. I imitated those around me. I tried on the Americanness now available to me, and although the fit wasn't perfect, I thought it would have to do, as I didn't see any other options. I rationalized that someone like me could never wear another identity without feeling it pull or pinch somewhere. I would have to learn to live with the feeling of discomfort. After all, what was a pinch or two compared to the corset I had been wearing all my life?

The second part of my plan involved putting the money I had saved working odd copywriting jobs into a bank account of my own, leasing a car, and renting my own apartment, where my then nearly three-year-old son and I would officially start our new life. In search of something affordable, I had found a two-room alcove under a gabled roof on the banks of the Hudson River for fifteen hundred dollars a month. I bought a mattress for one room; in the other room I put a cheap sofa, two chairs, and a table.

The apartment came with a view of the Hudson River and the Palisades Cliffs towering on the other side, behind which lay my former marital home, as well as my husband, who continued to move in and out of it as if nothing had changed, as if his wife had only just popped out to get groceries and would be back at some point to cook him dinner.

I hadn't really said good-bye before I left. My lawyer had advised me to leave the situation open-ended, as her intention was to slow down the process as much as possible, not only in order to establish a custodial precedent but also to buy me some time to get my book published, which she felt was our only real shot at coming out of this with even a small win. The legal situation for Hasidic women was so precarious and the only thing my community truly shrank back from was the harsh spotlight of sustained public attention. Yet the situation didn't feel open-ended to me, in fact it had already been a closed book for a while. Eli and I had been married for five years, but for the last two we had barely talked. Our lives had intersected only at brief points, such as Sabbath meals, and even then there had been other people around to serve as distractions. Having never truly gotten to know each other, perhaps we did not realize that we had been drifting apart. The new separation did not feel very different from the life we had led before.

When Eli asked me where I was, why I wasn't home, I was careful not to make statements about the future. I said I needed space, and since he did not understand this concept but was reluctant to ask questions, he simply accepted the explanation as if it made sense. He was convinced the separation was temporary; perhaps that was why he made no attempt to prevent me from taking our son with me. In his world, women could not survive without men, so why should I be any different?

It was in my interest, the lawyer had advised me, to create a lengthy separation period in which I was allowed to retain my child. To do so, I had to pretend that I did not yet have a clear intention to divorce, that I was open to other options. And of course, I could not reveal my intention to become irreligious. Instead, I had to slowly introduce small changes in my lifestyle while still remaining in the realm of what was acceptable. This meant still keeping a kosher kitchen, covering my hair when I went to meet Eli for his parental visits, keeping our son in a Jewish day-care center, and so on. Only later, when I had the security of this precedent, could I then truly relax and live the way I wanted to.

Yet even small changes felt momentous in the beginning. I was excited to be on my own. I celebrated my freedom in little ways. I arranged cheeses on a plate, the names of which were unfamiliar to me, invited a few classmates over for a small cocktail party, and felt like a sophisticated host. I went to the big library in town with its floor-to-ceiling view of the river and enjoyed being able to read unselfconsciously on the screened-in veranda. I took home enormous piles of books and stacked them proudly near the entryway for visitors to see. I was determined to catch up on all the titles I'd missed, titles that were an integral part of the secular canon. When I picked up a worn copy of *The Art of Happiness* by Epicurus, I recalled immediately a similar sounding word in Yiddish, *apikores*, and understood quite suddenly that the derogatory term for "heretic" that my grandfather had used to denigrate only the lowliest of characters must have been inspired by this author. By reading his guide to a happy life, I would be receiving an education directly opposed to the one I had received as a child, for happiness had certainly not been the goal in my community. By rejecting religion, I assumed, I must be choosing happiness instead, as if to reject night is to choose day. I read the text with eagerness, realizing, though, that a faint sensation of guilt and caution still accompanied the act of reading certain books, even then.

In addition to stocking up on taboo tomes, I also celebrated the everyday ways in which I now felt normal. Normalcy, as I had come to understand it then, was a life without proscription. The path to fulfillment of one's desires was direct, without any arbitrary obstacle blocking the way. All I needed was the vehicle of willpower.

But where was this vehicle, this inner resource, which seemed to come and go at random like a driverless train? At times I thought I possessed this force and it could never leave me; at others I felt as if it had never been there at all, that I had woken up from a sweet dream into harsh reality. The fluctuations between these two emotional states were so sudden, so frequent, and so intense that I soon realized in order to survive this period, I would have to enter a different emotional state entirely: that of numbness. Of course, I was lucky, since I had memories of similar times in which I had used this self-shutdown mechanism in order to survive, and now I slowly coaxed that memory to the surface again, understanding that the current challenges called for an unparalleled reserve of emotional control.

The nights were the most difficult, because nighttime is when one forgets who one is, reminded only in the morning. In those dark hours all is muddled and ungovernable. This is still true for me at times, even today. At night nothing is certain. Time is not fixed. One's life is not a concrete, linear thing, but a murky body of water about which nothing is known. No matter the mental exercise, this conviction, that all has been lost, cannot be chased away. How I feared those predawn hours! Isaac and I slept together on the single mattress, and when I awoke in that familiar panic it was only his steady, gentle breathing next to me that reminded me of the one thing that was still certain: that I was his mother. This meant something. I had a task; I could orient myself around it. This was the only thing that gave my life a sense of form.

Yet on those nights when I awoke to see the darkness stretched across the window, I looked over at my son, and though I was comforted by his presence I was also frightened by it. I was so young myself, and completely alone in this world I was struggling to be a part of. Already there was someone even more vulnerable beside me. I was responsible for the two of us; what sort of hope could there be for us, with both of us relying on my meager reserves? Although the middle hours of the night yawned like gaping chasms, I knew I just had to hold on until morning, because gradually, as the sun rose, this dreadful conviction of a hopeless future would inevitably dissipate, to be replaced by an enthusiasm toward all the day had to offer. The fear receded; it became something like background noise that I would eventually accustom myself to. I'd find distraction in the rituals of our daily life, in coffee, breakfast, and leisurely walks to the kindergarten up the hill. There would be things to do in this new world, with its new kind of time that I had to shape on my own, without the strict religious schedule that had once defined every hour, that broke up my existence into manageable fragments. Now time was an endless loop that I painstakingly cut into pieces with my own freely chosen schedule: food, kindergarten drop-off, college, kindergarten pickup, dinner, bath, work, bed. But the days would never again feel as angular and defined as they had before. The days behind me faded into nothingness; the ones ahead blurred into one another like a desert horizon. For Isaac, who had found friends at kindergarten immediately and had switched from Yiddish to English in a matter of weeks, this was not an issue. That old world had not yet managed to engrave itself onto his spirit. I felt a great rush in my heart when I observed him playing. I thought to myself, You've saved him! You've done it in time and now he will never feel the way you feel now. He won't know this pain. And even if you manage to do nothing more in your lifetime, you've already done enough just by accomplishing that. This revelation was a great comfort to me.

I didn't realize then how many lessons from my past I had unconsciously taken with me, or just how deep a mark the belief system of my childhood had left on me. Although I had abandoned the rules and traditions, I was still looking instinctively for God, searching for signs where there were only natural occurrences, wanting to believe that the raccoon that sidled out from under my front stairs in broad daylight was a coded message, left for me so that I could feel less alone. I didn't even know how to live without God. I had such an aching emptiness in my heart, and the great irony lay in how much more room there was for him now, in comparison to before, when he had had to take a back seat to all the rules and regulations. Before, God had been confined to the territories of prayer and ritual, now I searched for him in the ecstatic crescendos of poems and the gripping spasms in classical music. Often when I found something that looked or felt like perfection in an art form, it felt like I had found him. I would feel the recognition like an epiphany in my body, a powerful feeling that moved me to tears. I thought that the perfection that humans could create must be proof of the existence of God. After all, hadn't my teachers always said that within each of us was God, in the form of a spark he had given us that we had to nurture into a fire? The challenge was how to find that spark within myself, and what to make of it.

But there was also no certainty anymore, not the kind I had felt as a child. God had been distorted into something beyond comprehension. In this way, my old yearning for God battled with this new voice in me that urged me to reject him, to free myself of him. I remembered Epicurus, who in his list of preconditions to happiness had said, "The irreligious man is not the person who destroys the gods of the masses but the person who imposes the ideas of the masses on the gods. . . . The masses, by assimilating the gods in every respect to their own moral qualities, accept deities similar to themselves and regard anything not of this sort as alien."

At Sarah Lawrence I met so many atheists. There was a kind of irony in how passionately they tried to convert me. I was the perfect candidate for enlightenment. There were many earnest conversations over coffee in the canteen, debates over cigarettes on the lawn, in which they tried to pass their wisdom on to me, a wisdom I often perceived as cold comfort. One atheist with horn-rimmed glasses and greasy hair said to me once in an off-hand way that the argument for the existence of God was like the argument for a false reality. Sure, it was possible we were all living in a computer-simulated video game, he posited, but until any evidence to that effect was presented, it was more sensible to concur that such a reality was highly unlikely and therefore not a viable part of the argument. To him, whether or not God existed was irrelevant; the fact that doubt presented itself rendered the answer moot: he didn't need God, so why bother?

I remembered feeling my own derealization as a child, when I feared that I was the only person with real, absorbing desires. How frightening it had felt. What if you lived in a video game and you knew it? How could he hide himself so effectively from that possibility?

Earlier that year I had enrolled in a yearlong workshop for creative nonfiction, planning to patch together in that class most of my memoir, the first payment for which was now financing a large part of my existence. Deep down, I was afraid of the gargantuan task of writing a whole book. I had written so few things in my life. What did I really know about writing? A voice of self-reproach created a running commentary in my head as I attended each class, and I struggled to concentrate amid the internal clamor.

As part of the writing workshop we were required to print fourteen copies of a story we had written and distribute them to the other students at the beginning of each week. They would read them and give a thorough written critique. At the end of every week, the professor would choose one story in particular for an oral discussion. One week the professor notified me that my story had been chosen. On the day of judgment I sat in a sort of permanent cringe; I could hardly imagine what would be said about the glorified personal recollections from my childhood, peppered with transliterated Yiddish. This week I had sought to spare the readers the work of cultural translation and submitted something comparatively neutral. I hadn't wanted them to undergo the ordeal of trying to pronounce those foreign words out loud.

At first the students approached my material tentatively, perhaps reluctant to hurt my feelings. But then one of the star students in the class, a pale-skinned goth from Ohio, opened her comments to me by exclaiming, with great exuberance, "Deborah, I'm so glad you finally un-Jewed your work! All the pieces you submitted until now were really confusing, but this one I could actually understand." Her tone of voice was positively congratulatory, much like she was encouraging a preschooler for a colorful drawing.

The other students laughed uncomfortably, clearly sensing the loaded nature of the comment, but the teacher waved it away and swept the discussion onward. It was as if those words had never been said, but I sat there in shock, feeling as if I had been slapped.

I was gripped with the panic that all the experiences I had in me to share were the wrong ones. They weren't "universal," as my professor always said; they were little oddities existing at the very margins of society. I thought of all those great Yiddish poets and writers I had recently been unearthing from dusty stacks in the library that had long since been forgotten. The people capable of understanding them were mostly dead; those still alive had chosen a life without art, without culture—they blamed the ruin of their people precisely on those indulgences.

I didn't submit personal pieces for the rest of that year. A few times I met with my professor, who tried to gently encourage me to move away from what she termed my "young adult" voice, most likely her euphemism for simple language and a direct style. I did not bother to tell her that it was precisely those young adult books that had fortified my childhood and planted my best qualities within me. More than a decade later we would meet at a café under a cluster of bright green linden trees in a Berlin square and I would discover that our memories of this time were very different, that my professor only remembered how encouraging she was toward me, how she always knew that I was on the right track somehow. I thought of Lauren, the only student in that workshop who would later befriend me, and the gossip she described taking place behind my back, all those snipes about the inaccessibility not of my style, but of my content, and I wondered if all those young women now also remembered that scene differently. After all, the zeitgeist had taken a dramatic turn since then: the marginal had become central; the central had become redundant. If we would not say certain things today, did we still say them in the past?

At the end of the semester, when it was time to choose next year's classes, I skipped over the section on writing workshops in the course catalog. I made a point not to talk about my private life anymore, and I didn't socialize very much, but most probably I didn't fool anyone. I was afraid that when I talked, I would reveal the fact that I didn't have a real self. I desperately sought out the person I could become. I tried reflecting the expressions of those around me, parroting accents, mannerisms, and social behaviors. I took up smoking briefly because all the cool people at Sarah Lawrence seemed to be doing it. I would stand outside the library with Sharon, a friend from the masters program, watching her inhale the smoke effortlessly, and feel enormously aware of how the cigarette was tilted between my fingers, wondering if I looked natural holding it, wondering if I looked just like everybody else. I eyed Sharon's long blond hair and tanned skin with awe. Would I ever look that normal, that American? This self-consciousness accompanied my every move in public. Only when I was back in my state of complete aloneness did it slip off me, for there was no one to see me in my raw, skinless state except my child, and he already knew me in all my states, and always would.

After the initial celebratory mood that had colored the early days after my flight, a paralyzing mixture of fear, loneliness, and self-doubt had been brewing underneath my numbness. Six months had gone by since my departure, and it had finally dawned on my family that I wasn't coming back. To avoid their manipulations and threats I had changed my phone number and withdrawn even more into myself, afraid of being followed or discovered. But even though I knew I didn't want to be pulled back into the past, I wasn't very confident that there was a place for me anywhere else.

I was in the outside world, but I wasn't *in* it, not really. I felt like a displaced person, as if I was looking at a photograph of a scene I remembered being a part of, but I couldn't find myself in it. In my dreams I was always searching for a spot on a map where I knew I lived, but I was unable to find the street. Somehow I had been erased.

Since leaving, I had begun to see life as an enormous grid, a cross section of human connections. Every man and woman

I encountered appeared as a plotted point on an intricate map, a map indiscernible to the eye but obvious to my sensitive perception. There were lines drawn between these people and their close family members, and longer lines rushing through open tunnels on the grid to anchor friends, neighbors, lovers, even acquaintances. Wherever I looked, I saw the invisible threads that connected people; every person seemed to have their grid firmly in place. I had been dislodged from my grid. I wondered how long I'd survive without one of my own, and whether it was even possible to rebuild one from scratch. What if I was doomed to forever linger in the no-man's-land between points, feeling as if I was fading into nothingness with each passing hour? There were hardly any people in my new life; I had simply not had the time to get to know anyone yet. Filling the space around me with hearts and minds would take years, and even then, there was no guarantee I would ever be able to trust and rely on them like I would on family. The worst part about that was knowing that if something happened to me it would take a long time for that to be discovered. For some reason, this often worried me, the idea that I'd be lying somewhere decomposing someday.

It's not that I was lonely, not in that traditional sense in which I yearned for company. After all, if I really wanted to, I could have conjured a companion or two. I actually preferred to be alone. It meant I had to be less aware of my faults, of the ways in which my life was still lacking. Besides, I had occupied an enclosed mental space my entire life. In a world where neighbors reported on one another's sins and friends betrayed one another to win the approval and accompanying benevolence of the authorities, trust was a luxury I had never been able to afford, not with my host of transgressions that needed to stay hidden. Perhaps I had subconsciously sought out this new, post-departure solitude, because it was, after all, the only condition that felt familiar to me, and therefore safe.

Growing up we had a saying in Yiddish that essentially translates to "a cow out of the stall." It was used to describe a Hasidic Jew who had left the community, likening the person's behavior to that of a cow suddenly let loose after a lifetime of imprisonment. It was believed that such cows were most likely to charge madcap down a hill to their deaths. Hasidic rebels reportedly indulged in wild, drug-abusing lifestyles that inevitably ended in ruin, similar to the cow's doomed trajectory. Freedom posed an especial danger, the adage emphasized, to those who had never previously experienced it. This saying, scornfully evoked when the conversation turned to the subject of the few known rebels in our society, irritated me greatly as a child. Didn't the phrase do more to point out the failings of life in a stall than the dangers of freedom? Wasn't it clear that the cow would have been better off grazing freely in the first place?

One Sunday morning I drove to the anonymous parking lot near the Tappan Zee Bridge where I normally picked up Isaac from his father. We were still kind to each other then.

"We weren't like the other couples," he said to me that morning. "They all fought like cats and dogs, but we didn't."

I sighed. "That doesn't mean we were happy." I thought it meant we hadn't cared enough, but I didn't say it. "I want to be happy. Don't you?" He looked at me with blank, quizzical eyes, as if he had never even considered the idea.

"When will you come home?" he asked.

"Why don't you leave with me?" I asked. "You know we can't really be happy there."

He looked at me as if he was considering it for a second, and then the look in his eyes said otherwise. There was that word again, they seemed to say.

"What does it even mean to be happy?" he asked me.

He had a point. What did we know about happiness? We didn't even have a word for it in Yiddish. *Menuchas hanefesh*, my grandfather had said, or *harchavos hada'as*. Those terms meant happiness for him. A rest for the soul, a broadening for one's mind. But that was not enough for me. I wanted the pure essence of joy in my life; I didn't want to settle for the bit of peace or understanding that had satisfied him. I wanted to learn the art of happiness, and for that I had to become an *apikores*, a heretic or an epicurean, depending on which way you looked at the term.

"Have you ever heard of Quine's theory of the web of belief?" my professor had asked me during one of our thesis meetings. He explained that Quine was the first philosopher to challenge the idea that belief systems were built like pyramids. A pyramid, my professor said, would topple if sufficiently disrupted, but a web could adjust its margins without sustaining damage to its core. It was Quine who postulated that people could be exposed to ideas that challenged their web and simply adjust the web's margins to go on believing in the same way. In the end, no matter how well informed we are, we choose what to believe, he said.

There would be no more religion in my life, I knew. But neither could there be anything to fill the empty space it had left behind. I felt I would not be able to find anything in this world to hold on to. No matter how deeply those inculcated beliefs were engraved in me, no matter how deep the crevices left behind as I dug them out, I needed to learn to live with those empty spaces, because it was better to live in the truth than in the dangerous comfort of the lie.

But even that was a naïve thought. After all, I was a human being. The needle of my inner compass quivered without pause in its search for something, the nature of which I would not be able to pinpoint for some time.

2

VERZWEIFLUNG
פֿאַרצווייפֿלונג
DESPAIR

With college classes behind me, I was now truly adrift. This was the absolute emptiness I had always known would arrive, one I had managed to postpone until that moment. I have not often attempted to revisit this phase in my memory, and now that I try, I discover how difficult it is to recover, perhaps because I knew while the experiences were still occurring that I would never actually want to remember them. Even then, when they were present realities, I was storing them deep in the forgotten reaches of my brain before they had the time to develop into stockpiled recollections. I was pushing my own life away from me as if each moment were a layer of dead skin that I could peel away and be rid of forever.

It is troubling to me, when I try to go back there now, how I find my thoughts spinning in circles, uncertain where to land in that murky storage space. Intent on finding purchase somewhere, I fixate on a tree. This method has worked for me before. Many of the most vivid memories of my childhood seem to bloom around the presence of a particular tree, even though the neighborhood in which I grew up was not exactly overflowing with arborous specimens. This says something perhaps about how memory itself can function like a growth, with a root event that germinates into a network of subsidiary issue. The tree I recall now was a rather sickly locust, growing out of a small, sandy pit in a stone courtyard on the Upper East Side of Manhattan. I suspect it is no longer alive today. I used to think that the death of that tree would spell my own doom, but now I sometimes wonder if perhaps our fates unfolded at the expense of each other.

The locust tree is the first thing I remember seeing from the window of my next apartment. It was a scrawny tree with leaves that had turned brittle by late August, which was when I moved into the third-floor walk-up apartment behind a Lutheran church on a Lexington Avenue corner. I spent hours in my new home just sitting at the kitchen window, which faced the courtyard between the church and the tenement building, staring at the dried pods dangling in clusters from its branches. It was the only growing thing left for me to look at now. From the windows in the other rooms I could glimpse chunks of high-rises in the patches of view that were not obscured by the neighboring buildings, a strange, geometric puzzle of gleaming metal silhouettes seen through a network of shafts and alleys. In every direction I looked my sight was arrested by walls. So I preferred to sit in the kitchen and stare inward at the frail and slender locust instead.

The tree was only just tall enough to unfurl a small coronet of branches into the square patch of sunlight, which settled for a few hours each day into that small cleft in the row of Manhattan rooftops. Its dangling pods reminded me of the acacias my grandmother had occasionally pointed out to me during our

Sabbath afternoon strolls through the quiet streets of Williamsburg. Though she loved all trees, acacias were her favorite species, and when I first visited Budapest so many years later I would indeed discover entire avenues completely cloaked in ancient rows of them, leaning toward one another to form a lacy canopy that filtered the sunlight into shifting patterns on the ground. On the few occasions we spotted one in our Brooklyn neighborhood, she seemed so overjoyed that the markers of the acacia remained embedded in my memory and I became adept at recognizing them even then. This is how I knew that they were easily confused with locust trees, an invasive species in New York; indeed, locusts were sometimes called false acacias. Now I couldn't help but contrast this meager "false acacia" that was the central point of my vision to the conversely resplendent tree that had extended its copious branches into my childhood bedroom. Outside the Brooklyn brownstone in which I had grown up, a towering sycamore with a massive trunk and a wide radius of thick leafy branches had dominated the sidewalk, its limbs reaching through the bars that covered my window and scraping against the grainy stucco beneath, as if unaware of the limitations presented by its urban surroundings. The dense thicket of leaves obscuring my view had given me the romantic illusion that I lived in a tree house, its branches a buffer against the more grating noises of the city around me. Now this buffer was conspicuously and comparatively absent; my new home stood naked in a sea of towers, and my restless nights were punctuated by the whirl of sirens, endless honking, and the jarring thuds made by trucks rattling over potholes as they hurtled down Lexington Avenue to make their deliveries during the predawn hours. If anything, that tree in my courtyard represented the inverse; it had been cowed by the urban infrastructure around it. I became convinced, the more I looked at it, that it was a bad omen, that I too would be cowed and weakened by this ruthless milieu I now found myself in.

Of all the ways in which I had dreamed and fantasized about a possible future "outside," I had never imagined myself here. Of course, I had been aware as a child that Manhattan, although practically inaccessible, was geographically close. The skyline had glittered like an array of cut-glass shards behind the foreboding gray expanse of the East River, promising to be everything that my world was not, but also threatening, in its shimmering, shape-shifting glory, to be a mirage, an optical illusion that could transform into something more menacing up close. Now this cryptic vision had become the concrete maze in which I lived, an important legal address that I would use to secure my freedom. There was an irony in the fact that my freedom would come to me only by living in what felt like, on particularly bad days, a tightly packed open-air prison.

I mean this in a quite practical sense, having experienced 9/11 and knowing of the consequences for the city: the closing of bridges and tunnels, the shutdown of public transport, the sold-out supermarkets, which as a result of delayed deliveries couldn't restock fast enough, the breaking down of phone lines and jamming of cellular signals. And of course I would later see what havoc Hurricane Sandy wrought, when downtown Manhattan was without electricity and residents of skyscrapers found themselves trapped on high floors, as elevators ceased functioning and the stairways to be used in case of emergency had little to no illumination. It was always clear to me that the people living in New York City were particularly vulnerable, as it is a city that is hard to survive in on a good day, but nearly impossible to survive in during a catastrophe, be it man-made or by nature's hand. It is precisely that knowledge that renders one a true New Yorker, I had learned, because testing fate by staying was what made one a local, as opposed to those who fled every time the situation threatened to worsen. Yet I had never before been so painfully aware of the treacherous nature of my current geographical positioning. Naturally my thinking was interwoven with the childhood belief that cities that hold God in contempt were slated for retribution, like the city of Babel, whose people tried to build a tower that reached all the way to the seventh heaven and God himself; as a punishment he fractured the people's speech into a million different languages, so that none of them could understand the others, and their doomed efforts to coordinate resulted in the toppling of the tower and the destruction of all. Manhattan fit into that religious archetype of hedonistic, idol-worshipping cities that populate so many of the biblical narratives, and if I feared catastrophe, it is because I feared being swept up in that wave of divine fury, without access to a place on an arc as refuge, or even a hill from which to observe the apocalypse below. I felt trapped in a primal way, subconsciously fearing that when the hand of God came to sweep the sinners from their comfortable perch, I too was condemned to get caught up in the swell, simply by association.

For some Manhattan will always remain the city of unlimited possibilities, of endlessly exercised freedoms, but for me the city was never able to live up to its more advantageous promises. Perhaps it was a question of timing, or perhaps, as I later came to suspect, it was that the clash in value systems between the spiritual empire of my childhood and the materialist kingdom I was so suddenly confronted with was so extreme as to be permanently irreconcilable.

After all, I didn't choose to move to Manhattan that summer of 2010. I had been advised by my lawyer to do so, shortly before my studies at Sarah Lawrence had drawn to a close. The next phase of our legal strategy was due, she had reminded me. The necessary separation period was on the official record, a custodial precedent had already been achieved, and it was time to try for an actual divorce, in the process of which I would have a chance to establish my parental rights. Whatever case there was, my lawyer had informed me, it would be tried in the county of the child's residence, and since my son had been living with me, I wanted to be safe from the corrupt judges voted into place by the Hasidic community, notorious for repeatedly deciding against those who chose to go up against their primary constituents. However, after carefully considering the court system, and where exactly we might land in it, my lawyer had concluded that I needed to try to guarantee as much as possible the assignment of a liberal judge to my case, someone who wasn't afraid to go against the community, someone whose decisions had been fair in the past. These judges, my lawyer said, primarily sat on the benches in Manhattan.

Initially I perceived the news mostly as a blow to my budget. I had followed a very strict financial plan until that moment, using my book advance for *Unorthodox*, my memoir of growing up in the Hasidic community and my decision to leave it, to meet my basic monthly expenses, and covering unforeseen or extra expenditures with small side jobs. Moving to Manhattan would mean a drastic increase in my monthly overhead, no matter how much I downsized. Of course I knew of the difficulties in finding affordable housing in Manhattan, which was ludicrous when you considered what even passed for affordable there. Polly, a classmate at Sarah Lawrence who lived in a cramped three-room apartment in a Tribeca high-rise with her husband and child, had told me about her neighbors paying four- or five-thousand-dollar monthly rents for smaller spaces. I remembered the words of a professor at Sarah Lawrence, who had asked me to reconsider my decision to leave. "Divorce is already the number one poverty predictor for women in America," she had warned me. "How do you think you will manage, being so young and without family?"

I hadn't confided these fears to my lawyer, and I wasn't planning on letting her see my apprehension. I already felt disproportionately guilty for being a pro bono recipient of her advice, normally prohibitively priced, but even more so I was worried that her small confidence in me would waver if she realized that my own poise was simply a thin pretense. As I was even then still a woman of some sort of faith, I left my lawyer's office on that day convinced that I would indeed move to Manhattan and somehow it would all work out. Though I had despaired of finding God under the auspices of any religion, and similarly abandoned the search for a secular equivalent, I still thought of my life as a story then, and stories were the one thing I still believed in. Their structures seemed to me to reflect immovable natural laws, like the golden spiral, and although I knew stories to have moments of chaos and confusion, in the end things always seemed to tie together rather neatly, and probably it was only a matter of time, I felt, until I would begin to see the threads in my own narrative come together and feel the fabric fit snugly around me once again. One could say I had a spiritual faith in the unstoppable momentum of narrative evolution.

And then, as if this faith was a thing to be naturally rewarded, a miracle did indeed occur; that is to say, I found the small two-bedroom apartment with a view onto the church's courtyard and the spindly locust tree growing awkwardly in the middle of it, and I was naturally convinced that it was the work of some higher power. The sexton of the church, a tall, fair-haired man named Schultze, had met me for a short interview and promptly offered me the apartment for two thousand dollars a month, a rent that normally wouldn't have gotten me a studio in Harlem. There was still eight thousand dollars left in my bank account from the book advance I had received. I knew that wouldn't last me longer than three months in Manhattan, and I did not have a long-term plan for life at my new address, but there was this strange and stubborn faith, and the old, deep-seated belief that people who had faith were rewarded. Perhaps these convictions would do more to cripple me than help me.

I packed my few belongings and drove them into the city over the course of several trips. A van service delivered my mattress and sofa. In order to sweeten the deal for Isaac, who had recently turned four, I purchased a new Lego set, hoping it would distract him from yet another change in his short life. Being much smarter than me, he did not fall for this ploy. As soon as we got out of the car he realized what was happening and refused to enter the building. He screamed and cried; he shouted at me that he wanted to go back home; he hit me; he pulled wildly at my clothes; he said he hated me; he quivered with a panic and fury that was outsize and yet exactly right. I understood with perfect clarity in that moment that I was failing one of the primary maternal obligations; I was proving unable to provide him with a stable home environment.

In the end, I carried him up the three flights, sadness and shame erupting from the pit of my stomach to form a bile in my throat while I struggled to keep hold of his flailing limbs, wincing as his yowls echoed into the landings. I unlocked the door to our new apartment and we practically fell into the hallway, my muscles relaxing in relief. His temper tantrum escalated; I sat him on the sofa and he jerked away from me, kicking and punching the sofa cushions, and because I felt helpless to offer him comfort, I sank to the floor and started to cry as well. The weight of my disempowerment fell suddenly like a block from above, and I buckled under the blow. My shoulders heaved in relief then, as all my own suppressed fear and grief escaped as if from a pressure valve. There it was, first the blessed emptiness, the freedom from the nonchalance I had been feigning to myself and others, the conviction that leaving wasn't so dramatic after all and my life was now ordinary and common. Then, here was the truth I had been avoiding, swarming in to take its place: the fragility of our standing in the world, my fearful lack of resources both practical and internal, the impossibility of anchoring onto anyone or anything.

Isaac looked at me, perplexed by my own heaving, ragged breaths. His tears stopped. As I continued to gulp and wheeze through my own sobs, he crawled into my lap, put his thumb in his mouth, and promptly fell asleep. I held him in the dimly lit, cheerless room, looking out the window at the labyrinth of brick, steel, and glass and the patch of flat gray sky visible above it, feeling mentally and bodily how lost we were in this new world, with its eight million inhabitants clawing at survival, the supply of which was more than usually limited. We were well and truly alone, my son and I, and our story might very well end here, I knew, in this city, where keeping a roof over one's head was an impossible battle, and where people like me disappeared into the sinkhole of failure every day. A rough blade of panic had been unleashed from within, and it would saw at my nerves for many years to come.

Terrible moments pass if you are willing to wait them out. The practical things in life need doing; they intrude insistently into the grief-induced paralysis until one grasps at the rope provided and hauls oneself up and out. To enable a perception of stability, I made endless to-do lists; looking at them gave me the much-needed sense that there was still purpose to my existence, and purpose was important because it gave my life form and texture; it was an antidote to the tyranny of terrifying nothingness.

Isaac was first on my list. I needed to return some sense of normalcy and routine to his life as soon as possible. He needed friends; he needed stimulation; he needed structure. So I would enroll him in preschool, but since my current temporary custody agreement dictated that Isaac had to attend a private school with Jewish affiliations, and I was still maintaining the pretense of an observant Jewish life, I made an appointment at a Modern Orthodox primary school not far from where we lived, hoping to apply for a need-based scholarship. With the submission of my application, I had to appear before a board to qualify for sharply reduced tuition. The board consisted of three middle-aged Jewish men, all scions of prominent, moneyed, upper Manhattan families. I was unprepared for the first question they directed at me.

"Tell us something, why are you here? Why don't you put your son in a Satmar school, or at least a Hasidic one?" the board member asked, looking from my application to me and back. "After all, that's where you come from, right?"

I would have thought the answer to that was obvious. Nonetheless I tried to suppress my discomfort and answer the question politely. "Well, because I'd like for him to have a high school diploma someday. I want him to have a chance at a real education and the opportunities that come with it. Isn't that something any mother would want for her child?"

"But why us?" he countered. "Why should we take responsibility for you? You're not part of our community, after all."

The implication was clear. Funny how that cliquey group mentality that I had sought to escape seemed to exist everywhere else as well. Everybody was an "us." Would I always be an outsider, no matter where I went?

I took a deep breath. I steadied my voice. When I answered again it was in a tone of exaggerated humility and respect.

"*Chas v'sholom*," I said, a Yiddish expression, the equivalent of "God forbid." My hand was on my heart. "It's definitely not your responsibility. I have faith that everything happens for a reason. If for some reason my son goes to public school, I know that will be because he was meant to. That won't be your fault." Of course I knew that public school was the ultimate evil, even here, among the more cosmopolitan Jews. Nobody wanted the blame for that on their celestial record.

One of the men, his expression indignant, raised his finger as if to lecture me, but his colleague reached over to touch his arm, restraining him. He turned to me and said I could go; the board would deliberate and apprise me of their decision. The following week, Isaac started kindergarten there. Although the teachers were kind and he was able to form some tentative friendships, he became more and more guarded each time he entered the building. He was starting to realize the differences between himself and the other children and beginning to understand that he would be punished for those differences. Much like the world we had come from, this new world of wealthy Jews was a similarly conformist environment, in which we were now marginalized not only because of our poverty, but also because of my youth and my status as a single mother, and because my Jewish background was not like that of the other families. The Upper East Side congregation was composed of people with similar incomes, backgrounds, and ideals; in a way it was as uniform as the world we came from, if not more so. I had taken Isaac from one oppressively homogenous environment and plunked him down into another. How could I sentence him to the same childhood experience when the whole purpose of everything I'd done was to save him from it? Was it the case, I worried, that we could never hope to find a community, Jewish or not? Once an outsider, always an outsider. That's what my teachers had said about those who didn't fit into our community. Failure to fit in promised to be a permanent disease. Deep down the fear that the maxim held truth gnawed at me. I couldn't accept that my fate, never mind my son's, had already been decided. I told myself this was all temporary. Someday soon the divorce would come through, and then we would really be free to start our lives over, on our terms. We'd find somewhere they didn't make us feel like we didn't belong.

The next item on my list was finding a job. I dutifully filled out applications and printed résumés, but it was well-known even at Sarah Lawrence that getting a job that paid enough to survive in New York City involved having the right social connections to set you up with desirable unpaid internships so that you could work your way into a good position someday. It was just after the financial crisis of 2008, and I had never heard of anyone getting a decent job, one you could actually live off, straight off in Manhattan by applying for it the old-fashioned way. Nevertheless, it was clear I had to do something. God helps those who help themselves!

Did I already know back then that some stories just as easily end in disaster as they do in triumph? Today I know that the only structural law of a narrative is that it have a beginning and an end, whatever their nature might be.

As I waited for responses from the companies I'd applied to, I tried to keep myself occupied during the hours when Isaac was at school. I found cafés where they let you sit for hours while sipping the same cup of coffee. I brought a book with me but often peered past its pages to watch the young waitresses bustling about; they were my age, and I wondered at the lives they were at least partly financing with this job.

Some days I rode the subway all the way down to the lowermost tip of Manhattan and then back up, simply to pass the time. At first, I used my perch to regard the denizens of the city, feeling as if they were part of a theatrical display that was touted as the great reward for the high price of living there. But gradually, as the months passed and the weather changed, and as I watched those who moved around and past me, I became aware that I had slipped out of my story. I noticed all the stories that were constantly taking place around me, and they were a sharp contrast to the distinct emptiness and stagnation in my own life. I could glimpse a person and immediately I would perceive the narrative that they were a part of. My imagination would fill in the blanks; I could envision where they came from and where they were going; I guessed what they did for work and who they would have dinner with that evening; and I realized that because

I had exited my narrative structure, I now was stuck in an inert space, where my life could no longer develop or move forward, as I was missing the connections to people and places that would normally serve to propel movement.

For a reader (I do still primarily identify myself as one) this is a particular devastation. Since I have always valued nothing so much as the sacred act of infusing meaning into chaos, it was all the more painful to realize I had been squeezed out of the space in which narratives can germinate. I remembered then how as a child I slowly came to the realization that just like all those characters I was introduced to in my clandestine reading sessions, I too was a character, as were all the other people around me, and it occurred to me then that it was up to me to become the main character, the protagonist of my story, for if I sat idle I was doomed to play the small role that had been allotted to me, thereby sacrificing the story to someone else.

I had been so hungry for the form of autonomy that would allow me to construct my own narrative that I had catapulted myself beyond any framework that could contain my story. In fact I had landed in a kind of narrative vacuum. Because I had burned all my bridges before reaching the other side, I was now stuck in the ether between active and passive, a character in literary limbo.

At this time in my life, I began to drift away from books; the act of reading became a painful reminder of my limitations. I had sustained myself during my childhood by reading, not just because of the simple joy inherent in the act, the escape into fantasy, but because those books were proof that a life could be actively lived, not simply unspooled on a predetermined loop by an impersonal hand. Books had planted within me the desire to truly inhabit my life, and now that I had finally broken out into the world in which I was free to do so, it was crushing to discover that I could not simply pick up the thread of a new story and plunge into the plot with the reins firmly in my grip. I was still stuck in that same position as I had been then, forced to live vicariously, by reading, or by watching others as they navigated the tangible lives they were immersed in. But what I really wanted, what I had always wanted, was to live, and to finally set aside the act of wishful observation.

Life is made up of people; I knew this much. There are no stories without characters. People create movement and growth; without them there is only stagnation. But there was the problem of making friends in my new environment. I had looked up some old classmates who I knew lived in Manhattan as well, but I soon realized that the primary binding factor in a Manhattan friendship was a common denominator of personal net worth. This is not to say that any of my Sarah Lawrence acquaintances now judged me or rejected me for being poor; it was rather that my being poor inconvenienced them and made friendship difficult in practical terms: when they suggested lunch at a restaurant or a trip to the salon, it was simply impossible to say yes, knowing the exorbitant prices that were standard at such locations. It wasn't their fault that they could afford to do things that I could not, but eventually they tired of having to think of things to do that didn't cost any money, especially when it was much easier to simply go out to the restaurant they wanted to go to in the first place, with a friend who could afford it. So I steadily lost the few opportunities for friendship that presented themselves; my economic hardship hammered in my loneliness until it was a permanent, immovable fixture.

As time went by and no job prospects materialized, the

numbers in my bank account began to dwindle dangerously. I tried to stretch the money even further than I had before, living off seventy-nine-cent bags of white beans and forty-cent marrow-bones that I cooked with plenty of spices for flavor, just as my grandmother had taught me. I rewarmed it for each meal until only the burnt scraps were left. I wonder now if Isaac noticed, based on the changes to our diet, that I was worried about food. I wanted more than anything to hide my fear from him, to spare him the burden, but I think very few parents manage to do this completely when they are in a difficult position. Today I observe his relationship to food, the way he asks about our next meal, what it will contain, and when it will arrive, and naturally I wonder if this vague worry about future sustenance can be traced back to those days when I actively worried about us going hungry.

I had known hunger as a child, but never this kind. The hunger I had experienced then had been largely emotional. Always there had been freezers stuffed full of meals and sweets, and my grandmother in the kitchen whipping up dishes for me at midnight if I came out of bed with hunger pangs. Never had I known what it was like to skip a meal, except for those few religious fasts throughout the year, and even then we had celebrated at the end with such incredible feasts that I had almost enjoyed those twenty-four hours of restraint. I considered them worth it when confronted with the fireworks that exploded on my tongue at the first taste of food after sundown.

But our relationship with food had always been strange; I remembered that much. I had this image in my mind still, of my grandmother sitting on a chair in the corner of the dining room nibbling for hours on a chicken bone, lost in a dream, inattentive to my questions, to my curious gaze. She emitted little moans as she gnawed at the bone, perhaps sounds of pleasure at the taste, but there was something horribly sad about those moans as well, as if she was remembering a different time, a time when there had been nothing to eat except subpar remains. What else could explain her desire to suck the marrow out of spindly chicken bones when we had a house full of food?

She had always spoken of hunger. It was what she used to get me to lick my plate clean at every meal, guilting me into eating even if I wasn't hungry, by reminding me of the time when she hadn't had enough. She seemed to be trying to teach me to eat while I still could, as if that great, bottomless hunger that she had experienced would come again, and that I could ward it off by eating more, compensating in advance for future lack.

But I was hungry now, and those meals that I had once eaten to the point of distension did not serve me. Hunger is a special torture, but fear of it is worse, and I had been raised to fear hunger more than anything else. Truth be told, looking back I understand that I didn't actually go hungry during this time. Perhaps the quality of my food was less than desirable, perhaps the variety that appeals to us was lacking, but my stomach was full. It was the fear of that great threat my grandmother had described that gnawed in my belly like a beast, making me believe that the worst had already happened. And although my stomach was full, I tossed and turned at night as if I had gone to sleep on an empty one, and each morning I was awake far too early, fighting the endless hollow of fear that was nighttime. I watched as the sun rose as if from outside the haze each morning, its insistent beams illuminating every particle in the smog, reflecting off every glistening trail of dog urine trickling along the pavement. Even the Upper East Side, with its famous broad avenues lined with gleaming shop windows, its squares of gray asphalt trod on by designer-clad residents in dark sunglasses and red-soled shoes, could not be spared the excrement this city produced. It labored to hide its garbage and scrub its sidewalks to no avail. It seemed strange to imagine that this noisy, dirty, odorous place had once captivated my imagination and populated my dreams. I would have liked, for just one day, to walk in the shoes of someone for whom this city was an endless thrill. Perhaps the change in perspective would have melted my resistance.

After I dropped Isaac off at school, the hours loomed in front of me expensively, time I couldn't afford to pay for, and I walked the city aimlessly to stem the panic. Up Lexington, down Park, up Madison, down Fifth and into Central Park, up to the reservoir, down to the boathouse, back onto Museum Mile and through the hushed side streets with their expensive belle epoque town houses. One day as I made my way home via Park Avenue, traversing the land of doormen, valets, and chauffeurs, I saw a strange sight that has stayed with me in perfect clarity until today. Two policemen were standing around a prone body that lay outstretched in front of the grand entrance to an elegant, forbidding condominium building. They seemed to be trying to determine if the homeless person in question was dead or only sleeping. I had seen this before; normally the policemen, having been alerted by the private neighborhood guards, would shake the homeless person awake, insisting he change his location. Hours later they would most assuredly be called to pry him from his next spot, but such was life if you were homeless in New York City. You weren't allowed to loiter, but there was nowhere to go, so you loitered as long as you could. I spent so much time then thinking about homeless people because I was convinced it was only a matter of time before I would join their ranks. This particular person wasn't showing the slightest response despite the increasing rudeness of the prodding by those policemen. And then suddenly, the door to the building was swung open by the uniformed valet, and out paraded a tall, slender woman with a veil of long, shiny platinum blond hair, her long legs tucked into knee-high black leather boots with sharp stiletto heels, strutting as if on a catwalk on the way to the chauffeured town car lying in wait. In those brief seconds I took note of her crocodile-skin bag, her sable coat, the way her chin was lifted up and out as if propped up by an invisible brace, and I deduced in seconds that she was wearing probably thirty thousand dollars' worth of clothing. I watched in disbelief as she stretched a long, spindly leg over the body of the man lying on her street, as if he did not exist, or rather, as if his existence was nothing but a silly inconvenience that others would dispense of for her, before disappearing into the cavernous town car only a moment later, the door shutting behind her with a resolute thud. Off they sped into the traffic, and the police continued their poking and pushing as if nothing had happened.

This terrible image would come to represent the city of New York to me. I would see such performances repeated in various forms all over Manhattan, but it is this one that remains crystal clear in my mind, like a video playing on repeat. In their absolute indifference to the reality of human suffering in the immediate vicinity, these ostentatious displays of wealth that I was suddenly confronted with seemed to confirm what my upbringing had led me to believe, namely, that wealth was immoral, that it was the root cause of all evil. I came to see New York City as ugly because of its emphasis on wealth at the expense of all else, and this ugliness depressed me. I lost the ability to be enchanted by the small beauties in life because they had become eclipsed by the all-consuming ugliness of a capitalist paradise.

On that day, as the rich woman sped off in her town car, I turned away, feeling sick. Across the street from me was an enormous Catholic church, its doors open, and without thinking I crossed at the intersection and fled into its pews. In the silence and emptiness of the church I found a respite from the ugliness outside it, and to alleviate the hopelessness growing within me, I began to escape regularly into the many imposing churches that lined these affluent streets, simply because, unlike most synagogues, they were left open to the public every day. I was not seeking religion, but there was a kind of salvation in the silence to be found there, in the cool darkness of those empty stone buildings.

I visited many churches, both Catholic and Protestant, although I preferred the Catholic, with its smells of incense, its flickering candles, its clergy members moving soundlessly over stone floors in their mysterious robes like magician's capes. I frequented the cathedrals on Fifth Avenue, or the Anglican church of St. Thomas More on Ninety-Fourth Street, where dark wood wainscoting recalled an English manor and a priest bustled around the pulpit without ever glancing toward the dark corner where I sat under the eaves. I spent entire days sitting in churches, feeling ensconced, safe from the overwhelming chaos of the city. Very often, I drifted into a kind of trance and would awaken from it hours later without being able to account for the time that had passed. Perhaps those were my first periods of meditation. I marvel now at how my instincts functioned during this period, seeking out coping mechanisms to see me through that difficult transition.

What if, I wondered as I sat in the back right corner of St.

Ignatius Loyola, *God was still there after all? What if he had been there all along, in the silence, in the aloneness, in me? What if I needed to get rid of everything, every last thing, in order to find him?*

I began to fantasize that I was finally on the right path toward God, that by being stripped of every comfort and crutch, I would come to know the truth about him. I remembered the stories I had been told about the *lamed-vav'niks*, about how they had achieved ultimate closeness to heaven by renouncing all earthly consolations. Perhaps I had been onto something all those years ago. Perhaps the spirit of Leibel from Oshvar did indeed reside in me.

———

On most evenings, after I had put Isaac to bed, I would run myself a hot bath in the hope that it would relax me enough to make sleep come smoothly, instead of in the fits and jerks characterized by the ever-wakeful state of my anxious brain. My white-tiled bathroom was small and cramped, the tub custom-made to fit into the awkward, narrow space, but there was a tapered window on one end that I usually propped open as ventilation. On one particular evening in the spring of 2011 it had become warm enough to keep the window open during my bath, and as I emerged from the water after dunking my hair for washing I was startled by a sound, that of an otherworldly singing, which at first seemed to me music playing from a device, and yet was too diffuse and vibrant to be confined to a recording. I soon deduced it was the church choir practicing across the courtyard, the weather having allowed for them to prop open some of the slender panes in the large stained-glass windows as well. I listened to the quavering tones that trailed intermittently toward my ear, and that old conviction in me vibrated to life again along with them. I thought, *this is a sign, if there ever was one.* I dried off, put on a robe, and went to the kitchen window to see if I could glimpse the choir from that vantage. I could not, but the disembodied voices floated into the apartment fuller and more tangibly now, as if on a magical current of air.

I observed the locust tree below me then, as it had just begun to flower again despite the odds, and took heart in some small way at its persistence. The church choir continued to sing, songs I did not know or recognize, with words I could not single out or understand, but as they sang, while I stood at the window listening, I felt moved, as if by very old, deep-seated forces, to pray. This would be my last prayer, although I could not know it then, and in retrospect I can now identify this same ecstatic comingling of outer and inner stimulants that led to all my previous beseechments. That is to say, in all the moments in my life in which I was moved to engage in spontaneous and effusive prayer, I entered into a state just prior to the action that can only be called drugged, much like the way I feel today after a glass of wine. The world seems to recede into a passive, benign state, and my emotions soar forth as if the canal locks have been released. Each time it seemed that forces within and without were conspiring with each other to bring me to this spiritual precipice, from which there was nothing to do but leap.

The act of suicide is not wholly unrelated to that of prayer. In the appeal of the spirit to God there is the feeling, even the conviction, that the querent abdicates responsibility over his being and his life to God; with a suicidal leap the jumper abdicates it to death, but both acts are driven by the underlying impetus of having nothing left to lose.

Back then, as I sensed myself leaping into the void that these two acts have in common, with my stomach lurching as if I truly was in free fall, I remembered the husband of my high school teacher, a follower of the Breslov movement, which propagated trancelike prayer under the influence of supportive drugs. It was later said that after embarking upon a spiritual meditation on the rooftop of the synagogue, he had in the heights of his exultation leaped unknowingly to his death.

This was the price that prayer demanded of us. It was not enough to appeal to God from a secure vantage point; no, prayer wanted from us the willingness to take a risk, to make ourselves vulnerable. Only then would a higher power extend itself for us—when we had extended ourselves for him. A prayer wasn't some chant one mumbled perfunctorily, or even thought or felt inside one's own consciousness; it was an act that possessed body and soul and afflicted both with intense spasms of devotional subjugation. One who prayed in earnest invited the spirit of prayer to settle within him and occupy him from the very center to the outermost margins of his being. For this reason we had also learned to *shuckle* while praying, which was the art of swaying back and forth energetically in order to help the process along.

But on this particular evening, at the age of twenty-four, I prayed the same way I had as a child; I addressed God again as if he was an old friend, as if he was quite tangible, somewhere out in the beyond listening, his character exactly how I had always imagined it, distracted yet benevolent. I formed the invocations silently, the words looping through my mind like a calligraphic engraving, as if by doing so I was inscribing them into the ether. As I murmured the words to an old and favored psalm, an image of my younger self sank suddenly and heavily into my consciousness, before I could defend myself against its onslaught.

There I was, twelve years old, sitting outside the principal's office. Even at that age, I was still getting into trouble for reasons I couldn't quite understand. This time I knew the rabbi would call my grandfather, my grandfather would call my aunt, and I would get weeks of lectures and intense supervision because of something I said, or wore, or did in school without noticing. I recall myself sitting on that hard wooden bench as if it were yesterday, my shoulders hunched in a posture of defeat, looking down at the scuffed floor while I felt my eyes stinging, threatening to spill over in a deceptive portrayal of guilt, hoping in my sad and weary state that justice might intercede to put an end to this unfairness. And so I started to pray, that one prayer, Psalm 13, which I often repeated many times in succession in a superstitious ritual whenever I found myself in difficult situations. I've memorized it by now, this glorious hymn with its dramatic language intimating a powerful narrative, its assertive statements assuming a close and direct relationship between God and his supplicant. I whisper the Hebrew words to myself now:

How long, O Lord, wilt thou forget me forever?
How long wilt thou hide thy face from me?
How long shall I take counsel in my soul, having
sorrow in my heart by day?
How long shall my enemy be exalted over me?
Behold thou, and answer me, O Lord my God;
lighten mine eyes, lest I sleep the sleep of death;
lest mine enemy say: "I have prevailed against him";
lest mine adversaries rejoice when I am moved.

But as for me, in thy mercy do I trust; my heart shall
*   rejoice in thy salvation.*
I will sing unto the Lord, because he hath dealt
*   bountifully with me.*

And then, sometime after the twenty-seventh or twenty-eighth iteration of the psalm, the door to the office opened, and it was not the rabbi standing there but the secretary, saying the principal was too busy to see me, and I should head back to class. Oh, the joy I experienced on that short walk back to the classroom, knowing I had been saved from certain punishment! How to describe the wonder in feeling that with my prayer I might have reached over some looming wall to something powerful and magical on the other side that could save me.

Now, all these years later, I searched within myself once again for that spirit, rendered lost in the process of my alienation, because I was clinging to the belief that somewhere in me there was still that ability to manifest the impossible, to sense the invisible, to tap another dimension. I conjured the filmlike images of my desperation, those portraits of ruin that had often haunted me, playing them once again before the gaze of God so that he could fully grasp how tenuous my situation was. Was this not my special power after all, the power to invoke a response through emotive description? My prayer, the first after a long period of silence, felt like an important interview that I could not afford to fail; I needed to impress upon God the urgency of my need in order to not squander the opportunity of his audience. Should I be able to do so, much in the way I had done when I was twelve and desperate for succor; should my desperation today prove as authentic and pure as it had then, then surely now I too could arrange for my salvation.

Soon I felt exhausted from the effort, much in the way that prayer had exhausted me as a child, as if I sensed the spiritual store emptying and knew that with each great effort to reach God the human being was left taxed. There was only a limited amount of spiritual energy in an earthly creature, it was clear, and mine had not been replenished in quite some time. After I finished my prayer I waited for a while at the window, as if hoping for a celestial response, or at least a subtle signal, but nothing happened, at least nothing as concrete as on that fateful day in school, when the secretary stood in the door like an apparition and it was as if Moses had parted the Red Sea before my eyes.

Slowly the effects of the stimulant wore off, and the high began to wane. The choir stopped singing, and in the comparative silence everything seemed mundane once more. Although I went to bed fantasizing that when I woke up the next morning, things would be entirely, magically different, my moment of supplication at the window had already begun to seem vaguely ridiculous and childish. Within me it was as if the very last cinder of faith had been consumed in the furnace of prayer.

After that, around once a week or so the tones of the choir would waft toward my window like the aromas that drifted from nearby chimneys, but no answer to my desperate entreaty presented itself. I did receive a job offer as a secretary in a small dance studio, which paid only enough to cover my monthly grocery bill, and though I took it for lack of something better, feeling I needed to do something to stem the panic and emptiness, I was more aware than ever how urgently I needed to meet the gap between my meager income and the exorbitant rent. During my work hours I was often so distracted by fear as to be rendered practically useless at my job. Yet I continued to repeat my mantra to myself, which I used as a psychological defense against the waves of anxiety hurling themselves at the walls of my spirit; I made myself the promise that I would endure. It was not as if I had ever thought that these years would be easy, I reminded myself. I had not been deluded about the challenges that lay before me. I would suffer gladly under the notion that it was all temporary, that eventually I would figure out how to live the life I wanted, the one I had given everything up for. One day, it would all become clear; it would be thrown into perspective. One day, all of this would just be a story, I told myself, trying to diminish the roller-coaster experience I was having into a predictable dramatic arc.

———

It was around this time that Isaac began coming home from school withdrawn and irritable. It had already become such an effort to project calm around him to protect him from my fear that his new moods threatened to destroy all my efforts. At first I worried they were a sign that he saw through my facade completely, that I was failing at my most important task. But then I began to discover strange bite marks on his arms during bathing, or bruises on his body when I changed his clothes, marks that concerned me, as they did not strike me as the normal signifiers of playground roughhousing, but when I asked him about them, he stiffened into further reserve. I eventually coaxed it out of him that there was a bully in school. I had been somewhat prepared for this moment, having been bullied as a very young girl myself, and like most mothers perhaps, I had always preferred to imagine my son as one who would not bully others; therefore, it stood to reason that he would at some point fall into the role of the victim. Life seems to force us into these oppositional roles, as if we have to choose between the two and cannot simply refuse to participate in the duality.

I tried to give him advice about how to handle the bully, perhaps standard American parenting advice in this regard, that is, to communicate to an adult what was happening and to trust that he or she would solve the problem, which was official policy in most preschools in New York City. But the next time I picked up a tearful Isaac from school and asked him if he had followed my instructions, he insisted he had, wailing with frustration at the injustice, for his teacher had done nothing, he said, even though he had done exactly as he was told, even though he had done the right thing. In fact, he told me, she had seen it happening and had failed to address it, instead sending Isaac for a time-out, in a sense punishing him for reporting the violation.

Concerned, I made an appointment to speak with the teacher about this. She was a young woman whom I actually liked, as she seemed kind and thoughtful and, unlike the clientele at the school, not necessarily from a wealthy, privileged family. She seemed uncomfortable during our meeting, saying only that since she had not witnessed the events that Isaac had reported it was difficult for her to address the problem. Had she seen the marks on him? I wanted to know. She had, but again, having not been a personal witness, she found it hard to exercise her authority freely. The conversation was going nowhere and I felt vaguely frustrated, sensing that there was something I was missing, a piece of information that I wasn't privy to. But there was no way of proving that my gut feeling was rooted in reality and not in stereotypical maternal angst. I implored the teacher to keep a special eye out for such incidents in the future. I was clear about our situation, trying to impress upon her that the two of us were too vulnerable at the moment to withstand any extra challenges. I felt certain I detected sympathy in her response, but she was careful to remain neutral in her language.

Shortly after, I received a call from Isaac's school while I was at work. I was to come get him immediately, the staff director informed me, as he was causing a major disturbance. After having been sent to the principal's office to be disciplined after an altercation, she informed me, he had climbed under her desk, curled into a ball, and refused to respond to anyone.

"Have you considered the fact," she asked me in her haughty tone of voice, "that your son might have psychological problems?" Within that sentence was the inevitable accusation, packaged neatly and conveniently: Had I considered the fact that I was damaging my son by forcing all these changes upon him, by imposing my vulnerability as a young and impoverished single mother without support, in such a way as to be irreparable?

After this sentence I did not hear much. By the time I hung up I could feel my carotid pulsing, hear its throbbing in my ears. I rushed across town with my heart in my throat, the whole of me reduced to my lioness instincts, ready to swoop in and rescue my cub from the enemy. This is the only way I can describe myself on that day. My experience of being alive was reduced to that of an animal, blood rushing through the places in me where thoughts and emotions normally competed for space, my brain a pulsing white heat sending electric charges through my limbs. When I arrived at the school building I did not stop to speak to anyone. I charged into the staff director's office without so much as a hello, reached under her desk to scoop up the rigid, unresponsive body of my son, and swept out of the building as quickly as I had come, the calls of staff hurrying behind me falling on deaf ears.

Once outside, I headed straight to Bellevue Hospital, Isaac still in my arms, his hands clasped around my neck, his head buried in my shoulder. He clung to me so hard I could feel his nails digging into my skin. I was going to Bellevue because I knew they had an emergency child psychiatric department of superb repute, and I needed to call the school's bluff. It was the only way to make sure the school understood that they weren't dealing with an easily intimidated, helpless young single mother, but with a woman who would stop at nothing, come hell or high water, to protect her child.

On that particular afternoon the waiting room at the child psychiatric emergency unit was relatively empty, and the receptionist looked curiously at my son as I filled out the intake forms, seemingly wondering what we were doing there, as at that point Isaac had calmed down and was sitting quietly next to me. Moments later, a doctor came to see us, and after I explained the situation briefly, he indicated that he would like to see my son privately before continuing the discussion. He went with Isaac into a special intake room, which had a door with a window so that I could see inside as Isaac sat on the rug and tentatively explored the toys that lay strewn about, but I could not hear them talking. I sat outside and waited, and while I did so the animal instincts that had taken over earlier began to recede. Now the feelings of outrage and helplessness and frustration began to surge in, and suddenly I doubted my actions as rather rash and extreme.

Thirty minutes later the doctor emerged with Isaac, and both seemed surprisingly cheerful. Isaac was smiling and he seemed to have completely forgotten the events of the day. The doctor shook my hand warmly, saying he thought I was doing a wonderful job raising him and that I should be very proud of myself.

"So he's okay?" I asked uncertainly.

"More than okay!" he answered boisterously. "A perfectly healthy child, obviously very intelligent, doing exactly the right thing in a bad situation."

"Oh," I said, surprised to actually hear my suspicions being confirmed, realizing that until that moment, although my instincts had been powerful, I had still doubted them.

"Would you mind waiting here a few more minutes?" the doctor asked kindly. "I would like to call your son's school."

I nodded wordlessly, burning with curiosity. I watched him walk into his office and close the door behind him. Isaac sat down on the rug to investigate the toys that lay in the middle of the room. As I waited, I thought about the times when I was bullied as a child and punished for it, because it was always easier to punish the child with no parents or family members who would stand up for her or make a fuss on her behalf, and I comforted myself with the knowledge that at least in this department Isaac was not lacking. Vulnerable and disadvantaged as I might be, I had never failed to show up for him, I had always been there when he needed me, and perhaps that doctor had a point after all; perhaps I wasn't doing as badly as I feared at this motherhood business, because after all it wasn't about money or social position, but about priorities.

The doctor returned once more. This time Isaac didn't even look up from the Lego city he was building.

"So, I spoke to the staff director," he said, "and I don't think your son will be having any trouble in school anymore." He smiled easily as he said this.

"How can you be so sure?" I asked, wondering at his ability to make such broad guarantees. "What did you say to her?"

"Oh, just that I would be notifying the board of education the next time I got a whiff of their practices, and that the way they are running their school could get them shut down."

I was baffled as to what practices exactly he was referring to. Was it an empty threat, done as a kindness to me, or was he referring to something specific? Most of all, I wondered what Isaac had told him in that room. As we walked out into the late afternoon sunshine bouncing off the glass panels of the surrounding buildings, I noticed Isaac's unmistakably jaunty gait. His body language was carefree, and whatever he had told the doctor must have relieved him in a way I couldn't. Perhaps he hadn't been able to burden me with the full truth, as if sensing I couldn't handle it, but had felt that the doctor was the right person to turn to.

Regardless of the exact details, things were indeed very different in school after that, just as the doctor had promised. Isaac no longer came home with marks or poor moods. The staff director spoke to me with a new and unparalleled deference, constantly inquiring about how Isaac was doing, as if needing validation that he was indeed content and thriving in the classroom. And still I couldn't make sense of what had happened exactly, of what had transpired in that fateful phone call between her and the psychiatric fellow, until about six weeks later, on the last day of the school year, when I had arrived to pick up Isaac's things. I was about to leave when his teacher called to me from the school entrance.

"Ms. Feldman," she said, "I just wanted to tell you how sorry

I am for what happened with Isaac this year. I hope you know how bad I felt, being in that position. I never thought, when I was studying to be a teacher, that I would ever have to go against everything that I was taught, against every instinct . . ."

My gut tightened. "What do you mean by that?" I asked carefully.

She seemed to pull back slightly, her eyes searching mine as if to test the limits of my knowledge. "Well, you know about the other child in question, the one Isaac was having problems with . . ."

"What do I know?"

Her gaze seemed to register that in fact I did not know.

"I just hope you can forgive me, Ms. Feldman. I was only trying to keep my job and make everybody happy. I would never want to hurt a wonderful child like your son. He really is a good soul."

"What would I need to forgive you for?" I asked, sharply this time.

Her eyes teared up slightly, and her voice turned to a whisper. "It wasn't me, you know. It's the administration. We're a private school, you know; we run on donations . . . If I'd alienated the school's biggest donor, it would have cost more than just my job. Who knows?" she continued. "The school could have collapsed."

And there was the explanation, the one I had failed to fully intuit, but one that a Manhattan doctor familiar with the landscape of children's schools in this city would have quickly grasped, after years of experience at a hospital like Bellevue. In this city, it was normal and common that children who were bullied by the sons and daughters of generous donors were punished instead of their tormentors. In this city parents who paid for their children were more valuable than parents who loved them.

———

Already in June, the starting point of summer vacation for private schools, the city began to empty, first just on weekends, but after the Fourth of July the lethargy was palpable. As the asphalt streets baked under the relentless sun, the air moved in sluggish whirls, pushed along only by traffic. The secretions of air-conditioning units dripped relentlessly onto the sidewalks, which were trod on not by purposeful urbanites but rather by disoriented summer interns and small-town tourists who could only afford to visit Manhattan during this season, when most apartments were sublet while their inhabitants escaped to cooler, calmer locales.

Isaac would have three months of summer vacation, and his father and I had agreed to split that time equally. Isaac and I whiled away the early weeks in the still bearable weather exploring the parks and playgrounds, escaping into the cool air of museums when the afternoon sun reached its apex. In my first year at college, a Sarah Lawrence professor had taught me the trick of offering to donate instead of paying the standard admission. As soon as I said, "I'd like to donate," there was immediate recognition in the eyes of the ticket seller, and I was surprised by how little embarrassment I felt at plunking down two nickels for our tickets. After all, the purpose of the law was so that New Yorkers could regularly visit the facilities in their own city; what was the point of living here, after all, if everything the city had to offer was closed off to the less fortunate? Mayor Bloomberg would attempt to eliminate the policy a few years later, to the chagrin of many.

But then we were still allowed to make our way multiple times through all the exhibits at the Metropolitan Museum of Art as well as the Museum of Natural History, and it was gratifying to see how Isaac never tired of exploring those rooms, asking questions and positing his own theories about the artists and their techniques. He was becoming someone quite interesting, I realized as I observed him, and it pained me how difficult it was to see past the fog of my desperation to the personhood he was developing.

In mid-July I would have to hand him over to his dad, and then what? Would I still have the strength to wake up every morning and pretend that my life had value if he wasn't there to remind me of it? I was afraid I would lose the only thread tying me to some kind of narrative: that of mother.

During those weeks I eventually came to the decision that I too would leave Manhattan for the period in which Isaac was to stay with his father in cooler, greener upstate New York. Not necessarily because I had somewhere better to go, nor to escape the city itself, although I had certainly been yearning to do so since I had arrived, but because of a very practical reason that had occurred to me as I had observed the seasonal changes the city was undergoing: namely, financial opportunity. Since there was nothing keeping me bound here for the next few months, and I had finished my manuscript and only the copyediting remained, why not rent out my apartment for two or three times the rent I was paying, like everyone else was doing, and go somewhere, anywhere, cheaper? Then I could use the money I earned in those six weeks to stretch out my budget so that it covered me until late fall instead of summer's end. It was clear that no other miracles were about to happen to ensure my extended survival, so perhaps a trip to some foreign destination would provide the right setting for a wonder I had not given up hoping for, in the depths of my heart, since that evening at the window when I had discharged that final prayer.

I will admit, I had an idea of where I would be going already. A month earlier I had stumbled across Jean Baudrillard's *America*, and although I was yet unaware of the great tradition started by de Tocqueville, that of the European tour of the New World, I already identified as a refugee in the country of my birth, and I felt a compelling need, after a lifetime in the *shtetl*, to experience the full expanse of the United States up close the way Baudrillard and many others had done. I needed to "discover" America.

My grandmother had always said that America was simply the next place to which we had come, a stop on the winding diaspora route. One day it would be replaced by the next point of refuge, she was sure. In this country I was simultaneously citizen and immigrant; this dichotomy was reflected in the relationship between my individual and communal identities. The community I had been raised in was one of exiles, and since I had been exiled from them, did that mean the double negative could cancel out my alienation? Could I become an American?

One day, I needed to believe, my divorce would come through, and I would no longer be forced to live in Manhattan. I needed to plan for this eventuality of a future elsewhere. Perhaps this plan would give me strength to continue; perhaps by choosing my goal I could give myself something concrete to work toward and hope for.

Where was this unknown place in which my happiness could sprout? Baudrillard had started in California, so I would start there as well. I placed an ad on Craigslist offering to rent my car out to anyone looking to drive from New York to San Francisco, figuring that with the money I would drum up as a result I could cover the cost of a plane ticket out as well as the gas, tolls, and expenses that would accrue once I was ready to hit the road and make my winding way back to the East Coast.

A young man answered the ad and came to inspect the car. I made a copy of his driver's license and passport, took down all his information, and added him to my insurance, and we agreed on a date for pickup in the Bay Area. It would take him around five to seven days, he estimated. He would take a relatively direct route but I should still expect him to put around four thousand miles on the car. For this he paid me 750 dollars in cash, in advance, plus security deposit. Around the same time, having placed an advertisement for my apartment as well, I chose two MIT grads from the hundreds of people who had answered the ad; they had summer internships at Goldman Sachs and were offering to pay almost four times the rent on my apartment even though they would barely be there because of the working hours involved.

I was nervous about leaving the only refuge to which I could retreat. It was unnerving for me to know that for the next six weeks, I would have no home, no steady address. But I was also impressed by how quickly I had managed to make the best of my situation, marveling at my own resourcefulness. I had raised enough money not only to cover my costs now, but to support myself for an additional three months.

On the day I crossed the Golden Gate Bridge the weather was a perfect summer dream, but the bridge itself was suspended in a cloud of thick fog, and I was immediately reminded of the biblical cloud pillar that had served as a guide for the Jewish people in their forty-year exodus through the desert. It was a shock to emerge suddenly into the bright sunlight again, but I pulled over on the side of the exit ramp and turned to look back at the strange cloud formation enveloping the bridge's statuesque limbs like an elegant shawl. I thought about how in order to receive guidance, one had to have the conditions in which such guidance would be at least noticeable. The slaves of Egypt had taken a risk, had wandered into the unknown. Then had come the pillars of cloud and fire and, at the end of their journey, the promised home. In my own small way, I was hoping that the risks I was taking would pay off similarly, that a path would be shown before me, inch by inch, mile by mile, as long as I kept faith.

I had already arranged, through old Sarah Lawrence contacts, to meet a woman named Justine for drinks and dinner at the pier; an acquaintance in New York had written ahead and informed her of my arrival, as I had asked literally everyone I even vaguely knew to connect me with as many people along my route as possible. I hoped this would provide me with some sort of buffer against loneliness.

At precisely seven p.m. I entered the restaurant and was promptly shown to a round table covered in thick white damask, with a candelabra casting a yellow aura in the dimly lit but cavernous room. Justine came in somewhat breathless ten minutes later, her short, brightly dyed purple hair all tousled, her long, flowing skirt fluttering around her leather-sandaled ankles. She sat down and turned to me, her eyes wide and warm behind green-framed glasses, and her smile so big it was as if she'd known me for years and tonight was a reunion of sorts. As waiters poured us glass after glass of wine I found myself telling her my life story, and it was almost frightening to see with how much sympathy she was responding. I felt guilty, as if telling her about my situation was a kind of burden from which no one could retreat, and that by doing so I was somehow roping people in against their will. But Justine's sympathy came from personal experience; although she had grown up in the Midwest, her own life story could be said to resemble my own, with its themes of flight and self-reinvention. But she was in her sixties and had long since found her peace. "You will too," she promised, "not because that's the way it always goes, but because you're strong, and you won't give up until you've found it. I can recognize that in you."

Before dinner was over, as I explained I had to leave in time to make my couch-surfing appointment before my hosts went to sleep, Justine asked why I didn't just stay with her. Her husband was away on business, and she had a big house on the beach just south of the city with lots of extra room. Moreover, she had to leave for a trip soon and there were two cats that needed to be cared for while she was gone, so this was the perfect opportunity for me to get to know them and decide if staying was an option.

Justine pointed out her little red Mini Cooper in the parking lot and suggested I follow her in my car. We drove down Highway 1, quiet at this hour but beset with stretches of thick mist, past the hazy beaches of Pacifica and around the hairpin turns of Devil's Slide, where I struggled to keep up with the Mini as we jostled around the sharp curves, but soon we had arrived in a tiny town named Moss Beach.

The house was large and light filled, lined with floor-to-ceiling windows and built on stilts almost like a treehouse, overlooking the ocean on one side and the forested ridge on the other. In the center of the house was a large woodstove that Justine used as heating on chillier days. She was a writer who spent most of her time in that remote house, she explained, working on her magnum opus. She had once lived in the city but left the urban life behind to live here with flowers and animals and fog tentacles, so she could retreat into the active space that was her mind. Like me, she felt assaulted after spending too much time in a city. Her thoughts needed more room to grow. "It takes most of us too long to realize that the mainstream formula for happiness might not fit and that we have to find our own," she told me. I thought about mainstream ideas of happiness. New York promised that if you had a fat bank account everything would be wonderful. What did America promise? Would money matter as much everywhere else as it did back home?

During the next few days, we took walks alongside the ocean, and the beaches there were always empty. The stretch of sand in front of Justine's home was ringed in rocky ground upon which grew diverse and colorful species of moss, stretches of yellow and purple and green, after which a slight strip of sand gave way to slate-colored waters. Here and there a harrier hawk swung low to the ground; a scrub jay squealed frenetically in the brush. As we walked, I experienced for the first time the peace inherent in total isolation, and noticed how the first ideas of my future had begun to germinate quietly within my imagination. If I was to find a real home someday, I thought, would it be like this, surrounded by trees and water and birds, my identity allowed to grow into itself without being shaped and molded by any community of humans?

Back at the house, I sat on the veranda for hours without any interruption, remembering those Sabbath afternoons in which

I had lain motionless on our porch, eyes closed, listening to the uncharacteristic stillness and to the sounds of bird and breeze that had been allowed, only on that day of rest, to come to the fore. I remembered the cherry blossoms that would fall like swirling snow in the spring, the blue jays that came to peck at the seed my grandmother had prepared, and I thought about my grandmother then, and her ability to create for herself a sense of home in a foreign land, by planting the species of flowers and shrubs that she remembered from her childhood, in an attempt to create a familiar island for herself where she felt at peace.

That garden had been a sanctuary for me as well, when I was a child growing up in my grandparents' home. It was probably the only real garden in pre-hipster Brooklyn. It was the early 1990s, and most people had cemented over their backyards to keep away the weeds. My grandmother had made an agreement with the neighbors on either side of us: she would take care of the little plots of land behind their houses if they, the owners, allowed her to plant whatever she desired there. And so she did, growing strawberries in the damp, rich soil that lay just under the thick refuge of ivy filtering all that wonderful light that hit the back of our brownstone in the afternoons. She planted fat pink climbing roses so that they used the chain-link fence marking the perimeter of the yard as a trellis; the thorny stems climbed higher each year, inextricably intertwined with the metal. Crocuses and daffodils came up in late winter, and gorgeously colored tulips popped up in clusters in early spring, followed closely by brilliant blue irises and delicate lilies of the valley.

She had a real eye for landscaping—the garden was divided into three rectangular sections, each delineated by carefully trimmed white-edged Swedish ivy and bordered on the corners with broad-leafed hostas. Slabs of rock were laid in between the sections and at the borders to create a walking path, and little tufts of moss grew between the rocks. It was a magical place, so well cared for that it gave back generously and graciously each year. I had read Frances Hodgson Burnett's classic by then and begun to pretend that it was my own secret garden. When I stood among the rustling leaves and smelled the delicate fragrance of the flowers, the incongruent urban cacophony was muted and remote, the sounds of honking cars and droning airplanes softened by wind-tossed stems and whispering petals. The ivy beds were like cushions that absorbed and suffocated the ugly sound of the city. In my imagination, it was as if invisible walls had gone up around the garden, and I had fallen, like Alice in Wonderland, into another plane of existence.

Every year, catalogs would arrive from Holland, offering nothing but tulip bulbs, and my grandmother and I would pore over the varieties and talk about which ones we might like to try. We'd survey the potted African violets on the windowsill to see if they were ready to be transplanted, but we'd leave the geranium cuttings until summer. There were always exciting plans to be made in the spring, and a summer of surprise growth to look forward to.

One morning in 1999, my grandmother and I went downstairs to check on the plants, and I watched as she fingered a strong-looking sapling that had sprung from the middle of the garden, just past the line of shade cast by the porch overhead.

"What is it?" I asked, thinking it was something she had planted last year, wondering if perhaps we could expect another rosebush.

"I made a mistake," she said, looking crestfallen. "I thought it was just a weed."

"What is it?" I asked again, more curious this time.

"It's a loganberry tree," she said. "I don't know how I missed it. I was surrounded by them as a child. I should have recognized it instantly."

Immediately I understood her consternation. It was too late to do anything about it now—she might have been able to tear it out when it had still been a shoot, but a tree that gave fruit could not be cut or pruned. It is against Jewish law to hinder a fruit tree's growth in any way.

She had to let it take over her garden, and as the years went by, it did so, eventually towering over our second-story porch. It dropped purple splats of berries for three years, until it became permissible to pick and eat them. As the tree grew, it became hungry and greedy, stole nutrients from the soil and light from the sky. Year by year, the other plants began to die. The tulips grew fewer and fewer in number; the irises disappeared completely. My grandmother saw this, and although she never said anything, I watched her make fewer and fewer trips to that garden she had once cherished. Eventually, the ivy became so neglected it grew over those carefully laid paths, and weeds began to crowd the borders and infiltrate the center of the garden. These were no mild breed either; they were the thick, broad-leafed stalks indigenous to Brooklyn, hardy plants that needed hardly any time at all, it seemed, to grow as tall as trees and drown the garden completely in darkness. When I saw that the weeds would not be addressed, I went downstairs to rip them out myself. I had no knowledge of gardening; my grandmother had taught me only to love flowers, not how to take care of them. With bare fingers I pulled and tugged on each insidious weed, feeling with every success that there were already new ones growing to replace those that had been excised. My grandmother came out onto the porch and watched me work, thinking I was doing it to please her.

"You don't have do that for me, little lamb," she said, using her traditional term of endearment. But I wasn't doing it for her. I was desperately trying to rescue the only realized fantasy of my childhood, the one beautiful thing that had marked my upbringing in this otherwise godforsaken corner of Brooklyn. I pulled furiously, my vision blurred by pollen irritation, my nose stinging from the pungent odor of weed juice spilling onto the earth. I finished the whole backyard, and when I was done, the garden looked as if a massacre had taken place there; the weeds had left gaping holes and depressions in the ground. Never mind, I thought, those would fill. I was older by then, making money of my own from babysitting; I could plant new things in the holes to replace the weeds. Hydrangeas would be nice, perhaps some bleeding heart. I would buy weed killer. I would keep pulling them out if it killed me.

I made my way over to some young climbing roses, shriveled and drooping sadly where the twine had come loose. I found the rusted edge of a metal tie used to affix the bush to the fence and tried to force the stems back into their original upright position, to no avail. The tie snapped back, its jagged edge tearing into the skin of my palm. Blood sprang from the gash, but I bit back my scream so that my grandmother wouldn't notice. I hadn't thought to ask for gardening gloves.

How I wanted her to come down then and work alongside me, just as we had always done. Those times seemed gone forever. No matter how hard I worked to fix it all, I knew my grandmother had given up on the garden, and my grandmother did not change her mind. She had learned to detach from the things she loved because she had experienced so much loss in her life already.

It was from her that I must have inherited that deep-rooted ability to detach. It hurt to love things now, I had discovered, even though I wanted to love without being afraid of disappointment. I wanted to be able to invest my energies over and over again, but what was easy, what was familiar, was the act of cutting—cutting off, cutting out, cutting away. When would I be able to stop trimming at the edges of my life, gnawing it down to the bone, and start building it?

I had already begun to miss my grandmother then in the garden. Even as I stood next to her while she cooked and scrubbed and sang tremulous tunes, I longed desperately for the woman she had been before loss and tragedy had sanded her down. After I left, it felt as if she had already died, and her spirit hovered over me like a guardian angel.

Perhaps in this memory lay the answer to my question. Perhaps I too would have to carve out a home for myself in a territory that would always be foreign. Perhaps I too needed a garden, and the refuge that came with it.

———

I stayed at Justine's house for three weeks, a time in which I truly felt ensconced in a sanctuary, far away from the real world that I would soon have to return to. There were no social interactions, but there were long walks and time to read books, and lots of hours focused on the manuscript edits that needed to be approved. I managed to postpone all my fear about the future.

I left San Francisco in early August to give myself enough

time to complete my trip. I passed through the flattening land-scape of Sacramento and the other interior California towns, then the initial dryness of the Sierras, and soon I was racing to catch the sunset at the Utah-Nevada border, where the Bon-neville Salt Flats lay just west of Salt Lake City. I got there just in time. I crossed the state line and parked in an empty lot that seemed to serve as a station for freight trains, one of which stretched down the tracks as far as the eye could see this late in the day. Looking back at the receding brown mountains, I saw the sky above and between them pulsing bright pink, the clouds streaks of orange and purple. I had caught the sunset at its apex. Off to the east, a lone Joshua tree stretched up from the flat landscape against a quickly darkening horizon. The rest was all salt mud, looking almost like an enormous ice floe in the dis-tance, reflecting the vivid neon sunset so blindingly that the effect was Narnia-like. The roaring sound of wind rushing over the flats filled my ears; the dazzling silver surface mesmerized me. I felt like I was in another galaxy. It was like no other vision I had seen or imagined, and for the first time on my trip, I felt floored by the place I stood in, unable to communicate or relate to it, feeling my foreignness emphasized suddenly. What a strange, wild, and enormous place this country was.

I drove past the darkening flats along a quiet highway, into the compact, symmetrical skyline of Utah's capital. I slowed down only as I passed the Mormon headquarters, because I no-ticed a group of women congregated outside, dressed in long pleated skirts and high-necked shirts, their hair modestly slicked back; they could have easily been mistaken for the peers of my youth. If I talked to those girls, would they be like the girls of my childhood, thinking and acting in chorus?

The next day I drove through Utah's hill country, where

clusters of modest mountains huddled under the scant cover-
age of stunted conifers. After three hours I seemed to cross an
invisible line in the sand as I descended yet again into the
purple-veined skin of the desert, looking back at the fertile
landscape that had so bluntly come to an end behind me. I
drove on for five hours straight, in what felt like nothingness,
on a one-lane road, and felt grateful for the red pickup truck in
front of me. Its Utah license plate made me feel more comfortable about traversing such a long stretch of uninhabited and
inhospitable land.

This is America, then, I considered, this vast stretch of emptiness that lay between the coasts. I drove the rest of the way
through Utah's parched southeast region feeling an urge to re-
join civilization. I relaxed slightly once I ascended into the
winding, mountainous roads of Colorado's ski country. I passed
the perched chalets of Vail, noting the elegant, manicured gardens and contemporary vacation homes with a sense of guarded
relief—this at least was familiar in the sense that luxury will
always be familiar to a New Yorker. By the time I hit Denver
traffic, it was two hours past nightfall. I stopped at a roadside
bar called the Grizzly Rose, where a neon sign outside announced that it was ladies' night. That meant free drinks.

The women who were square-dancing on the polished
wooden floor wore very short shorts and tube tops, and the
length of leg between hem and cowboy boot inevitably boasted
a smooth, dark tan, but what stood out the most for me were
the large, gem-encrusted crosses dangling wildly over tightly
compressed cleavage, the ostentatious display of piety in jarring
relation to the overall atmosphere of drunken hedonism. Those
girls in long skirts outside the Mormon temple had made sense
to me; I had recognized in their garb the same severe lines as

in the clothing of my own childhood. I would always connect religion with the modest concealment of women's bodies, with the stilting humility of their movements. I was flummoxed by what felt like an irreconcilable contradiction: here were people clearly advertising their devotion to Jesus while engaging in what seemed to be some kind of bacchanalian ritual. America just didn't add up.

My GPS said it was a sixteen-hour drive from Denver to Chicago, but I did it in twelve, stopping only once for gas, chips, and beef jerky. What a thrill it was to find myself again on a booming highway, a silvery skyline thrusting powerfully ahead of me! It could easily have been Manhattan; the traffic was similarly aggressive, and the New Yorker in me swerved confidently through it. I gaped at the impressive architecture as I followed the directions to my friend's address, which turned out to be a brownstone very similar to the one I grew up in, tucked into a small side street a block away from elevated tracks, like the ones I heard rattling through my childhood dreams every night. It could have been the same neighborhood. Instantly I was soothed by a false sense of the familiar.

I visited the famous sculpture *Cloud Gate*, known as "the Bean," and made my way through the Art Institute. As I turned a corner from a room filled with Manets and Boudins, I found myself suddenly face-to-face with a famous Nazi propaganda poster, *The Eternal Jew*. The familiar image, that of a wizened, humpbacked Jew holding coins in one palm and a whip in the other, set on a bright yellow background, seemed discordantly out of place in a museum of art. Nothing could have prepared me for its assault on my consciousness. Underneath the poster was a description of the temporary exhibition of Nazi and Soviet propaganda posters from World War II.

I stepped inside the room, which was quiet, lined with brown carpeting that muffled my footsteps. Dimmed as if in a theater, spotlights shone softly on the yellowed posters stretched and displayed in glass cases on the walls. Many of them contained Jewish symbolism juxtaposed with images of horror and evil; always there was the ugly face, with its hooked nose, its piercing eyes peering from under thick, dark brows, and its menacing scowl.

I moved from poster to poster, feeling as I progressed through the exhibit that each one resonated with something inside me, that in every image was something recognizable, something horrible yet true.

It is this that terrifies me about the stereotypes I learned growing up, and the ones I'm still incorporating as I make my way through the world as a new sort of wandering Jew—that there is always a speck of truth packed into the core of each accusation, and that I will never be able to fully rid myself of that self-affront. I did not want to leave my world only to be forever chased and haunted by the identity it bestowed on me. I had been raised in America without knowing what it was to be an American—it was that problem that I had hit the road hoping to resolve.

Here in the Art Institute, it felt as though the rest of America was involved in discussing the influence of Jews in art and culture, but that the physical Jewish presence was concentrated only in negligible pinpricks throughout the country, a speck here and there, except for the powerful communities that coalesced into a blob on the East Coast. Here in Chicago, I felt I wasn't even real, but just an apparition. I felt keenly that I had no identity other than the abstract of the Jew; I could pretend to blend in, but it would be a false construct that would deflate immediately.

I left Chicago that night, anxious to return to New York, vowing never to venture out into the unwelcoming territory of greater America again. The sun set over the flat, impoverished plains of Indiana; Ohio and Pennsylvania passed by me unnoticed in the night, because I drove intently without stopping, until I crossed the Verrazano-Narrows Bridge at dawn.

To get to Manhattan, I drove through Brooklyn, and even in those early hours, the city was sweltering and stagnant in the summer heat. Although the streets teemed with spectral memories, nothing about New York City struck me as particularly welcoming on that day, for I had come home to that familiar and unescapable feeling of homelessness; I had flung the door wide open to a paucity of roots that had only been emphasized by my journey across the country, forming a bowl of emptiness in my soul. My grandmother had always said that it was bad luck to present an empty dish; she had filled any borrowed container with gifts of fruit or cake. "No one wants to open the door to an empty container," she had said. In abandoning every reference in my own life, had I opened mine to just such a ghastly vision?

3

HANDLUNG

האנדלונג

ACTION

Manhattan in the early fall seemed softer, more harmless somehow. As the last of the sticky heat faded, and the frenzy of the temporary summer infusion waned into the more solid and reliable tempo of routine city habits, I began to recognize the locals again: the women under polka-dotted umbrellas sloshing through those brief, cooling rains in their multicolored Hunter rainboots, pulling the umbrellas shut and looking up as the sun, infinitely kinder now than in those past months, winked briefly from behind a patchy cloud cover. Transitional weather in New York had always been a delight to me, those thunderstorms and hail squalls that came as fast as they went, the way the air positively vibrated with change and movement. Now the city swung ahead at a pace I could recognize, and as the familiar autumn gales arrived to pluck the leaves from their branches, strangely I felt relief. I had wanted to forget about the trip, forget that the summer had ever happened, for I had learned something frightening during that time that I was not ready to face, and yet it was something I still could not quite articulate to myself.

Nonetheless, looking at my bank account now gave me an unmistakable thrill of satisfaction. For it truly was a miracle, to look at my account balance and see numbers on a date where I had long since expected to have arrived at empty. And although technically the miracle had come from myself, it was difficult to draw the line between circumstances that arose from me and those that were stimulated by other factors. I had learned as a child that God could act through oneself or others, and a part of me did not trust that I alone was capable of this magic. If what I had once considered impossible had become real, then it was not me who was responsible. Such tremendous inversions could only be attributable to God.

I moved through my life quite muddled in those days, because everything around me seemed to be suddenly encased in spiritual auras, charged with negative or positive energy, and it was as if I was trying to tune my own aura until it was just the right degree of receptive. Now it was no longer about signs or signals; now everything was shot through with invisible potency. The desperation of the last year had finally delivered its impact; now it was as if my mind had fallen under the influence of a low-dose psychotropic drug. In search of the supernatural, I had lost the thread connecting me to the prosaic.

———

I floated through September and October on what felt like a cloud of spiritual intoxication. Everything that had seemed terrifying to me last autumn now seemed exhilarating instead. My whole life seemed like an unreal adventure, a game in which the cards could be played in an endless variety of ways, where nothing was at stake. This euphoria was likely purely internal insofar as no one around me seemed to notice it. Isaac certainly did not seem affected by it, but nonetheless there is no denying the rapturous mood that enveloped me then; when I look back, all my memories from that short time seem swathed in a brilliant haze. I hardly need to point out that I was bound to come crashing down from this artificial high very soon, and so I did, as I paid November's rent and realized that, once again, I had no money.

I remember meeting my agent on one of those days, a day when the trees were mostly bare, the sky gray, and the wind chilling to the bone, a day when I felt the pain of my anxiety once again in a primeval and bodily way that made me feel dirty and ashamed. I did not know then that I was at the beginning of a pattern that would last a long time for me, a pattern in which I was flung to the most agonizing depths by fear of failure, only to vault to ecstatic dizzying heights each time I was saved by a hairsbreadth from the jaws of ruin. On that day, as I handed her the edited manuscript to pass on to the publishing house, I asked her when I could expect the next portion of the advance, which was due at manuscript delivery, it said on my contract. What this meant, my agent had explained, was some sort of official notice that the bureaucracy would churn out once the manuscript had survived every critical eye and had been pronounced ready for print. She couldn't predict when the next advance would come through, she said. Best-case scenario, the official acceptance process took two months, bureaucracy included, and ideally I'd be above water again in the new year. But be forewarned, she said; nothing happens quickly at a publishing house. And then, seeing my miserable face, she softened and said to me, "Why don't you just get a job? You know in my day I'd walk into any shop on the street and ask if they were hiring!"

I wanted to laugh, but the situation was too serious for that. In her day. Before the internet, when there were jobs to be had everywhere, and nobody was saving them for someone they knew or had networked with, when employment had been a given and educated people from middle-class origins didn't live on the street with their yoga mat from a previous life doubling as a sleeping bag. What reality was this woman living in? How could I make her understand? I couldn't. She had amassed her fortune and had been about to comfortably retire before taking me on as a last client. Even if I described my situation to her in detail, it could never feel real to her. She would never be able to feel it in her body the way I did.

I walked home from our meeting feeling lonely and resentful, especially because my agent was probably the only person in New York City who had all the information necessary to fully grasp my circumstances and yet was able to employ the distance of professionalism to remain insulated from them. For her it was only important that manuscripts were delivered, contractual promises kept, and of course, her percentages earned. I reminded myself that even though I had managed to sell a book on spec at the height of the late-aughts recession, as a total unknown at the age of twenty-two, this didn't translate into any commercial value. I recalled the meeting we had with my editor recently, where she had solemnly informed us that although *Unorthodox* was a very "niche" title, they were going to go ahead and order a very generous run of eight thousand, as a gesture of good faith. It was obvious to my agent, as she explained to me later, that eight thousand was the absolute bare minimum number of copies a big house like that would order.

Naturally that meeting had accelerated my decline into horrid self-doubt and the gnawing anticipation of certain downfall. For I regarded the book as my only chance now, the only possible way that my situation could change from something barely resembling survival into relative, fundamental stability. I needed someone else to believe in the book I had written. I needed more than a little bit to tide me over; I needed a boost up into the echelons of the middle class, the feeling of a floor, however thin and weak, below me.

I collected Isaac from school, where, at the very least, he continued to reap the benefits of the demonstration I had staged a year before. He had really settled in among his peers, even made some friends. We rode the bus uptown to our apartment, where I warmed up mac and cheese and we settled on the sofa and ate it together. I watched him eat, looked at him as if for the first time, for he had grown so much in the last year. He would be six in the spring, and next year he would have to start first grade, although God knew where. This school was only a preschool. Most of the children there went on to Modern Orthodox day schools. But I couldn't possibly live out this lie much longer. I was hoping that by the time we reached that point, I would have a civil divorce and Isaac could attend any school he liked. Of course, I'd have to get him in, and without money, how would that work? Off I went again, thinking in panicky circles that led nowhere, that simply closed in on themselves until they became little imploding fireworks of despair.

I looked at his silky blond hair, the dimple in his left cheek that I so loved, the big blue eyes that he had gotten from his father, eyes that had made me so happy when he was born, because it was exactly those features I had wanted him to inherit from the man chosen for me, the all-American coloring that would perhaps guarantee him more ease in his own skin than I would ever have in mine. I knew Isaac would be my only child. I would never get to a point in my life where I felt safe enough to take on this wholesale responsibility for another human being. It occurred to me in that moment that because I was young and had already given birth, I would be an ideal candidate for egg donation, something that had often been advertised at the Sarah Lawrence campus, college-educated young women being especially valuable products in the portfolio of any private fertility clinic. My intelligence had been assessed, my fertility had been proven, and perhaps my Jewishness could even prove valuable in this case. I knew that most rabbis had decreed that a child born from egg donation would be seen as Jewish only if both the carrier and the donor could prove their Jewish ancestry.

Yes, it was an abject bodily exploitation, an invasive procedure that would have both physical and psychological effects, but unlike the other forms of exploitation available to me it was both fully legal and well paid. Not regulated, but not forbidden either. And did I have any other choice? I could not afford to wait for miracles any longer, to live in that airless limbo. I was tired of constantly being forced to walk up to the edge of that cliff, of having my limits tested to the extreme. There would be no miracles. This time, when I conjured up the money I needed to keep going, it would not be God acting through me. It would be my body producing sustenance, in the most corporeal way possible.

The great irony in this undertaking lay in the fact that although I would offer my body up for utilization, it would for the first time in my life be my own decision to do so, and therefore it was also doubly sad, for this was one of the reasons I had left after all, to free my body as much as my mind, and I had not thought to find myself in such a situation, where once again I would have to offer up my physical self for inspection and use by others. Yet my resolve was fierce, and with it a small sense of that previous satisfaction returned, for I knew in that moment that I had the reins in my grip again, and with it the knowledge that I would always be ready to do whatever it took to maintain that grip.

———

I visited the clinic on Fifth Avenue the next morning. I sat among older, well-heeled women, my cheeks red because I knew how obvious it looked, me among them, and I was mortified by the unspoken yet acknowledged public display of my poverty and desperation. And yet, I admit I was surprised that every woman in that room, coming from privilege and the education that usually comes with it, had been able to suspend whatever ethical principles they might have had for the chance to have a baby. I could not ignore the different tone and cadence in the voices of the doctors and nurses who interacted with me when I compared it to the way they spoke to those slim, smooth-browed women. When I left the office, after having taken all the requisite tests and left the vials of blood and bodily fluids with the nurse, I stepped out into the windswept street as if into a different world. Now it was clear that there were two layers in this world, the upper and the lower, and the latter only existed to be utilized by the former. My body was my last resource, and once again, even in this new life, I longed to be outside it.

Later, when I was living in Germany and mentioned having donated my eggs, my revelation was met with the shock Americans might have exhibited had I spoken about prostituting myself. Yet while prostitution was a legitimate vocation in most European countries, it was paid egg donation that was illegal. It was as if things were the other way around, as if I had betrayed myself more abjectly than I could have imagined. Had I not comforted myself by saying at least it wasn't prostitution? Later, dealing with the medical aftereffects, I could no longer see clearly which was the truly lesser of the two evils. After all, I had known so many women in New York who had prostituted themselves informally, through nebulous underground networks, for extra cash or nice clothes—basically an easier lifestyle. And many more had done so just to survive. It wasn't that radical. It was practically part of the culture. Was my decision to donate my eggs a part of that generally exploitative culture as well?

The syringes filled with hormones arrived via special refrigerated delivery, along with detailed instructions. The period of injections would last two weeks, at the end of which I would have to administer a special trigger shot, and forty-eight hours later the aspiration procedure would occur. The manual explained that I should pinch a fold of skin in my stomach and keep it pinched until the entire vial had been injected. I should expect bruising to develop at the site; should this make future injections painful, I should just choose another location on my abdomen. I was warned that if I developed any symptoms, such as abdominal pain, bleeding, and so on, that I should call the clinic directly, but go straight to the hospital if this happened after clinic hours. The guide did not explain the origin of such symptoms, or their likelihood.

I looked at the long thin needles and was surprised at how they failed to elicit the anxiety that injections had always sparked in me. When had I become this person who had abandoned all her old fears as if they were luxuries she could no longer afford? The first injection went in fine; I didn't really feel much of the needle itself with the flap of skin squeezed so tightly between my fingers, but the cold fluid oozing underneath my skin was painful; I had to go slowly, pushing it in drop by drop until the vial was empty. But I felt relatively normal that day, as well as the next; it was perhaps only on the fourth afternoon that I began to notice a vague sensation of swelling in my pelvis. Even then, I told myself that the process really wasn't half as bad as I expected, and perhaps it was after all a very small sacrifice to make for such a generous paycheck. A few days later the vague swollen feeling had turned into an unmistakable heaviness, as if I was carrying small rocks in my abdomen. By day ten the rocks were big and hard; their weight pulled me forward so that it was hard to stand up straight. In my reports to the clinic I described this sensation but was told it was normal, a result of the ovaries filling with follicles. "Normally, human ovaries never reach a size larger than that of a walnut within a woman's lifetime. Yours are now expected to grow to the size of, say, an orange." I shuddered at the image, and the telephone slipped from between my clammy hands. If ovaries could never naturally reach the size of an orange, wasn't it safe to assume that they probably shouldn't?

That night I was awoken by a sharp pain in my pelvis. I tossed and turned but it did not go away, only growing more insistent with each change of position. I knew the instructions said to go to the hospital, but I did not want to leave Isaac alone, so I called a friend who I knew would be woken by a vibrating cell phone and explained that it was an emergency, could she come and watch him? I didn't offer any details, but twenty minutes later she was at the door, at which point I was dressed and ready to hobble the few streets over to Mount Sinai's emergency room.

Once there I tried to explain about the egg donation and how I had been instructed to go to the hospital if I exhibited these symptoms, but I quickly noticed that the nurses in charge of the intake were nonplussed, as if they had never handled this scenario before or been prepared to do so. They called for a doctor, and I discerned from his aimless questions that he too had never had a case like this, that is, never treated an egg donor, and was completely uncertain as to the protocol. He went to look something up and came back to tell me I might have OHSS, that is, ovarian hyperstimulation syndrome, and that although this was an identified syndrome, not much was known about how or why it occurred, or what the short- and long-term consequences of it might be, and that the most important thing was to rule out ovarian torsion, so he would be ordering an ultrasound. As he said this to me, I got the distinct impression from his curt tone and dismissive body language that he saw me as a student who had taken a silly risk for some spending money. He didn't imagine that there could be deeper reasons for such a decision.

In the ultrasound room the technician kneaded away on my pelvis and acted similarly confused when he finally realized that those grapefruit-size spheres were my ovaries, remarking that he had never been in this circumstance and couldn't recommend what should be done, but that something like this could not possibly be beneficial for my body. I detected the fine layer of judgment in his voice, but I was still concentrating on the word "grapefruit." Hadn't the woman said orange? Wasn't a grapefruit bigger than an orange? They sent me home in the morning and told me to call the clinic, as they had more experience with such matters. The doctor didn't think torsion was an immediate threat but couldn't be sure.

At the clinic they gave me an appointment right away, and we ran through another ultrasound on their fancy, expensive machine. The doctor said not to worry; everything was fine: I was doing great and producing lots of eggs. In fact we could go ahead and do the trigger shot already and schedule the aspiration. I was relieved to hear this, as I couldn't imagine how it might feel if my ovaries got any bigger than they were now. After the aspiration they would surely go back to their normal size and everything would be as it was before. I was anxious to get the procedure over with and move on. I thought I would simply forget it ever happened and all would be okay again. At the sight of my paycheck, everything would be worth it, I imagined.

On the day of the procedure I took Isaac to school, after which I was picked up by one of those chauffeured town cars that normally patrolled the wealthier avenues. I was driven to a private surgery, where an anesthesiologist first injected fentanyl to create the initial relaxed and sleepy state, then created a port for the anesthesia that would put me to sleep during the process. I was escorted to the gynecological table and instructed to count backward from ten. I felt the anesthetic burn a trail up my arm but I only managed to count to three before falling into the darkness.

When I awoke I was lying in the recovery room, and the first thing I noticed was the euphoria, that incredible, incomparable, indescribable feeling of absolute, groundless well-being that is apparently common during the period when fentanyl slowly leaves your system. The nurse came over to ask if I'd like anything to eat or drink, as I'd had to fast before the procedure, and I gazed at her as if she was a guardian angel.

"You did really great," she said with a smile. "I think they got about six dozen out of you, if not more."

I smiled and thanked her as if it was a compliment. It was only later, when I was home in bed huddled in a ball with the most painful cramps I had ever experienced (I told Isaac I had a bad stomachache) that it occurred to me that six dozen was an inordinately large sum. Hadn't they told me they would try to produce around six in each ovary for a total of twelve? Of course my ovaries had been the size of grapefruits! Of course I had been "hyperstimulated"! I suddenly deduced that I had been intentionally overdosed.

Horrified, I started researching this online, reading reports on forums from women who had been through similar experiences. I learned that this was an unfortunate yet common deception in the industry, and since egg donation was not yet regulated in the States, it was technically not illegal to mess with the hormone dosages. Some survivors had started a group and were petitioning Congress to establish clear rules for the procedure so that donors were more protected, but as of now, we were guinea pigs to be experimented with on a whim, and no thought had been expended as to the consequences. A few years later I would read the articles of the former donors with ovarian cancer who were fighting for research into the link, but even then no regulation would have been instituted.

The clinic was so pleased with the results that when I arrived to pick up my check for ten thousand dollars they asked me if I would consider donating again in two months. "No!" I said, my tone conveying a horrified reaction.

"But why?" the doctor asked, seeming honestly surprised. "The procedure went so well, and you clearly have excellent fertility."

"You overstimulated me!" I said. "I produced that much because you gave me too high a dose of hormones. How can I trust you with my health when you would do something like that, just to create more funds? I'm still a human being; I'm not a machine you can optimize to get better results."

"Well, I . . ." she sputtered. "I don't think . . . I mean . . . we gave you the standard dose for a woman your age. After all, you had your child at nineteen, but you are twenty-five now. Your fertility changes a lot during these intervening years. We had to assume that you weren't as fertile now as you were then . . . It's not an exact science yet, you know. But if you donated again, we could adjust the dose, now that we know . . ."

"I will never donate again," I said, my voice steely. "And I will certainly never recommend it to anyone else."

Perhaps standing up for myself was supposed to bring me some vindication, but it didn't. In the end, they had gotten what they wanted from me. All I had to show for it was the check. I looked at it now, standing on the pavement in front of the imposing office building in midtown: a one with four zeros behind it. Now I understood why egg donation paid this much. They weren't just buying your eggs. There were buying your life.

I would suffer from inordinately painful, erratic cycles for years following the aspiration, from the sporadic throbbing of twisted ovarian ligaments that would disable me for days if not weeks. My body would never be the same again, as multiple doctors in Europe would later confirm. But although the shocked looks on their faces would remind me of the humiliation and debasement I had been forced to stoop to, simultaneously it would bring with it the reminder that I had been willing to suffer and sacrifice in order to survive, in order for my son to continue to blossom in his new life without being hindered or sabotaged by my failure to sustain him. The shame would always be mixed with a kind of perverse pride, and for a long time I didn't even try to explain, because I was convinced that nobody could possibly understand the complexity of my circumstances or emotions. Perhaps this still is the case, although now I do discuss it occasionally, because I've reached understanding on my own, and it turns out that is enough.

God is like a crutch that you lay down only to discover that your legs had been functioning just fine all along. I was determined to try to stop seeing the world through some mystical lens, convinced that I would be best served in the future by clear sight, no matter how few comforts this might seem to offer.

On the morning of December 25 I got into my car to take a rare drive around the city. I was not expecting the postapocalyptic landscape I encountered as I zoomed down the FDR Drive. I did not spot a single car on the highway, or a single moving boat on the East River. Up the West Side Highway it was the same. A trip that would normally take me more than an hour took twenty minutes. Winding through the narrow streets of Soho, usually packed with chic shoppers, I saw only gray shuttered storefronts and metal trash cans tossed wildly about by the wind.

The emptiness was chilling in a city like Manhattan, which I had only ever experienced as wildly, permanently frenzied. It underscored, intensely, how out of place I was in this world, because it showed me quite concretely that every other human being had somewhere they belonged right now, and this was the full scope of my aloneness, not simply a rarity, but an alien aberration. In that moment, I felt that my very self was an empty vessel, unmoored and floating in deep space, trapped outside the bounds of life.

In the afternoon I went to pick up Isaac from his father. This time Eli looked at me searchingly and said, "It will be three years soon, since you moved out. You're not coming back, are you?"

I shook my head no, this time knowing that the answer was true, in every fiber of my body, because I had drawn a line between myself and my past simply by enduring the plunges of the last few years. The suffering itself was like a brick wall that barred return.

"So can we get a *get*?" he asked. I supposed he was thinking about remarrying. To do so in the Jewish community he would not actually require a civil divorce, only a religious one. Technically he could also acquire it without my consent, but that process was costly and time-consuming, as it required a *heter meah rabbanim* (literally permission from one hundred rabbis).

"Yes, sure, when the civil divorce comes through I'll go with you to get one." My lawyer had informed me that the *get* was protected in the state of New York and its conditions subject to that of the civil divorce. I myself didn't care about obtaining a religious divorce, since I wasn't planning on staying observant, although he couldn't know that. And it was one factor in the small amount of leverage I had, since it still mattered to him, although I had to wonder, as lately his appearance had been changing. First his beard got shorter and then disappeared completely; then the *payos* were cut shorter and shorter until they were practically invisible little tufts, like sideburns.

"Okay," he said, "we will go to the table and mediate." I was delighted he was willing to skip a court battle.

The lawyer was very happy to hear about the conversation. We had landed in an ideal situation, she said. I had managed to placate the other side, get them to let their guard down. Mediation was the goal, after all. She would prepare papers, send them to his lawyer. There'd be a back-and-forth for a while, but eventually we would reach a compromise.

"I don't want to ask for anything," I said. "Just primary custody."

"But, my dear, you are entitled to a minimum of child support! I don't think any judge will accept a mediation agreement with no child support; it's not even legal."

"Well, his income isn't reported, and I know he doesn't want that dredged up; it's my bargaining chip. I can promise not to cause any trouble for him. And technically a judge can't order a percentage of an income that doesn't exist, right?"

She reluctantly agreed, although she worried that I would later come to regret this decision. Once the agreement was on paper, she said, it would be close to impossible to sue for support later, should, for example, our circumstances change. But I wasn't worried. I had learned that I could rely solely on myself no matter the situation. That was always better than having to depend on someone else, and I was ready to face my future on exactly those terms. I walked home with a spring in my step, feeling that freedom was just around the corner. Who knew? I could be living elsewhere by next summer! I eased into a new and cautious optimism.

———

In February my publisher started sending me on interviews. I received no training beforehand. I was simply instructed to meet up with various people at various places and times. My agent informed me that I was not in a position to be picky, as I should be thrilled with whatever morsels of press interest I could muster. So I didn't feel empowered to ask why I would be giving an interview to the *New York Post*, the trashiest tabloid in the city, nor did I understand that their headlines were echoed in distorted form in other tabloids around the world. I also didn't know how to talk to journalists then. I spoke to them the way I would to a friend and was not prepared for my statements to be presented in convenient, misleading fragments, wholly out of context in order to portray a more newsworthy, salacious image. The way I had always approached any form of authority was still deeply influenced by my childhood; as I had attempted to seduce God with naïve directness, so I approached the lesser gods of journalism with the same faithful intentions.

Overnight I experienced that typical American invasion of "fame," as Baudrillard had put it, that instant and total erasure of anonymity that knocked me completely off-balance and robbed me of any orientation as it trampled over me and in doing so ripped the layers of my personality off with it, leaving my brutally skinned self raw and throbbing underneath. My ability to determine my sense of self was gone; I now existed solely within a publicly imposed framework and was subject to its dictates. During this time of my life I would learn that fame can represent the greatest loss of freedom of all. Had I not already had the experience of living in a world where everyone seemed to know better than I who I was? Yet none of the limitations I had experienced prior felt like they could compare to this all-encompassing psychological net in which I was now hopelessly tangled like a fisherman's squirming catch, held up to the scrutiny of connoisseurs before ending up on some communal dinner plate.

But that *New York Post* interview, although humiliating to read, unleashed a wave of attention that crested even before the official date of the book's publication. Barbara Walters, also a Sarah Lawrence alumna, called to invite me on her nationally syndicated talk show *The View*, a show that my editors at Simon & Schuster informed me was watched by more than twelve million people, and my editor's voice quivered with excitement as she relayed this information to me on the phone. The situation had changed drastically in the last week; suddenly my book was no longer niche, but clearly capable of appealing to a wide audience. My publishers were practically beside themselves with excitement and nervous shock. After all, we did not have enough books printed to meet that kind of demand. Although an order had been placed in response to the flurry of preorders reported after the *Post* interview appeared, it would not be ready for another few weeks, and even that sum would not be enough to meet the kind of demand that followed an interview such as this one.

On the morning of the official publication day, the day I was scheduled to appear on the show, my lawyer called me.

"I have bad news," she said.

I gripped the phone hard, my knuckles turning white. "What is it?"

"Eli's lawyer called. I think he is religious; I guess he saw the *Post*. He says he will be encouraging his client to pull out of mediation and sue for sole custody. He sounded like that was his idea of just punishment for your behavior. It's ridiculous. I told him he has no chance in a Manhattan court with that kind of position. But if Eli sues, it means we will have to go to court, and it could take years and end up costing you a lot, so even though you could win, it's not something I would advocate. Do you think there's anything you can do to make him back down?"

I took a deep breath and steeled myself. "You can call his lawyer back right now and inform him I'll be on *The View* today at twelve, telling an audience of twelve million about his threat. Ask him if that's what he wants. If he wants me to keep quiet about the custody case, he needs to have the papers we've agreed upon together signed by eleven."

She let out a sigh. "Phew. Okay. I will try that and let you know what happens. Are you sure you are ready to call his bluff?"

My hand hurt from clenching the phone so tightly. "I'm sure."

In the studio a makeup artist worked on my face and hair while I sat nervously in the salon chair, watching my phone. At eleven thirty I was in the green room with the other guests, and still there was no news. I began to mentally formulate an appeal for custody suitable for national television. Only when I had been picked up by the studio attendant to be brought to the side of the stage did my phone finally ring. It was eleven fifty.

"It's signed!" my lawyer screamed into my ear, laughing. "Holy hallelujah, you're getting a divorce!"

I thought I might faint right there on the stage steps. But I handed my phone to the attendant, composed myself, and walked up. I gave the interview I had prepared, as if in a daze.

An hour later my editor called and informed me that we had sold fifty thousand ebooks in one hour. I called my agent to tell her the news.

"How can we have sold so many ebooks?" I asked. "I thought you told me they don't sell as well as real books."

"Well, we don't have any real books. Didn't you know? We sold out almost immediately."

Three days later, the *New York Times* bestseller list had me at number two on the combined print-and-ebook list, solely as a result of ebook sales. I had been getting angry messages from people all over the country who had trekked to bookstores to buy the book only to come up empty, with booksellers unable to even offer a date on which the book might become available. It would take three weeks to restock the shelves again, during which time we continued to sell electronic copies and remain on the bestseller list as a result.

It was a whirlwind that would last for months and then would only partially ebb. Suddenly I was juggling multiple interviews each day. My new recognizability was jarring, not only on a general level, but in the way I was accosted while standing in line for a cup of coffee or sitting with my son on the subway. The frightening thing was that I could never be certain if the person approaching me wanted to praise me or condemn me. When so many people have all these caricatured ideas about you, be they positive or negative, you start losing your grip on your own carefully cultivated sense of self, and instead you begin to glimpse yourself only in the mirror of their projections. Soon I was receiving threats of harm from members of my community; someone forwarded me a conversation in

Yiddish about whether it was permissible according to *halacha* (Jewish law) to kill me in the name of God. Uncles and cousins I had only had minimal contact with as a child suddenly wrote me letters inciting me to kill myself. I stopped being able to eat or sleep. I needed, more than ever, to finally get away from New York.

Soon it would be possible, for there was money in my bank account now. Enough for a long time. My life had changed overnight, only the new version was not necessarily more attractive than the old one. I was invited to exclusive parties and posh locations; I found myself surrounded by important and famous people and a crowd of underlings and would-have-beens who worshipped them. Money had legitimized me, and suddenly everyone wanted to be my friend. Although I could not have predicted it, I was more devastated by this new social capital than I had been by my enforced solitude. This social world felt false and dangerous, and I could not, would not believe that this was the other option, that this was the form of consolation others seemed to settle for. Surely there was something better out there, something deeper and more meaningful. I had not forgotten my promise to myself to seek it out. Soon. The divorce had been filed in court; it was a question of weeks before I received the judgment.

Indeed, on the eve of Passover 2012, a holiday I no longer observed but the spirit of which I nonetheless still understood, my lawyer emailed me my signed and stamped judgment. "Now you can get married!" she had written. "Just kidding!"

I was free. I was truly free. On the eve of a holiday that celebrated the liberation of the Jewish people, one Jewish woman had been declared liberated. Now there was nothing standing in the way of me and my future.

Well, nothing except the standard requirement that I live within an approximately two-hour radius of my ex-husband's stated address, as Isaac's father still had his usual visitation rights, as before. We had meticulously agreed to weekends and vacations, and that Isaac should not have to face an arduous commute between the two of us.

Nonetheless I would take what I could get. I drew a circle on the map, with Eli's home at the center, and looked at all the possible locations within the two-hour limit in every direction. To the southwest there was New Jersey, a state I was familiar with and had no desire to live in, full as it was with Orthodox Jewish communities where I would be easily recognized. Up north were the Catskill Mountains, where I had spent my summers as a child and to which Hasidic Jews flocked in the hotter months; I remembered my time in the boggy summer camps, flies swirling in tornado-like clusters over puddles that never evaporated in the wet and humid heat. In the southeasterly direction there was Brooklyn, full of hipsters and artists now, but also the place from whence I had come, and I could not bring myself to go back. And directly east lay Westchester County, that rich enclave where I had attended university; that could hardly be an improvement on Manhattan. I traced my finger farther up, northeast past Westchester and Duchess Counties, cutting diagonally across the Hudson Valley up to the Appalachian ridge, the old mountain range flattened and softened by time, and stopped at a little triangle of country on the borders of Massachusetts, New York, and Connecticut. It lay at the very edge of my permissible radius, nestled at the foot of the Berkshire Mountains. I knew this place; in fact, I had been there once before, on a brief visit to one of my only college

friends, Lauren—well, actually, to her parents, who were lawyers in New York, Jewish in name only, and kept a house in the
woods to escape to on weekends and vacations.

I remembered Lauren's family quite distinctly, for I had asked
her father what caused him to identify as Jewish, since he didn't
seem to observe or practice any of the usual rituals, nor did he
seem to have any connection to Jewish culture. Yet when asked,
he insisted he was.

"That's simple," he had answered me. "I guess I've just always known if Hitler were to come around, he'd be knocking
on my door too." That was enough for him, and enough for
most of the Jews I had encountered since then, just a basic
knowledge that what was binding them all together was this
shared hypothetical vulnerability, this giant what-if. It was the
ultimate equalizer, the thread that could bind someone like me
with someone like his daughter, despite the differences in class,
income, and education.

I now recalled their sixties split-level on the peak of a thickly
wooded hill, the way the front of the house was in the perpetual shade of the birch forest, while the rear with its wraparound
veranda boasted sweeping views of the valleys toward the west.
On particularly clear days, the Catskills appeared like thick
smears of bluish paint on the distant horizon. I recalled that
fleeting trip to the area, and my longer visit to Justine's house
in California, and since it was clear that my choices still were
relatively limited and likely to remain so, why shouldn't I at
the very least take a drastic step and leave civilization behind
me? I could find a cheap year-round rental in the northwestern
corner of Connecticut. I would have my peace and quiet, and

Isaac would go to a great school. He only had one month left at preschool; one more month in Manhattan, and then it was good-bye and good riddance.

I went with Eli to the Beth Din of America to perform the *get* ceremony as promised. When we arrived, I was surprised to discover that the *sofer*, the scribe, was Hasidic. I realized then that among the Modern Orthodox there was clearly no one qualified to serve in that role; the Hebrew script required to make religious documents official and binding was a complex calligraphy that took decades to learn. Should a mistake be made, I knew, the scribe would have to start from the beginning.

The *sofer* asked me for my maiden name, and when I gave it, he nodded his head sagely. "I'm from Williamsburg too," he said in Yiddish, speaking over the head of the court officiant, or *rav*, who wore a small, inconspicuous yarmulke but clearly did not understand a word we were saying. "You were married to this guy?" the scribe inquired with raised eyebrows, looking at my uncovered hair and jeans and then at Eli's large black kippah. "I can't believe it. A girl from Williamsburg?"

The *rav* interrupted him, reminding him that we only had thirty minutes to complete the process before the next appointment. The scribe bent over his work, scribbling furiously as the *rav* dictated the details. We were required to confirm our identities; this entailed giving our full Hebrew names as well as those of our parents. The rest was communicated in Hebrew between the *rav* and Eli, while I stood off to the side and waited to play my small role in the process. When the documents had been completed, the *rav* folded them and presented them to Eli, instructing him to repeat the words he was saying. I then had to hold out my hands while Eli dropped the *get* into them, saying to me in Hebrew, "I now pronounce you free for any other man."

I bristled at those words and laughed sarcastically. "Now walk away," the *rav* instructed sternly, pointing to me. I took a few steps backward. "Now bring the *get* to me." I placed it on his desk.

"You can go," the *rav* announced, waving us away with nary a glance in our direction. "You'll each get confirmation proof in the mail." And that was that.

Eli moved to shake my hand once we were in front of the building. "Did you forget?" I asked. "We're divorced now; we can't touch." He chuckled uncomfortably and put his hand in his pocket, instead nodding to me. We said our awkward good-byes and parted ways, he walking up Broadway toward Penn Station to catch the train out of the city, and I walking south to the subway. The marriage was now over in all respects. Perhaps this was the beginning of something for both of us. I hoped he would find happiness too, I thought, for I understood that anything I achieved in my life could be seen as coming at his expense in some way, and the only way for me to feel truly free, in the sense of mental and emotional ties, was to know that he too had moved on and found his own path.

———

It didn't take long for me to find a house in Salisbury, Connecticut. I chose an old converted barn situated on one of the many lakes in the area, ringed with wilderness.

I made an appointment at the small private school in the area so that Isaac could interview for a chance to attend first grade there. In June I drove upstate with him, and it was evident that he too relaxed as soon as we arrived in the calmer countryside. At the interview I had to let him see the principal alone. After it was finished, she told me that everything seemed fine and that Isaac would be welcome to attend, but there was one strange thing. Apparently he had been forced to learn to write with his right hand, even though he was clearly left-handed. As a result he had developed a less-than-productive and improper approach to penmanship, which would have to be corrected by slowly training him to return to his lefty instincts, as well as teaching him the left-handed technique. It was important, the principal impressed upon me, that Isaac use the summer to practice as much as possible, so that he would be on the same level as the other children when he started school.

Left-handedness had always been viewed with suspicion in our community; I remember my grandfather saying, "A Jew does everything with his right hand." In all the laws that governed our daily life, from how we washed our hands to how we tied our shoes, everything began with the right hand. This had powerful spiritual significance; left-side orientation was associated with the devil.

Of course, I had not dreamed that such practices would also be instituted in Modern Orthodox schools, certainly not to the extent that a left-handed child would be forced to write with the right. After all, it was nothing but a silly superstition. I felt so relieved that Isaac would be attending elementary school in an environment free of such arbitrary stupidities. He was about to have the education I had always dreamed of. The school was a charming gabled country house on an enormous sunny meadow; it even had its own golden retriever, who greeted each child with a paw shake every morning. It was small and cozy and everything that Manhattan was not.

While Isaac went to his father for his share of the summer vacation, I prepared for the move, closing out my current rental contract and signing the new one, packing up the few things I owned and acquiring the things I did not, and by August I was settled, just in time to pick up Isaac and show him his new home.

It was a glorious month. Isaac, then six years old, swam in the lake that abutted our property every day. We lay on the dock and peered over the edge to see the sunfish and perch sheltering beneath. He collected snail shells; he tried to skip rocks but rarely succeeded; he spied on rabbits making short work of leafy plants. Every evening the sun would set in magnificent colors over the water, the lake would seem stiller somehow, and the world would get very quiet. I watched, pretzel-legged on the grass, as the last of the pink glow faded and the crickets assumed their nightly routine. The madness of Manhattan seemed very far away.

I was finally living life actively, I thought, the way I had dreamed, and I knew just how lucky I was, but in some ways my brain was still stuck in the past. I was having bad dreams every night, waking up each morning enveloped by feelings of dread, and I panicked secretly when in groups or crowded spaces. None of this was consistent with the calm and fulfilling existence I had begun living. When I finally went to a psychiatrist that fall, to receive a formal diagnosis on the list of mental illnesses I was so sure I suffered from, the verdict of posttraumatic stress disorder seemed almost anticlimactic. The Hasidic sect I grew up in was a community living with a pooled inheritance of residual trauma. Although I was reminded of that every time I thought to feel resentful or deprived, I came away from childhood with the knowledge that nothing would ever be as bad as it could really get. I learned that even at my lowest point, I could still have a lot. At the very core of my character, underneath the self-doubt that came later, is the legacy I inherited from the people who raised me. As sure as if it were etched in stone, I know I am a survivor. This is the primary identity I inherited from my war-ravaged grandparents, from my ancestors who survived centuries of persecution in Europe, from my people who wandered in exile for millennia. This is how I think of myself, first and foremost. Yet how was I to access that reserve of strength? How was I to be more than just a survivor and learn to actually live? I wanted desperately to enter the next phase, the space beyond survival, but I felt stuck, as if survival was the only mode in which I was capable of functioning.

The fact that I failed to find contentment at that point in my life was a source of great shame and anxiety for me. I thought to myself one night as I lay awake yet again at three a.m. that I had always felt that niggling fear that my birth was a mistake, like a computer glitch that left me permanently disconnected, with no ability to form real and lasting connections. The system that everyone else used had always seemed unreachable, but perhaps, instead of bringing me closer, leaving had rendered that system permanently out of reach.

I remembered one of the articles the *New York Post* had printed about me, when the scandal around my book had erupted, in which members of my family had been interviewed. My uncle, the same one who regularly sent me poorly spelled death threats and insults, said to the reporter that, in essence, all of this had always been my problem, because I had simply "lacked happiness." This, despite all my family had done for me, he said. They had arranged a marriage to a good man, he said, spent thousands on a wedding. Clearly I was abnormal if, even after all that, I lacked happiness. Certainly this attack was less vicious than the ones my uncle lobbed at me in assumed privacy. Phrases like "ugly horse-face" should have stung more, but it was the "lacked happiness" comment that had eventually led me to my first real therapist; it had hit that deep and sensitive nerve in me that had always throbbed with the fear that in some undeniable way I was marked for unhappiness from the beginning.

If only I could understand why. Although I lived in a nice house surrounded by beautiful nature, and Isaac was as happy as I could have ever imagined in his new school, and we finally had financial security, my body still quivered with the same fear as before, as if any moment now all of this would prove a dream. My days became efforts in distracting myself.

My first friend while I lived in New England was Richard. He had just moved into his new studio when I met him in the early autumn of 2012. Tall and slender, with red hair, freckled skin, and a high forehead, he wore linen pants, aviator sunglasses, and wide-brimmed straw hats. He was a contemporary figurative artist, he told me; the work that hung on the walls of his atelier seemed to have been transported from some mysterious and magical castle. A crucified man, a baby suspended in a cold fireplace, a woman drowning in a bathtub, smoke rising from candles that had just been extinguished.

Richard and I had something in common; we had both left something behind us, for he had grown up dirt-poor in a trailer park in Georgia and had reinvented himself over the years into this elegant, well-read painter veiled in the mystique of having recently returned from Europe. He had nourished himself, like me, by reaching for the realms of poetry and literature. But even now, in this new incarnation with its impressive résumé, he felt mismatched, he explained, when he contrasted his work with the mainstream values of the art world. I had read Émile Durkheim recently, and the word "anomie" came to mind immediately when he said this. Perhaps I impressed him with this knowledge, with my recently acquired ability to drop words like that, for it was the beginning of a close and unusual friendship. Both of us had broken irreparably from something and were in pursuit of some kind of true self, but instead we both felt farther than ever from this goal. We comforted each other in our shared state of exile and alienation, made tangible by the fact that although both of us had finally become financially independent artists, neither of us could compare our lifestyles with the extravagant opulence that lay all around us, in this rarefied region where our neighbors were Kevin Bacon and Meryl Streep.

What was wonderful during that time, a truly blissful distraction, was being able to learn more about the art world, about which I was insatiably curious. Richard was my particular escape at that time; a non-Jew hampered only by a past steeped in poverty, he had scrambled his way up the social ladder and had experienced access to the very top rungs, which I knew by then were not necessarily defined by money but by a kind of access to deeper, more valuable riches that took a lifetime to attain. I could not reinvent myself the way he had, for even if I changed the way I spoke or the way I dressed, I did not have the basic genetic traits required to project the kind of sophisticated waspy eccentricity that he did. I would always be seen as a Jew trying to camouflage myself.

Although this divide existed between us, and in our own

way, we were each aware of it, our commonalities seemed to supersede it, and over time I began to see him as a brother, if not in blood then in spirit. I spent hours sitting on the sun-warmed wooden floors of his studio, leafing through the thick, glossy pages of his many art books, marveling at the high-quality prints, while he sat at his easel and dabbed light onto dark canvases. I was introduced to the full oeuvre of Rembrandt, Vermeer, and Hammershøi, but also names I did not know, as diverse as Eugène Carrière, Gabriël Metsu, Andrew Wyeth, and Caspar David Friedrich. As he worked with a practiced hand at a sketch, he told me about Klimt and Schiele, about Rodin and his mistress Camille Claudel, about Renoir and his muses. He had learned everything there was to know about the history of art, and I soaked up his stored knowledge. He talked about his time spent studying at the New York Academy of Art, which he had attended on scholarship, and immediately I recognized the phenomenon he described, of being patronized as the poor, uneducated student, tolerated only in name, to preserve the image of the arts as accessible to all. His attempts at creating something outside that acceptable frame were ridiculed at best, rebutted at worst. After a period of frustration, he had written a letter to a controversial Norwegian painter named Odd Nerdrum, known for bucking contemporary art values in a similar fashion, asking if he could study with him. To Richard's surprise, Odd had accepted him as a student.

Richard showed me Odd's work then, and it surprised me that the techniques I had just learned about, characteristic of the Dutch Golden Age and Flemish Baroque, could still be used by a living artist and not seem derivative or recycled. The images in those paintings, despite the way they were created with lush layers of thick oil paint, looked nothing so much as futuristic and primeval to me at the same time. It was as if a caveman had collaborated with a painter from an unknown era still to come. I listened to Richard tell me stories of his adventures at Odd's with a touch of jealousy, although it was still wonderful to live vicariously through him. He used his unparalleled photographic recall and his gift for visual description not only in his paintings, but also in the way he told stories, waxing eloquent about people and places in the way I had become accustomed to experiencing solely in nineteenth-century literature.

He told me about taking that trip to go study with Odd, how it had been his first time out of the country and how overwhelmed and ignorant he had felt at the beginning. But once installed at Odd's giant house in France, with its tremendous fireplaces and French doors—details I could actually envision because he had integrated them into his many paintings—he had realized that there was a whole community of people already there who felt exactly the way he did, in the sense that their aesthetic ideals did not match up with what was accepted in society. Odd had called it the Kitsch movement; it was supposed to be some kind of protest against postmodern art philosophy in that it embodied an aesthetically humanist position in what Odd saw as an anti-humanist technological society. Artists who were acutely sensitive to this experience were drawn to Odd and his ideas, finding a home among people who similarly identified as pariahs in the art world.

As I looked at the various works produced by Richard and his peers, I recognized the experience of marginalization and alienation as strong themes, and I was touched in a way I had not previously experienced in my visits to contemporary art museums. This kind of new old art reminded me of how I still insisted on filling my bookshelves with the literature of long-dead authors, while each season brought a new cornucopia of contemporary titles that I often had trouble telling apart, as they all seemed to echo one another in style and approach. In many ways I hungered for a past I still felt anchored to, a past in which artists' individual voices were more distinct from one another, braver in their search for the truth, clearer in their depiction of it.

In the end, Richard had become one of Odd's best and most renowned students. The work he produced under Odd's tutelage went on to gain international attention and catapulted him into a world where collectors and art critics fawned over him and galleries competed to display his work. It was a sharp contrast to the tepid reception Richard had experienced in his early days, when his ideas were dismissed because he lacked the credibility of education and parentage. I identified strongly with this reinvention, as I saw it. Both of us had experienced sudden and complete transformations in our lives; I too had burst onto the literary scene completely unprepared and did not quite know what to do with my success.

Richard had stayed with Odd for an unusually long time, traveling with him to his estate in Norway and then back to Paris, and during this time they slowly developed an intense master–student relationship. Odd had then entrusted Richard with his estate in France for three years, during which time Richard had painted furiously. By the time I met him, he was avidly preparing for several exhibitions, all scheduled to take place within a three-month period. He invited me to join him on a trip to his upcoming show in Paris. I had never before considered actually traveling to Europe. It had always felt like a place in a fairy tale, a mythical realm. But I did not hesitate to accept the invitation.

After dropping Isaac off at his dad's for the Passover holiday, I boarded a plane with Richard. I remembered when I had met Eli for the very first time, nearly seven years ago, on the day we got engaged; he had told me about taking a trip to Europe with his father and his many brothers, about how they had traveled across the continent by van, stopping only to visit the grave sites of rabbis strewn across Europe, where they would place stones on the tombs, light candles, and pray. I had been horrified to hear that on a trip like that he had not seen anything but graves. We had talked about going back there ourselves, but that had never happened. I had mistakenly assumed that he shared my desire to see the world, but in the end, he didn't have any interest, and that was what had prevented him from any forays beyond the cemeteries—not the lack of his father's permission.

But it was also true that Eli never understood my obsession with that faraway point of origin, one that every family in our community could be traced back to. For the people who had raised him had been born in America and did not speak of it. Only I had been raised by someone from that first generation, someone who remembered the Old World and the way things were before everything changed. And although my grandmother had always been convinced that there was nothing to go back to, I knew I needed to see that for myself.

I did not know then, when I first emerged into the golden light of the city of Paris, that it would be the first of many trips, that I would develop an unexplainable addiction to this entire continent that would consume me until I finally submitted wholly to its call. I still thought of it as a brief fling then, a romantic affair to be had and then released, with only the rosy memories lingering onward. Even then I looked at the city with hungry eyes, as if I would never see it again.

Every American comes to Paris and feels small, I'm sure of it. We've been taught that the French do everything better than us, and no matter how carefully I'd selected my wardrobe for the trip, or studied up on the gender of French nouns, I knew my Americanness was clear and conspicuous, and I felt inferior. I envied Richard his command of the language, the way the words rippled as they tripped off his tongue, the way he even seemed to have adapted the body language and facial mannerisms of Parisians. I imagined he blended in completely. Years later, after I had been living in Berlin for five years, we would reunite once again at a Paris café. I realized then that his French was rendered nearly incomprehensible by his American drawl, and I marveled at my own grasp of the basics, which seemed to have sunk in as if by osmosis. But by then I would be a European. Now I felt overwhelmed by the weight of this continent, where everything was terribly strange yet somehow exactly right.

We strolled through wide boulevards, Richard tilting his head up toward the sun, his hands tucked casually into the wide pockets of his linen pants, looking for all the world as if he was at home here, while my head ricocheted from side to side as I tried to take in every detail. A part of me felt the most simple, childish thrill when I thought of my younger self and imagined telling her she'd be strolling down the Champs-Élysées one day. Why, she wouldn't have even been able to pronounce the name of the street!

Soon we descended into the cool tunnels of the RER station, where we boarded the commuter train that would take us to Maisons-Laffitte. When we emerged into the downtown area of this famous horse-racing suburb, I recalled it was the place where Hemingway went to gamble in his memoir, *A Moveable Feast.* This town did not look all that different now from how he had described it. Here there were no sidewalks, only unpaved ground; horse's hooves marked the depressions in the grass. Magpies pranced fearlessly in the green, and dandelions grew at the borders of gated estates.

Odd's estate was on a beautiful wide street, from which one could see across the Seine to the hills on the other side. Only his self-portrait, overlaid on a ceramic tile, marked the address—there was no name on the bell. The gates swung open slowly for us, and we walked down a path bordered by lush trees into a small clearing from which the house was finally visible, a grand château with shrubs and trees growing with wild abandon all around.

Inside, the house had been emptied of furniture. In each opulent, high-ceilinged room, Odd's work had been hung; a tour of the entire house yielded a veritable lifetime of achievements. Although Odd was in his atelier in Berlin for the duration of the exhibition and would only be returning tomorrow to organize the transport of the work at the closing of the show, his four children, two sons and two daughters, milled about providing guests with information or a glass of champagne. They were all in their teens, with glowing skin, Scandinavian bone structure, and ethereal blue eyes.

I walked from room to room, my high-heeled footsteps echoing on the stone floor. The work was mesmerizing; up close, its power to transform put all those books I'd leafed through to shame. I had become fascinated with Odd's work too, at this point. In real life, he was essentially exiled from his home country, after being dogged by political accusations of tax fraud. The Kitsch community was convinced this was a ploy to suppress a critical voice. It was clear to me, looking at his paintings, that Odd was certainly different in his worldviews than anyone else I had ever encountered. In one painting, a group of primitive-looking people sat and chewed on the limbs of a human corpse lying nearby, the landscape behind them a stony wasteland against an ashy sky; the implication was of a world too barbarian for ethical rules, or the performance of them, to hold water.

Soon the guests were asked to gather in the main room, where a composer from Avignon named Martin Romberg had prepared a concert for the evening. A cellist and a pianist started to play, and as they reached the high notes, I could hear the return calls of chirping birds in the dusk. Just then, I looked around me at the crowd of people that had gathered, and I realized suddenly, with a lurch in my gut, that the house was full of Aryans, with angular bones and fair coloring, as my grandmother always described. Norwegians, Swedes, Austrians, Germans—of course the people most likely to be interested in Odd's work would be those ethnically related to him. My heart started to race. Was I the only Jew here? I wondered. Had anyone noticed? I fled the house in a panic, trying to slow my breathing in the dim light of the outdoor terrace. What was wrong with me? Why couldn't I just be a person among people? Was it all an illusion, one that had been planted in me, or was it real? I asked myself. And more important, how could I ever know for sure?

We slept in the apartment of one of Richard's patrons, I on a red velvet sofa in a study lined with artwork, he on an air mattress in the living room. The next day we headed to Odd's house again, this time to welcome him back from Berlin. The inner circle had gathered in the kitchen to prepare dinner. Kristoff, the Austrian who showed Odd's work in his Oslo gallery, and Helene, his wife; David, a Kitsch painter from Venice; and some of Odd's more prominent students. Bork, Odd's eldest son, milled about in an expensive-looking suit. I was not much use in the crowded kitchen, so I made my way into the grand sitting room, where my favorite of Odd's pieces was hung: *Volunteer in Void*, a figure suspended in a mythical galaxy. As I perched on the edge of a trunk, contemplating the large work, Aftur, Odd's only brunette daughter, entered the room.

She approached me and in halting English asked, "It is true that you are Jew?"

I froze. I felt at once accused and singled out, but also as if a small and delicate bird had accidentally landed on my finger and I must not scare it away. "How did you know?"

"Um, because of your nose?" Aftur said innocently, asking if she got it right.

"Who told you that Jews have noses like mine?"

"My father. My siblings always called me the Jew, because I have brown hair."

Aftur looked like Liesl from *The Sound of Music*, with straight-edge razor-sharp cheekbones, a delicate jaw, and piercing blue eyes. Her teeth shone like pearls in two neat rows when she smiled, a dimple just barely emerging from one hollow cheek.

"You don't look Jewish to me at all," I said, laughing. "So take comfort in my expert opinion."

"My father is one-eighth Jewish," Bork informed me, joining the conversation suddenly. Trembling with excitement as he spoke, he told me that when he was in school, his peers often called him a "fucking Jew." He said this to me as if to equate his experience with mine, as if it was the common ground we shared.

"Yes," his younger brother, Øde, chimed in, "and then they tell us to get gassed." He said this rather chummily, as if we had all been through some charming rite of initiation and now belonged to some special, exclusive club.

Myndin, the youngest daughter, all platinum blond tresses and translucent complexion, piped in as well, asking, "Is it true you grew up Orthodox?"

"Yes," I answered once again.

"I saw a movie about that," she said eagerly.

"Oh really? Which one?"

"*Witness.*" And she smiled, as content as a cat waiting to be petted.

I explained the difference between Jews and the Amish, in slow, deliberate English so that Myndin would understand. The situation devolved into a barrage of questions about Hasidic Jews from all of Odd's children. In the middle of it all, Odd and his wife, Turid, arrived; I heard them clattering into the front hall. Soon, Turid was standing at the edge of the circle, listening, asking questions. Odd barreled in and out of the room at intervals, his dramatic, Harry Potter–like robes gathering the dust on the floor. "I hear you are quite the rebel," he said as we were introduced. "You are the wandering Jew!" He lifted his fist as if to demonstrate some icon, like the Statue of Liberty.

I remembered the Norwegian family we had met at Richard's gallery. The daughter was a painter studying with Odd; the grandmother had once been a very successful artist in her own right, she told me, but had retired. She had reached out to caress my face, and I had flinched slightly at the invasion, although I didn't draw away, perhaps because I had been taught as a child to endure many cheek pinches from elderly women.

"You are a Jew?" she had asked then, in an almost adoring manner.

I had chuckled uncomfortably and drawn away from her hand. "How can you tell?" I had asked sarcastically.

"You have such a beautiful Jewish face," she'd said. "When I was a child, I had a Jewish friend, but we had to smuggle her over the border during the war and I never saw her again." Her eyes glazed over as if she was remembering something distant yet burdensome.

These episodes would be the first of many I was to encounter during my visits to Europe. It struck me then as strange that this fetishizing of my Jewishness felt no different when it was ostensibly positive than when it came in the form of ignorance and anti-Semitism. Everyone wanted to define me by my Jewishness, while I struggled to define myself outside of it. Each time I thought I had arrived at a consensus, someone would come along with a comment like that, and I would lose my carefully constructed balance. It was a precarious identity at best, this one that I was building.

Later the next day I found myself in a café by the Arc de Triomphe, gazing at the enormous empress trees leading up to the Place Charles de Gaulle, which were in resplendent pinkish-purple blossom. As I finished my *café sans lait*, I felt a lump in my throat, remembering how my grandmother thrilled to the blossoming trees each spring, calling out their names as we passed them, explaining to me what made each species unique and special. Cedar was prized for its aromatic wood, acacia for its delicate yet strong leaves. An occasional linden tree would remind her of Europe. How she would have loved Paris, I thought. How sad that she never got a chance to visit.

When I was a child, I had watched my grandmother light the traditional Jewish *yahrzeit* candle every morning on the same table, where it would burn for twenty-four hours, until the next one was lit. It was a grieving custom, but in this case the expression of it was subversive. It was not permissible to mourn relatives who had passed so long ago—Jewish law limited the mourning period to a maximum of one year. After that it was considered imperative that the grieving move on; after all, one had to accept God's will. But my grandmother never stopped lighting those candles, and although she claimed that they were for this one or that one, I knew that the one flame represented the souls of her entire family, from her two-year-old baby sister to her seventeen-year-old brother, all of whom had been gassed in Auschwitz.

I looked up at the blossoming trees, the petals luminous in the sunlight, and asked myself, would my grandmother have even wanted to visit Paris? No matter how eloquently and nostalgically she talked about Europe, not once did I hear her express a desire to revisit. Was it all burnt landscape for her, a wasteland of murdered souls and spilled blood? Or did she feel rejected by Europe, in the sense that it had spit her out and sent her to America, refusing to recognize her birth as legitimate?

Either way, here I was, struggling with a portion of what she must have struggled with, feeling at once rejecting, rejected, and at home. It was a dizzying emotional cocktail, and I felt that something had been stirred within me.

4

WURZELN

װארצלען

ROOTS

Four months later I found myself in Paris again, having dinner with a young opera singer who wore a silver Star of David around her neck. I had met Milena through a group of Yiddishists in New York. Jewish herself, with a Moroccan father whose family had been rescued by Berbers during the war, and a Polish Ashkenazi mother also raised by survivors, she was conscious of the past without having any direct access to it, and had studied Yiddish as a way to connect to her heritage. Now she was preparing a performance of old Yiddish melodies and needed help with their reconstruction; hearing that I would be in Paris, she asked if I wouldn't mind singing them into a recorder for her.

The day after I arrived was the first night of Rosh Hashanah, and Milena took me to a Masorti synagogue (Masorti being the European equivalent of Conservative Judaism) for evening prayers. The rabbi was an Alsatian Jew, it was necessary for her to explain, because he, along with his wife and children, had a shock of platinum blond hair and pale blue eyes that I had never before seen in a Jewish community. They looked like a family of Scandinavian supermodels, not Jews. Meanwhile, some of the other attendees were of Moroccan ancestry, and the congregation alternated between operatic Ashkenazi prayer intonations and warbly melodies evocative of the Maghreb.

Milena did not speak English well, and I did not even speak tourist French very well yet, so we mostly communicated in Yiddish. It was my native language, but I had not spoken it since leaving, and pulling it back out from the depths of my memory where I had buried it, thinking it was permanently out of use, felt almost unnatural. But Yiddish was the birth language of the woman who raised her, Milena told me, one she had been studying for three years in private classes. Other Jews desired to be assimilated and indistinguishable from the other Parisians, but Milena didn't care about being indistinguishable, she said. She wanted to know who she really was; she wanted permission to be proud of it.

When the rabbi delivered his sermon in French, Milena leaned over every so often to deliver a summary of his points in whispered Yiddish. The other congregants eyed us curiously. I could tell that Yiddish wasn't spoken much around them. It had once been the language of these people, but it had gone the way of the ghetto, been obliterated from the European map. Only a dozen people were attending the service on that Rosh Hashanah, arguably the most important Jewish holiday of the year. Even the most lax of Jews show up at the temple to pay their respects on this holy day. I surmised that Paris simply didn't have many Jews left, and I wasn't exactly surprised, as I had always expected Paris to be a city wiped clean of Jewish remnants—in fact, it was something I had anticipated of all of Europe. My beliefs were only being confirmed.

After the service ended, Milena and I rushed to the metro to make it in time for a celebratory holiday dinner hosted at her aunt's garden apartment in the neighborhood of Belleville. We entered the house from the side, through a pair of sliding doors that opened onto a secluded, leafy yard. Inside, we found a brightly lit, noisy room teeming with people. Twenty friends and relatives were there in total, from all over the world. At least six languages were being spoken at once. Food was already being eaten and distributed, and while I noticed the familiar gefilte fish and pomegranate seeds, there were a lot of foods that looked exotic and unfamiliar. One man wore a colorful woven head-dress; others had knit white caps draped over the sides of their heads. Milena sat across from me and introduced me to every-one in French, but I couldn't find anyone to communicate with. The couple next to me was Israeli and spoke only Hebrew; the man on my right was Hungarian and spoke neither English nor Yiddish. Finally, a young woman across from me identified her-self as German, and I attempted to Germanize my Yiddish for the first time, just enough to be understood.

I looked around at the lively group and marveled at how I had believed, based on what I was taught as a child, that there was only one way to be Jewish, that everyone else was just fak-ing it. Even when I had widened my circle to include the Amer-ican Ashkenazi Jewish population at large, I was still faced with the same homogeneous approach to Judaic practice. It had never occurred to me that just over the Atlantic Ocean lay a whole new world of interpretations and traditions.

The next morning, I resolved to visit the old Jewish quarter in Paris. I biked nervously over the Seine, trying to avoid being knocked off the road by street traffic. I had never biked in a city before, yet here I was, biking in Paris! I felt like a girl in an advertisement for a French perfume.

By the time I made my way into the heart of the Marais, wide boulevards had given way to the narrowest streets I had yet encountered in Paris, so that when I looked up, the roofs seemed to cave in toward one another with only a sliver of sky visible above them. On the rue des Rosiers, a short cobble-stoned alley said to have been the original main street of the Jewish quarter, the air was redolent with the smell of fresh falafel. Everywhere I turned, tourists stood holding foil-wrapped pitas, trying not to drip tahini everywhere. After a quick look around, however, it seemed that falafel was the only thing remotely Jewish that the rue des Rosiers had to offer. I bristled: just because there was a Star of David on the store's awning didn't make falafel suddenly Jewish.

I walked my bike over to the center of the street, where it formed a T shape with a longer alley that led out into the rest of the Marais. I passed chic clothing boutiques and quaint bakeries that claimed to sell "Yiddish specialties" like knishes and rugelach. No one inside these bakeries could speak Yiddish or boast of any knowledge about where their goods were pre-pared or whether the recipes had been passed down or simply reinvented by French pastry chefs. Certainly the challah looked nothing like the fluffy braided loaves I had grown up with; they were simply brioche under a different name.

But at the center of the rue des Rosiers stood a small, unas-suming machine, looking almost like one at which you'd buy metro tickets. Its touch screen leaped to life when I put my finger on it. I could choose from a dozen videos, in French with English subtitles, which turned out to be testimonials collected from people who had actually lived on the rue des Rosiers, describing what life was like back when that street was the heart of the Parisian ghetto.

One of the videos featured an older man, identified as a professor now living in the United States, and in the interview he recalled the shame he had once felt when revealing his original address. "It was like saying you had failed to make something of yourself. The rue des Rosiers was a place of stagnation, where only by the pulling up of your own bootstraps could you hope for something better."

He's talking about a ghetto, I thought. I certainly knew of the lost ghettos of Europe and their conditions. Even the Lower East Side of Manhattan had once been a stagnant, stinking ghetto for Jews, the Irish—any poor, oppressed immigrant, really. And then it struck me: Williamsburg was a ghetto. I might have been raised in one of the last ghettos in existence. Although the original ghettos were mandated by society and the government, and Williamsburg had been a self-imposed isolation, the result was the same: a bubble, an invisible wall that effectively divided the lives of those on the inside from those on the outside.

The man in the video seemed both nostalgic and dismissive. He clearly had nothing wonderful to say about the rue des Rosiers as a place to grow up, and yet his voice was tinged with regret at knowing that the place of his birth was gone for good, never to return. It made me wonder what exactly I was mourning, having shown up here expecting something and feeling angry that anything remotely Jewish had disappeared. Did I want to bring the ghetto back? Of course not. But it would have been spectacular to have discovered a world in which, for once, I could find the familiar, could feel instantly at home. It was roots I was looking for, thinking that of all places, the ghettos of Europe would most likely feel like they were a part of me and my past. It would have been comforting as well to see some sort of modern, thriving Jewish life in its place, instead of this cold absence, this hollow commemoration.

I walked onward, toward the end of the street, where I had spotted a sign that read JUDAICA. But the shop was closed, and the posters framed in the window were crude and unflattering portraits of Hasidic Jews sweating and lifting dumbbells, part of a collection titled "Oyrobics." I flushed with shame at the insult, which still felt like it was being made at my expense, although no one could have connected me to those caricatures in the frames.

Then, suddenly, as I was about to bike out of there in a huff, I heard the most incredible sound. It was a *shofar*, loud and steady, coming from the upper stories of one of the buildings nearby. I raced toward the sound, shaking with excitement at the prospect of a real live Rosh Hashanah service in what had once been the Jewish ghetto. Could there still be a Jewish community in the Marais after all? Alas, I couldn't find an entrance to a synagogue anywhere on the street. Bystanders watched me zoom from doorstep to doorstep with bemused curiosity, the hands holding their falafels frozen in front of their mouths as they waited to see what would happen next.

And then I saw a young man, dark-skinned, with thick, curly hair covered by a small kippah, a knapsack weighing down his thin shoulders. "You're Jewish!" I exclaimed triumphantly. "Do you know where that sound is coming from?"

He seemed taken aback by my urgency. In broken English he said, "That's what I'm trying to find out. Wait here and I will ask the falafel salesman."

He emerged from the storefront a few moments later, saying

that he did not know where that particular *shofar* was being blown but that there were apparently two synagogues nearby. *Two whole synagogues?* I found myself following the dark-skinned man down a dimly lit alley and wondering about the likelihood of any situation that involved following a strange man down an alley ending in a happy conclusion. But a second later, there we were, in an archway that led to two doors, one to a Turkish synagogue, the other to an Algerian one. He went right, I went left, and suddenly I was behind a thick velvet curtain, in another world.

I should mention that I had decided to wear red jeans that morning, which, it occurred to me as I was entering, might not have been the smartest fashion choice given the circumstances. However, once inside the small sanctuary, I was relieved to find that all the people attending this service could easily be mistaken for a troupe of models on break between *Vogue* shoots. The women were tan, thin, and lustrously maned; their wrists were bedecked in bangles, their necks draped in silk scarves. The men were equally lovely and well-groomed. But after I had digested the scene, I noticed something else. There was a real service going on, with a rabbi on a *bimah* in the center of the synagogue surrounded by men in prayer shawls, singing songs I did not recognize, lyrics I could not place. All these people clearly knew one another; I was the only stranger. All the while I had been growing up in a Satmar sect in Williamsburg, these Algerian Jews had been practicing their own Judaism, as legitimate and authentic as their Hasidic peers, if not more so. How had I never realized that there might be Jewish communities all over the world whose practices and perspectives had nothing in common with my own, yet were just as connected to our shared heritage as any other?

As I left the synagogue, an old, wrinkled woman wrapped in a metallic-threaded shawl was lighting candles off to the side. In that moment, gazing at the flames she hovered over so protectively, I knew I had found a piece of my new identity. I had stepped back from my Jewishness enough to achieve some kind of global perspective, to grasp the diversity and complexity inherent in it. Perhaps I could be some kind of global Jew too, someone who could be open to everything it meant to be Jewish, who could discover the complete length of its broad and colorful spectrum. Why would I ever want to limit myself to one version?

———

Returning to New England this time, with its manicured lawns and white picket fences, its sporting goods shops and genteel country inns, I felt that familiar sense of discomfort more than ever. I couldn't recognize myself in America, or perhaps it was that I couldn't recognize America in myself, but it was startling to compare my return to the United States, and the flatlining of my emotions that accompanied it, with the experience I'd had each time I'd arrived in Europe, that immediate, reverberating sensation of making contact with something old and almost, but not quite, forgotten. To ease the impact of my arrival now, in the fall of 2013, I told myself that I would soon return to Europe, that even if I was stuck here, in a place that felt impersonal and foreign to me, I would make going abroad a regular occurrence. I supposed that my passion for the European continent would become simply a part of my identity, that my trips would instill the rhythm that would define my future life here, that I would be a "Europhile." Of course a part of me believed that if I had another chance to feel that incredible sensation again, maybe I'd understand what it was and how to prolong its influence in my life so that I didn't always have to arrive home to a devastating sense of loss, this ridiculous, incomprehensible misery that can only be described as homesickness.

During those months when I was bound by routine and obligation to stay still, I tried to find methods with which to stave off this painful yearning. Back then, I was convinced that this phenomenon pointed to a character flaw in myself, a restlessness that could never be assuaged. Only years later would I learn that I had been longing for a home I did not yet consciously know, though it was known to me on some level nonetheless. For when I finally found a place to stay, this gnawing feeling that had accompanied me all my life would disappear for good, and I would be vindicated against those who had made dire predictions about me, for there is really no greater triumph in my life than that of having found my way home. Now, however, I did not have the comfort of this vindication, and I felt much like a woman whose lover has gone to war, forced to console herself with occasional messages scribbled from the front. That was my strategy, then, to devour the entire canon of European literature, more specifically the literature of those who had written of Europe, recognizing it as some greater, magical entity, the consummate strengths of which were matched only by its weaknesses. Now for the first time, I stumbled upon writers I had never heard of before, writers who had not achieved any kind of widespread notice in the States the way those authors I had read in college had done, but whose works shattered and remade me in their clarity: Jean Améry, Gregor von Rezzori, Czesław Miłosz, Imre Kertész, Primo Levi, Joseph Roth, Mihail Sebastian, Salomon Maimon,

Tadeusz Borowski, to name just a few. I began to notice a strange pattern; that is, when I read the works of these authors, especially those of the generation that had survived the war, I had the oddest feeling that I was communing with the souls of the people who had raised me, that through these books it was as if my grandmother herself was speaking to me, as if my ancestors on all sides had reached through time and grasped me by the throat.

Around that time I came across a poem by Anna Margolin in an anthology of Yiddish poetry, and as I murmured its words out loud, following them line by line with my finger the way I had been taught to do with the psalms as a child, I sensed that it was not a poem at all, but an incantation.

> *All of them—my tribe,*
> *Blood of my blood,*
> *Flame of my flame,*
> *The dead and the living mixed;*
> *Sad, grotesque, large,*
> *They tramp through me as through a dark house,*
> *Tramp with prayers and curses and laments.*
> *They shake my heart like a copper bell,*
> *My tongue quivering.*
> *I don't recognize my own voice—*
> *My tribe speaks.*
>   —Excerpt from "My Tribe Speaks" by Anna Margolin,
>   translated from the Yiddish by Richard J. Fein

Instantly I knew the phenomenon she was referring to. I recognized that I too had been raised to be a vessel for others, a being through which the dead could live again. I did not have the privilege of possessing my own life, my own spirit; I had a debt to the people who had come before me, who had fought to survive so that my existence was possible. In my own story I had to keep their stories alive.

Each time I lost myself in the bygone world referred to in the texts I had accumulated during my visits to used bookshops, it was jarring to come up for air, to go about my daily life in this idyllic, prosperous corner of America, where everyone around me was fully immersed in a benign present, while a part of me always remained in that forgotten, drastic time.

———

In the early spring we celebrated Isaac's seventh birthday. The weather was unseasonably warm that week; I planned to host the shindig at my house so the kids could all run around out-doors. My mother, who at that point played only a marginal role in my life—a role that only diminished over time—took the train up from New York, loaded with party favors and bal-loons she'd found in a ninety-nine-cent store. I purchased the snacks and cupcakes.

The day of Isaac's birthday happened to be Grandparents' Day at his school, so I dropped Isaac and my mother off in the morning and returned home to blow up the balloons and make other sundry preparations. When I picked them up at lunch-time, they'd created a wreath together, Isaac being the designer and my mom wielding the glue gun. They got along well with each other, having none of the baggage that my mom and I grew up taking for granted when it came to our families. To Isaac, she was just my mother, just another person who loved him, and it was uncomplicated.

DEBORAH FELDMAN

Isaac knew that my mother hadn't raised me, but he never asked why. I would have liked for him to be able to take for granted that a mother was always there for her child, but I could already tell, by the way he clung to me, that he didn't see me as the immovable caregiver most children saw their parents as. He already sensed that I came from an unstable, cryptic world, and that made his world seem somehow less certain.

In many ways, I was a repeat of my mother's life. Perhaps that is why I'd always struggled with feelings of anxiety and fear when I was around her. Was I doomed to simply relive her life experience and pass it on to the next generation in an unstoppable cycle of misery? Her marriage was also arranged when she was a teenager. She too was forced to have a baby with a man she didn't love. While I was being raised mostly by my grandparents, she was working menial jobs to put herself through college, an act that constituted her final rejection from our family and community. My father had presented three wives with a religious divorce by the time she was able to obtain her legal one.

My mom and I couldn't talk about these things, even now—she rejected my every effort, saying it was too painful to talk about the past—but talking about books was our safe conversation, the one thing that bound us together. She told me about how she too used to sneak out to the library as a child, filling her days with books by British authors, like the Malory Towers series by Enid Blyton. She was a child of divorce as well, a symbol of scandal among her peers.

I had no doubt my mother was happy. Her life had begun as mine had, it progressed as mine had, and yet here she was today, accomplished, educated, and independent. Yet I wondered when she would trust me enough to finally talk honestly with me about the past and thereby grant me the closure I needed to allow our relationship to develop. Until then, we treated each other like mere acquaintances; our connection felt superficial and tenuous.

I had asked her recently, after exhuming the old file on my family's past, what she knew about her own ancestors, wondering not only if she could supplement the patchy documentation I had collected, but also if she herself had at one time or another been possessed by the same driving need to know more about bygone times in order to shore up her own development. "I've never had one iota of interest," she had responded sarcastically. "Why would I care about those people? They were ignorant and traumatized and I'm glad to be free of them."

Yes, she always made it quite clear that the past held no value or attraction for her, that indeed it was something to be fully erased from the record. But she was forgetting the contradiction inherent in announcing that to me, for I was very much a part and product of that past. By attempting to erase it, it was as if she were erasing me. How could she hope to have any kind of substantial relationship with a daughter who had emerged from that very mire she was determined to suppress?

At Isaac's party she designated herself the photographer, feeling more secure among the guests when she was behind the camera and occupied with a task. I watched her hide behind the lens, always hovering at the edge of my own frame of vision. How was it, I wondered, that it was so clear to me that I could have no hope of a future without making sense of the past, but it was something she could totally reject? What had caused me to turn out so different from her when I had inherited her genes, after all? It was as if, by abandoning me in her flight, she had amputated herself from that family tree I had drawn as a child. As a result, there was no hope of any relationship burgeoning between us.

I turned my attention back to Isaac. The party was progressing very successfully. That particular early spring afternoon had turned quite hot, and the kids changed into bathing suits and clamored to jump into the lake. I distributed the water balloons I had prepared and challenged them all to first stay dry for the duration of the throwing contest. I watched as Isaac ran around excitedly, cupcake icing smeared around his mouth, looking gloriously happy to be the center of attention. I knew how special it felt to him, to have all his school friends here to celebrate. We'd never been entrenched in a place or community; it was the first time he could feel a sense of belonging, even if I didn't.

———

At that point Isaac had already figured out that he was one of very few Jewish students in his new school in the rolling hills of New England, but I had always encouraged him to share his culture and heritage with his peers as much as possible. He brought traditional pastries to school on Jewish holidays and was repeatedly called upon to explain Jewish culture to his fellow students, and no one had ever made him feel less than proud of this ability. I was thankful that he could at the very least trust that most people wouldn't try to exclude or deny him anything because of his blood. But I also wanted him to understand that a form of rejection was a part of his history. How to explain that to him without scaring him? I would never have discussed the Holocaust with him at this age, or any of the other great persecution epics like the Spanish Inquisition, but I wanted to tell him the ethnic story of the Jewish diaspora, about how his ancestors lived under very different conditions than we do now. I decided to show him the movie *Fiddler on the Roof*, to explain to him what Jewish life had once been like, without exception—that it had taken a big war and a lot of change for us to live the way we were living now. As I watched him try to process that, I realized just how different the two of us were— I had never been able to see myself outside of that identity, and he was struggling to place himself inside it. Had we really made the break, then? Had I freed him from an imposed legacy and allowed him to define himself?

On his spring break, I decided to take him with me on my next trip to Europe, and we traveled to Andalusia, the famed origin of Jewish thought on the continent. He had been learning Spanish in school, and it was an opportunity for him to practice his language skills while I continued to investigate the emotional pull I felt, which was only growing stronger with time. I knew that Spain played an important role not just for Jewish life on the European continent but also for my own particular heritage. The mystical beliefs and traditions that had been nurtured and recorded by medieval Sephardic scholars had later been integrated and fused into the Hasidic tradition, and I had been exposed to customs and stories as a child that had sprung from this era. By visiting Andalusia, I was acknowledging that the roots of my heritage went much deeper than Williamsburg, deeper even than the Habsburg Empire, deeper than the mid-eighteenth century, when the movement of Hasidism itself had been founded. It was an acknowledgment of a root system widespread and deeply buried, a confirmation that my past was more than just an anomaly but a product of global vicissitudes. I wanted Isaac to be able to understand this, to have the basic comfort that comes with knowing that one has a place in history.

Between Seville and Granada we toured cities and towns; it was marvelous to be abroad with my son for the first time, like a dream I hadn't dared to nurture had come true regardless. I showed him the grand mosques and cathedrals that dotted the Andalusian landscape; we were transfixed by the flamenco dancers; we encountered mountain goats on rocky inclines with the bells around their necks ringing incessantly; but we did not come across anything remotely Jewish. This was the seat of Jewish life in Europe, I had said to him. It was because of the Inquisition and its consequences that Jews were scattered in all the countries to the north. But where was the evidence of this, the minimal tribute? Everything else was still here; evidence of Moorish and Muslim influences remained despite the Christianization process; only our traces had been wiped out, and this was disheartening.

I decided that we would travel to Córdoba by train, for I knew Maimonides had studied and written there, and I had read that a sculpture had been erected in his memory in a public square in the ancient Roman city where he had lived. When we arrived at the square it was clear this was now the center of a chic and expensive neighborhood. Like in Paris, when I had visited the Marais, this too had once been the Jewish ghetto, and now it was snooty and lined with overpriced boutiques. Nevertheless, the statue was still there, and when I pointed it out, Isaac danced excitedly around it. I still have the photo I snapped in that precious moment. There was no denying the simple joy inherent in that experience, just the two of us exploring the world and finally discovering something we felt personally connected to.

Farther down the street, my guidebook said, lay the old synagogue. Upon arriving, we stepped into the tiny room that constituted one of the only three restored synagogues in the whole of Spain. It was smaller than my first apartment had been. Etchings and carvings in the stone wall had been recovered, but otherwise there was nothing on display except for a brass menorah in a case on the platform.

"Why isn't there any stuff?" Isaac asked me. I didn't know what to say. We had been to so many lovingly restored cathedrals, all of which had been large and grandiose and had boasted many beautiful objects and artworks. He had a point.

"I'm not sure," I said. "Maybe because everything was destroyed and they couldn't find it."

The synagogue didn't take more than three minutes to walk around; that's how small it was. A box asked for a donation of fifty cents on the way out. I remembered the pricey admission fee to La Giralda in Seville and felt irritated at the comparison. At the Sefarad House across the street, a similarly low fee was charged—and like the synagogue, the Jewish museum was incredibly small, with limited offerings.

I asked the man working behind the desk if he was Jewish, or if anyone who worked there was.

"Unfortunately no, ma'am," he said apologetically in a strong accent, "but all of us care very much about the history of the Jewish presence in Spain and are working very hard in the interest of preservation."

"Are there any Jews left in Córdoba?"

"Very few. We used to have eleven, but then the rabbi's son went to England to study, so now we have ten."

I couldn't fathom how ten people managed to hold on to the idea of a community here. I had not come across any other reports of Jews in the region. Perhaps I simply did not understand how to approach the research process. Years later, I would return to Spain at the invitation of a Jewish community in Barcelona and learn exactly why I now found evidence of Jewish life so undetectable. But by then my understanding of Europe would have been transformed by years spent living abroad, and my reflections on these early visits would be tinged with embarrassment bordering on incredulity.

To be Jewish in Spain, they would explain to me, is synonymous with discretion and inconspicuousness. There was no nameplate next to the doorbell of their synagogue identifying it as such, and it was located in one apartment in a building of many, but this was not because they needed to hide; it was because hiding had become part of the ritual enactment of Jewish identity in Spain. The impact of the Marrano (Crypto-Jew) lifestyle echoed across the generations; it had been fully integrated into their traditions. Just because those traditions were no longer required didn't mean they would get rid of them. After all, traditions were not valuable because of their current meaning, but rather because of their ancient one.

Isaac was not discouraged by what the man had to say. He was very excited to explore the museum, and he raced ahead, calling to me when he saw something he wanted to show me. But I was very pensive as I walked through the small house.

I looked down at the one-sheet guide the man had given me. It talked about the history of Jews in Córdoba. We were now in what was still called the Jewish quarter, but according to the document, any homes that had once been occupied by

Jews were destroyed by riots in the fourteenth and fifteenth centuries.

On the way out, I pointed that out to the man. "So, if the so-called Jewish quarter was completely razed after the Jews had already been expelled, why still call it the Jewish quarter? Not even the ground I'm walking on is Jewish! It's been inhabited by Christians for centuries." He must have felt put on the spot. I'm sure no one had asked him that many questions, and I knew it was rude of me, but I was frustrated and couldn't help myself.

"It's called the Jewish quarter in memory of the people who lived here before, ma'am," he said patiently.

"But look around," I said. "This is now your cool neighborhood! This is your Soho, your West Village, like we have in Manhattan. Do you have any idea how insulting it is to have your trendiest, most expensive neighborhood invoke the memory of the people who were oppressed and tortured here? Spain has made no effort to reach out to the Jewish community or welcome them back. The right thing to do would be to give this neighborhood to them. No wonder there are only ten Jews left."

I wouldn't live here in a million years, I thought. It would make me sick. I walked out of the museum feeling flattened.

"You're upset because they don't have any more Jews here, right, Mommy?" Isaac asked.

"I guess so. But I also thought there'd be more to see. This was the biggest Jewish community in Spain. We've been touring mosques and churches everywhere—those weren't destroyed. Why couldn't they have left just a little bit behind for us?"

It shouldn't have felt so personal, I knew then, but it did

regardless, for in a way it was confirmation of what my grand-parents had always assured me, that there was a kind of prime-val drive to erase the existence of Jews, both in practice and in memory, and now I myself felt the threat of deletion, because without the past to mirror my present, I was forced into this floating rootless state and I deeply resented it. I wanted nothing more than to physically force the society around me to admit the truth, to admit that I was an integral part of their history.

I was ready to leave, but on the way out of the quarter, now mobbed with fashionably dressed men and women sipping cap-puccinos, I passed a small jewelry boutique. There were hand-made Jewish stars on display in the window. The jeweler was an old man who didn't speak English, but I pointed to the one I liked and he gave me the price. I laid the money on the table, and he opened the case and gently lifted the necklace from it. He looked at me and motioned putting it on, a questioning look on his face.

"Yes, I want to wear it," I said. I moved my hair to the side and allowed him to fasten the closure at the nape of my neck. When I saw the star come to rest on my sweater, it was as if I had tattooed myself with it.

I walked out of that shop with that star on my collarbone, not hidden under my sweater. I thought of Milena in Paris and I held my head high and walked down the street holding Isaac's hand, making sure to meet everyone's gaze. It was as if I felt I was making some kind of announcement to the world about who I was, a proclamation. I am Jewish, I thought, looking straight ahead. No matter what my life looked like, my roots were right here too, a thousand years back perhaps, but just as legitimate as theirs. After all, in my grandfather's library of He-brew texts had lain the tomes of the great Sephardic scholars:

Bartenura, Abulafia, Caro, Maimonides, Luria, Vital. The approach to thinking that these texts had imparted, with its circular and allegorical nature, had engraved them into our lives and our attitudes. It still played a significant role in how I approached problem solving, even today, and would likely do so for the rest of my life. The stories I had been told as a child, the myths and folktales that had filled my imagination, had been recorded here, and their threads burrowed through the loose soil of time to anchor me, through thousands of years, to foreign ground. My relationship to Europe was broad and multi-faceted, a heritage that both I and my son could claim.

When we landed back in New York the next day, I thought about that empty container, the one my grandmother had so feared, the presence of which I had sensed during my very first return to New York two years earlier, and I imagined that some-where at the bottom of the vessel, a hole had been plugged. They had said, those teachers of my past, that a vessel could only be filled with spirituality and belief, but I knew now that something had been placed in mine, and it wasn't that. The star I now wore was not a gesture of faith or a religious ritual; it was something deeper and simpler, a symbol of knowing one-self, of being whole in oneself. My grandmother had said that every container, so long as it had something in it, regardless of what, was worth opening a door for, and somewhere off in the distance I could just barely discern that a door had been opened, just a crack. I could sense a whole world beyond it, tugging at me with a magnetic force.

———

It's important to explain that although this attraction I felt to-ward Europe was very powerful, it was not easy then to define it as positive or negative. Although I longed to be abroad when I was in the States, and initially setting foot on the European continent was like a balm, I couldn't help but notice that after spending a few days there, inevitably, I experienced a rigorous emotional stirring, almost an agitation. Of course, this was easy to explain on some level; although Europe was the home of my ancestors and the lost Atlantis that served as the sole reference for my grandmother's *Weltanschauung*, it was also the place where the great catastrophe had occurred, the apocalypse that had nearly wiped us out, and my existence was predicated on the fact that my grandmother had managed, by a hairsbreadth, to survive. To return to such a place was in effect to risk one's own renaissance and obliteration simultaneously.

Some people speak of inherited Holocaust guilt. The children of survivors repress their feelings and squash their own dreams, I'd read. I had carried mourning with me all my life. I had spent nights lying awake picturing the faces of all those dead children, tormented by the idea of their aborted existence. Was I really here simply to replenish the family, as my grandfather had said? Was it up to me to birth their souls into the world so that they could live again? Or was it enough to retrace their path, so that they could be seen—so that their memories could live on forever in my spirit?

As a child I had often dreamed about being in the concentration camps alongside my grandmother. I awoke always knowing with certainty that I had died, or was about to die, and that this was somehow proof that I still wasn't strong enough, or special enough, to survive what my grandmother had endured. Compared to her, I was a whiny weakling. I would stand in front of the gilded, oxidized mirror in my grandmother's bedroom when she was away and stare at myself for hours, trying to imagine what I would have looked like on the brink of death, my skin clinging to my bones, my eyes sunken into my skull. What was different about her that she was able to emerge from the pit of human despair that surely would have swallowed me whole?

Did she believe in her inalienable right to life in a way I could never hope to?

Sometimes, when the house was empty and quiet, I had rooted through my grandmother's drawers, looking for clues. It was difficult to learn anything about her otherwise. I asked many questions, but my grandmother was rarely in the mood to talk the way the women in my community did, chattering endlessly about trivial topics to one another. Her answers were notable for their cryptic brevity. Instead, I gathered frayed documents and sepia photographs obsessively, sneaking into my grandfather's office to use the color copy machine before putting the found treasures back in their original hiding places. I kept a folder under my mattress stuffed with facsimiles of postcards, letters, and documents. I did not know why I felt so driven to color in the vague outlines of our family's past at the time, to the point where I far exceeded the requirements of that momentous school assignment, but I remember that the folder was one of the few items I took with me when I eventually left my community. I abandoned years of diaries and journals and personal photographs, but for some reason I rescued that folder from the musty basement where it had lain untouched for years. Those documents were my only connection to my roots, not the shallow ones that had been planted in New York, but roots that went far back into the earth on the other side of the ocean. I had not known then, when I'd left, that the folder would prove central to the task of rebuilding my sense of self; I could not yet have imagined that to have a future I would need to lean far back into bygone eras to buttress it.

Now I opened that folder for the first time in many years, leafing through papers written in various languages, trying to put together the story they told. I opened an old brown envelope, tattered at the edges, reinforced with brown tape, which I had found tucked between the Hungarian down comforters my grandmother stacked in the old wooden crib that had still sat in the corner of her bedroom, despite the fact that her youngest child was then in his thirties. There was an old passport, with a photo of my grandmother as a young girl, thick dark hair waving as if there was a breeze, pinned by a clip on the side where it was thickest. She had a tired smile on her face, like someone who had just completed a Herculean task, a long hike or swim. The date said 1947, so that task would have been an arduous recovery from typhus. She would have had to gain the weight lost in the concentration camp, grow back the hair, come to terms with the loss of everything.

My grandmother's passport did not have a shiny leather cover like mine does now. It was a simple folded sheet of card stock. It was temporary. It said STATELESS in bold black letters. It was the passport issued to her by the Swedish Aliens Commission after the war, when Hungary didn't want to recognize her as its citizen anymore, and no country wanted to step up in its place. Until her American naturalization, my grandmother used that declaration of categorical homelessness as her ticket across borders and oceans. She was, for many years, a displaced person who relied on the sporadic generosity of host countries and international relief organizations.

In the story of the Jews, I had learned, we are technically all displaced persons. The last time we had a home, my teachers had proclaimed, was before the Second Temple was destroyed in AD 70. Then God punished us by sending us into exile, or *galuth*, as we call it, and the diaspora happened. We were cursed with wandering; we moved from region to region, from country to country. Every time we settled into a comfortable routine, something would come along and shake the earth from beneath us. Crusades, Cossacks, Tatars, Nazis. The earth shook in 1944, and a few years later my grandmother came to America with her stateless passport.

Enclosed in the brown envelope was all the correspondence between her and the bureaucratic government agency in charge of her naturalization. She was addressed as DP3159057. At the time, she had told me, she was working as a secretary in Williamsburg. She didn't mention the company she worked for or what she did exactly, as a secretary, but she did mention that she shared an apartment with roommates on Hooper Street and that at night she was awakened by the cries they emitted in their terrible dreams. Everybody around her was haunted in the same way. So she gave her information to a matchmaker.

"I'm ready to start a new life," she had said. She wanted to have many children. She had just gotten her period for the first time at twenty-four years old, and she was relieved. She had lost ten siblings in the war. She would ultimately give birth to eleven children. She did not raise her kids with the same traditions with which her parents had raised her. It was a postwar generation, and if you hadn't given up on God completely, you were well on your way to the other end of the spectrum. She had married an avid follower of what was beginning to be an extremist movement. My grandfather, while educated and successful at a young age, was the only man she had met who insisted on keeping his traditional beard in the New World.

Later, their sons and daughters would grow up in a self-imposed ghetto led by rabbis who were trying to make sense of the Holocaust and appease the angry God that had razed the European Jewish population.

Over the years, my grandmother had paid little notice to the winds of fanaticism blowing around her home. At times when the community was in its grips and my grandfather brought news of tightening restrictions into his home, my grandmother waved it away and sang a little tune as she carefully frosted a hazelnut torte. I remember that the little things made her very happy. She prepared such beautiful and tasty food, food the likes of which I had rediscovered only recently, in the restaurants of Paris and Madrid, food I would recognize all around me later, when I was living in Europe and each visit to a restaurant offered an unanticipated trip to the past hidden in its menu items. The food I grew up with was regal and classic in the way people rarely cook anymore in the United States, and because food was such a central part of our world, it stands to reason that my attachment to it did not fade, even after I had left. I would seek it out as a doorway to common ground with the culture and history of an entire continent.

To my grandmother I had attached ineffable elegance, even then. There was no elegance in Hasidic life, but there was elegance in her, in her origins, in her story, and in her inimitable cooking. My grandmother was European, and though as a child I could not fully grasp what that meant, I imagined that it was something wonderful and otherworldly. I cherished the photos taken of her as a young woman in gorgeous hand-sewn dresses of silk and lace. I loved the way her slim ankles looked in delicate high-heeled shoes. There was something spectacular about the loveliness and poise she maintained even in her old age, a bearing that stood in sharp contrast to another photograph I had found in her drawer, the one of her being carried out of Bergen-Belsen on a stretcher by the British Red Cross. To embody beauty after you had endured the ugliest of assaults, that was magic to me. I surmised that there was something very powerful at the core of my grandmother's spirit.

My grandmother's passport gave her name as Irenka, Hungarian for Irene. It was not a name I ever heard her called, but then no one called me by the name on my birth certificate either. It was custom to have a secular name, to make it easier for the outsiders to relate to us. Better that than they should resent us for having to *break their teeth* over our Hebrew names. My grandmother's religious name was Pearl, a beautiful name that I had thought I would like to give my daughter someday, except that, I reasoned then, I would have a daughter too early for that. We didn't name our children after the living, like Sephardic Jews did. It would have to be my granddaughter's name.

Of all the passive and submissive women in the Bible I could have been named after, somehow Deborah had ended up on my birth certificate. No one in my family had ever had that name, and Ashkenazi Jews never give their children random names. The custom is always to name a child after a dead relative. Indeed, I was given two names at my *kiddush*, the Jewish equivalent of a christening for girls: Sarah and Deborah. I was called Sarah growing up. There were plenty of dead Sarahs in my family. Deborah was an afterthought, rarely mentioned. I never heard any tales told about an ancestor with my name. When I scoured the family tree I had managed to assemble through careful sleuthing, no one by that name showed up, even when I went back seven generations. Why Deborah?

In the book of Judges, which I sought out now in its English translation, Deborah is introduced with the words *eshes lapidus*. I knew it was common for people who appear in the biblical texts to be tagged in such a way, with descriptions following their names. "Wife of," "son of"—that's how they were identified in those days. The weird thing is, if the words *eshes lapidus*, or "woman of Lapidus," are to mean that Deborah is a wife, why is Lapidus never identified separately in the scripture?

Lapidus is a Hebrew word for torch or fire. It is not the mundane term, but a literary word, a term with elevated connotations. It is an unlikely name for a person. Scholars infer that the description of Deborah therefore translates to "woman of the torch," or "fiery woman," as opposed to wife of anyone.

Woman of fire, I thought, and smiled inwardly.

Nothing was beyond the scope of Deborah's achievement. She is undoubtedly the most empowered woman in Jewish history. She was a judge, a leader, a military strategist and commander, a prophetess, and an icon. The Greeks later put her effigy on a coin. She was revered for her beauty, her wisdom, and most of all her strength. Men tried to marry her, rabbis surmise, but she refused. So she was given the ambiguous affixation—*eshes lapidus*.

When I first applied to college, needing a legal name for documents, I had discovered that my birth certificate said only Deborah, and from then on, the Sarah was dropped. To me, Sarah was my old name, a name for a passive girl. Deborah would be my future.

Deborah, woman of the torch.

Centuries after Deborah's rule, Jews were still talking about her, but not necessarily politely. The group of rabbis who sat around a table in a synagogue and argued with one another about every word in the Bible, and who had the minutes of their meetings transcribed into a collection of work that would become the Talmud, made a point of belittling, with a pernicious determination, the few women who had made it into biblical history. They focused on Deborah with unreserved vitriol, for of the paltry group of women who received positive mentions in scripture, she is truly the only threat. Not just a holy woman, neither a mother nor a wife, Deborah broke every rule in the book by occupying a position that had only ever been held by men and would never again be held by a woman. She died untamed, although surely there were those who wanted her retired into a convenient marriage to sink behind the name of her husband into obscurity.

There is a particularly memorable passage in the Talmud that records a conversation in which rabbis compete with one another to mock the names of the female prophets. By happenstance, some of the women were named after animals, names designed to denote industriousness, a cherished quality in a Jewish woman. *Deborah* is the Hebrew term for bee, a hardworking creature. The rabbis poke fun at Deborah by attacking her name as vulgar and unsophisticated. But Hebrew, as a language, works in a particularly interesting way. Words are composed of three-letter roots, which have altered meanings based on suffixes, prefixes, and vowels stuck in between. The root of *Deborah* consists of the Hebrew equivalents for *D, B,* and *R*. This is the root word for speech. The Hebrew version of *H*, tacked on to the end of an action word, usually denotes feminine gender. Therefore, *DeBoRaH* would literally deconstruct as "she speaks."

These sorts of language gymnastics are a beloved sport of Talmudic rabbis. They spend countless pages indulging in a game called *gematria*, in which they use a code that assigns numerical values to Hebrew letters to draw connections between different words by showing their sums to be equal. The acrobatics involved to draw these complex conclusions are necessary because too frequently they are cited as the only evidence to support a rabbi's claim.

Hebrew is certainly a language that invites the obsessive code cracker. It is very layered, packing meaning upon meaning. Words often have dual or triple uses. The poetic nature of Hebrew scripture has allowed for centuries of conjecture and deconstruction not unlike that which I experienced in a poetry class in college. My grandfather understood this concept. He often warned me that, although we were living our lives according to a strict rabbinical interpretation of the Torah, there was a distinct possibility that we had a lot of it wrong. He was the first person to explain the concept of a metaphor to me. That's the thing about the Hebrew language, he said. You never know if you've picked the right meaning. It could be literal or figurative. The language could be deliberately obscure, designed to cloak a meaning that only someone with the right code could access. And codes can go wrong. You could be using the wrong key to crack it and get an entirely mixed-up result.

My grandfather was confident in his rabbi nonetheless. He reminded me that faith in the righteous was our insurance against error. If we had the right intentions in hand, it was ensured that God would modify his wishes to align with those of the saints leading us. Such reverence was there in heaven for our holy rabbis. The same holy rabbis had mocked Deborah, who had been chosen by God to lead the Jewish nation to extraordinary victory, who had been blessed with a reign of unparalleled peace and prosperity, and most important, who had been beloved by the nation's subjects and fondly remembered by them.

The author of the book of Deborah was clearly of a very different mind than the fastidious group who chronicled their highly subjective opinions in the Talmud. For now my finger traced over this sentence: "And Deborah rose, a mother in Israel, and spoke."

In the story of Deborah came my first opportunity to find a positive reflection in the Judaic mirror. In those early years after leaving, everywhere I went, someone or something wanted to show me an acquired perception of Jewish culture. A stereotype, a joke, a Woody Allen reference, countless such instances of a projected identity I had never been aware of, at least not as aware as I was of my existence within the framework of Jewishness I had grown up in. No one had ever mentioned Deborah to me, except in passing. The stories of Moses, David, and Solomon were told and retold gloriously, but somehow the women slipped from collective memory, and only their shadows remained.

I wanted to hold the memory of this overlooked woman aloft in a way that could not be ignored.

It's hard to explain why I started to feel closer to my grandmother in the years after we had last seen each other than at any moment during the time we spent together in my childhood. I had once stood alongside her in the kitchen and mixed bowls of cake batter and meringue, and perhaps we had talked of this and that, but even then I was yearning to know the person she had once been. By the time I came along, my grandmother's life had been greatly diminished. I never knew her in her heyday, when she was raising a family of eleven with aplomb, sewing her children's clothes by hand according to the latest fashions she spied at Saks and Bloomingdale's. She could look at a dress and instantly know how to make it; she didn't even need a pattern. Neighbors whispered that her rich husband gave her free rein, but they didn't know that the opposite was true. Despite his financial success, my grandfather didn't believe in spending money on material things. So she slaved away instead, and they kept up appearances.

My grandmother was almost a ghost to me then. Perhaps for that reason, her spirit seemed to accompany me on my way out. I did not feel the separation so keenly because I had always been attached to the memory of her, and that would never fade, no matter how far I traveled. Instead, by freeing myself from the bounds imposed on relationships by the Hasidic community, I was finally able to explore the person my grandmother had been. I opened that folder stuffed full of photographs and documents and started to piece together as much as I could, assembling a chronology of dates, places, and people. Yet there were many missing elements, and I knew I had to start at the beginning if I was ever going to get the full story.

She was the ultimate model of displacement for me. Her story of exile and wandering felt more urgent to me than the story of how she had settled into her new life in America, the only life I had known her in. As I experienced my own exile now, literally wandering around the world looking for a new identity, there was no one I could feel closer to than the memory of her young self, traversing rivers and oceans in search of a place to call home. I finally had permission to dredge up her past.

That meant traveling to northeastern Hungary, where she had been born and raised, and so, in the summer of 2013, amid an uncharacteristic heat wave, I emerged from the airport into the humid haze of Budapest. The capital of the northeast region was Nyíregyháza, and as an acquaintance of mine in New England had connected me with the president of Nyíregyháza's only college, he had arrived now in a chauffeured Mercedes to drive me there. A Hungarian novelist and poet in addition to university head, Zoltán had started studying English only a year ago, so we communicated in his broken, outmoded German and my Yiddish. It was painful for him, he said to me then, that with the mind of a novelist and the desire to convey all things beautifully, he could not communicate effectively with me. Although we understood each other just fine, I could feel his frustration. For me too it would always rankle to be hampered by a limited vocabulary, but this was also my fate in a sense, as I would never again be able to speak my native language to someone capable of understanding me, and every language I adopted, no matter how hard I toiled, would never serve me in the same way. Luckily, Zoltán had grown up around Yiddish speakers, and my odd turns of phrase and archaic grammar did not stump him.

"The second language in Hungary used to be German," he said, "but now it's mostly Russian. English isn't even on the table. Don't expect to be able to communicate with anyone directly," he warned me. He had found me an interpreter, someone who worked at the college but who had studied in America for a year. I was relieved to hear that.

We took a brief walking tour around the city. The banks of the Danube were inaccessible then, because of all the flooding—across central Europe, train lines were submerged and low regions turned into stagnant ponds. The Hungarian Parliament Building, normally the architectural pride of the capital, was covered in scaffolding; only its imposing white spires could be seen amid the extensive renovation effort. We retreated from the noisy dump trucks and work crews and walked down Andrássy Avenue toward the famous Heroes' Square. Zoltán had a story for everything; he knew every sculpture and statue. He'd mention them by name and ask me if I'd ever heard of this person or that, but all the names sounded equally foreign to me. Famous Hungarian poet, he'd point out; famous Hungarian artist; famous king; famous general; famous writer. I wondered if any of them were famous outside Hungary.

My first glimpse of Budapest—so different from Europe's other capitals in that it lacks both contemporary chic and the varnished grandiosity of antique glamour—was jarring. Immediately I sensed just how influenced my childhood milieu was by the Old World aesthetic I saw around me. The voluminous block buildings, their facades cracked and darkened with age, reminded me of the impressive synagogues that rose between the tenement buildings of Williamsburg; I especially noticed the various flyers posted at eye level, some of them new, others rotted to strips and pieces by time and weather. Williamsburg too had been covered with such posters, called *pashkevillin*; because we had no radio or TV, we had resorted to more old-fashioned means of communication and advertising.

We sat at an outdoor café in the blistering heat and drank some chilled Tokaji. Zoltán taught me how to toast in Hungarian. *"Egészségedre,"* he enunciated slowly—meaning, "To your health!" Later I would constantly ask him to repeat it for me, because invariably I would invert the syllables or contort the pronunciation. Very little of the Hungarian I had heard as a child seemed to have stuck with me. "Paprikajancsi," my grandfather had sometimes called me when I was being particularly mischievous. Although it literally translated to "pepper jack," Zoltán said, it was actually the name of a classical clown character similar to Punchinello. Neither of my grandparents had wanted any of us to learn their native language. Hungarian was used only when secrets needed to be kept or in heated conversations behind closed doors. It was the language of the past, to which we were not allowed any access. We were the future, and the future spoke only Yiddish.

We had a three-hour drive ahead of us to the great northern plain bordered by Romania to the east and Ukraine and Slovakia to the north, in which Nyíregyháza was only a small city in a rural outpost. Traffic thinned after we entered the Szatmár-Bereg region, an area that had once been part of Transylvania, and was now a poor and rural place. By the time we arrived in Nyíregyháza, whatever cooling off the rain had provided was gone. Only a few damp spots remained on concrete structures, and steam rose from the asphalt. Once upon a time, gracious town houses and courtyard apartments had lined these orderly boulevards, but no sign remained of the former elegance my grandmother had described. Nyíregyháza seemed economically depressed, barely recovered from the communist regime that had fallen more than twenty years past. There had been no revolution here, no revival—the city seemed to have satisfied itself with a few new coats of paint, evident in crumbling apartment blocks done up in cheerful Mediterranean colors as if in rebellion. We sped through the center of Nyíregyháza, a smattering of stucco houses with clay-pot roofs interspersed among the blocks.

I slept like the dead, regardless of the heat. I was awoken by a mourning dove burbling outside my window. For a moment before I opened my eyes, I thought I was back in Brooklyn. I recalled waking up early on July mornings in my grandparents' house to that same sound of mourning doves cooing in the tree limbs level with my window, the last refreshing breeze of the night wafting into my room. Then I squinted into the bright early light, remembering where I was. I sat up immediately, walking over to the open windows to glimpse the foreign world in which I'd arrived and confirm it was still real.

Outside, two ancient gingko trees flanked the entrance to the building. Up close, their leaves fluttered tremulously under drops of dew the size of nickels. Every so often, a branch would shake in the breeze, and the dewdrops would quiver and slide along the surface of the leaves, which righted themselves eventually when the breeze died. Along the paths carved out between the lush gardens and lawns were the acacia trees my grandmother had spoken of to me so fondly, their dainty, fernlike leaves gently filtering the sun so that it dappled the grass beneath in lacy patterns.

Here were all the plants of her childhood, some of which she had tried to cultivate in our little backyard garden, and as I walked around the campus, I began to recognize some shrubs and flowers with joy. These were no English gardens at the college. These were the kind of gardens you might imagine had grown wild here and only been tamed, just barely, as an afterthought. Bushes and plants grew riotously into one another's territory, and the grass in between was twice as tall as grass was usually allowed to grow in America. Willows and poplars competed for space, fat lavender shrubs lined the pathway, and tendrils of creeping fig wound their way around them. I heard another dove gurgle throatily on the branch above me. The atmosphere was lush and fragrant; the sun was already hot on my skin; I closed my eyes and inhaled deeply, trying to preserve the moment into an individually packaged memory, complete with vivid sensory details. It seems funny now, how we are never really in control of the moments that do stand out later, with their smells and sounds so immediate and evocative. Afterward, I would not be able recall this one at will; instead, other flashes would return to me, glimpses of dark, suspicious eyes in the face of a Roma woman wrapped in a bright red scarf; fat, unripe walnuts dangling from a leafy tree; two old men playing tennis on a cracked court while wives more than forty years their junior looked on from the sidelines.

Regardless, I was there now, in the world my grandmother had come from. These were her childhood smells and sounds. These trees had been witnesses, and this sun had warmed her on summer days like this one. I hadn't thought about how it would feel to be walking on ground she might have walked on, under a sky so distinctly different from the one that had seemed so far away in dusty, honking Brooklyn. My eyes filled at the realization, and my vision blurred into a smear of gold and green. Somewhere a lawn mower shuddered to life, and the sound of it made me start. I tried to draw the world back into focus again, watched as a magpie strutted by, a starling pecked at a crevice between the paving stones, and slowly, layer by layer, my surroundings imposed themselves upon me again like the infinitely delicate sheets of flaky dough that my grandmother had deftly layered to create her famous napoleon dessert.

On the way to Kántorjánosi, a blink-and-you'll-miss-it village twenty-five miles from Nyíregyháza, I was largely silent as Angelika, the volunteer interpreter, and Zoltán conversed. In my hand I held an old photograph of my grandmother's childhood home that had been taken by one of my uncles on a 1988 visit.

I had scavenged it during a childhood treasure hunt. Of course, I did not know the exact address, so my plan had been to drive through the village and see if any of the houses matched the picture taken twenty-five years earlier.

Not the most ironclad plan, I now realized, as we drove past cornfields, apple orchards, and carefully tended vineyards. The land here was very flat and stretched for miles around us. Every field was full of enormous, healthy crops, seemingly impervious to the unforgiving heat of summer. Had I been crazy to think I could just show up with a few photographs and my grandmother's past would magically materialize before me? Now that I had actually made it, something I never really believed would happen, it seemed silly, and I was scared to fail after having come all this way. I had wanted to accomplish something specific on this trip. I had thought that if I could piece together the journey my grandmother had taken before she landed in the lap of the Satmar Hasids, then perhaps I could put into context my own journey out and back into the larger world she had once inhabited. In a sense, I would be able to clarify my own displacement only in the context of hers. We are, sometimes, simply reduced to where we come from—if not in the most immediate sense, then in an ancestral one. I was convinced that the angst that flowed in my veins was a result of more than just my childhood; that it was part of a greater composite inheritance that I was only a fragmentary part of, and to quell it, I needed to find the old fractures and mend them.

Kántorjánosi had one main street, which split into two smaller streets after the town square, and a few dead-end roads. We drove through it so quickly, thinking it was bigger, that we had to turn around and go back once we realized there were no more houses. I scanned every house, looking in particular for the unique ironwork in the gate in my photograph, but all the houses looked similar, with stucco sides painted various shades of beige and sloping terra-cotta roofs. They were all gated and had their own gardens.

"I don't see it! Do you see it?" I showed them the photograph. I had a panicky feeling that I had come all this way for nothing, that we would never be able to identify the exact house, that it was probably long gone by now.

"Is it that one?" Angelika asked, pointing as we coasted by a decrepit house, its gate rusted and warped. I turned back to look, trying to compare it with the one in the photo.

"They all look the same!" I said. "How can I be sure?"

"Never mind," Zoltán said. "Let's go talk to the mayor and see what he was able to find out." He had called ahead to announce our visit and its purpose, and I looked to him in gratitude. What reason did this man have to be so helpful? We didn't know each other from Adam, and it wasn't as if it was likely that we would see each other again after this pilgrimage. What could he possibly be getting from this? I wondered.

The mayor's office was in a modest but new building that flanked the town square. Inside, some people were lined up in the hallway. They seemed to be waiting for some form of assistance or welfare. "Gypsies," Angelika said, translating from the old Hungarian term for the Roma and Sinti people.

The mayor's secretary seemed unnerved by our arrival. I could imagine how she might be put off by the idea that I was some arrogant American expecting them to drop everything and help me. She instructed us to enter the mayor's office and wait there for his arrival. Inside, we sat at a small table that was covered in a crocheted tablecloth like the ones my grandmother had used for her dining room table. She had told me stories of women who started preparing their own trousseaus from a young age, knitting and sewing their own linens. I wondered who had crocheted this tablecloth.

The mayor was a soft-spoken man who seemed a bit taken aback by all the fuss. I could tell that this town didn't get many visitors. He had found my grandmother's house, he told us— there was an old woman living there now who, he said, was quite popular in the town. She sat on a bench outside her house every day and talked to everyone who passed by. She claimed to remember my family, even though she was in her nineties.

"Does she remember my grandmother?" I asked Angelika to ask the mayor.

"Perhaps," the mayor answered. "She's a bit fuzzy, but she says she remembers some things. Shall we go to her?"

We walked a little ways down the main street, named after the Hungarian poet János Arany, all of us in a group, and neighbors watched from behind their gates, eyes squinting in suspicion at our ostentatious procession.

"The people in this town always had a good relationship with the Jews," the mayor said pointedly to Zoltán, instructing him to translate. "Hungarians in general are not anti-Semitic."

The mayor then talked to Zoltán about his plans for the city, obviously happy to have an official visit his small town, and Angelika whispered the translations to me as we followed. The economy here was farm-based, he said, but somehow the Roma population accumulated enough money to furnish their homes quite lavishly, and even I could hear the sarcasm in his tone. The mayor estimated that the region was now at least fifty percent Roma. But it had once been at least as Jewish, I thought to myself, and I wondered if he would have expressed a similar displeasure at that fact. I supposed it was easy not to trouble oneself with anti-Semitism when there weren't any Jews left to hate.

A dark-skinned woman with flared nostrils and hair dyed a flaming orange crossed the street in front of us, pushing a stroller loaded with black plastic bags. She paused on the other side of the road and gave us a blank stare as we passed. Soon we came to a stop in front of the decrepit house that Angelika had pointed to earlier. Now I looked at the photograph in my hand again and saw that it was indeed the right house, but very neglected. The house was actually two buildings: a living area in the front and a separate kitchen in the back. The front building had a badly rusted tin roof, and lichens had coated the terracotta roof behind it. Both roofs seemed as if they might slide off on either side at any moment.

Outside the gate, an ancient-looking woman with only one visible tooth sat on a bench, her arm resting on a cane. She was wearing a loose flowery dress that buttoned down the front, and her exposed skin was leathery and brown from the sun.

I was not the first one to come visit her, she told Angelika as soon as we were within earshot. She remembered a tall young man many years ago who had asked her some questions.

"That was my uncle," I said. "He took this picture."

I showed her the photograph, and she apologized for the condition of the house, explaining that she had not been able to do any necessary repairs. Yet the garden behind her was bursting with color, and I remarked on it. There were numerous carefully pruned rosebushes and lilacs poking through the rusted curlicues in the gate. In particular, a bench lined with potted geraniums caught my eye.

"Tell her my grandmother used to do that," I said to Angelika. "She used to replant the cuttings."

Angelika relayed the information, and the old woman smiled and responded eagerly.

"She used to have more things growing," Angelika said. "But now she is too old."

Angelika leaned in and started a conversation in Hungarian. I looked past them at the house. I couldn't believe this was where my grandmother had spent her childhood, in this tiny little village. The fashionable, cosmopolitan woman I knew couldn't possibly have come from such a far-flung, barren smattering of dwellings.

"So, she remembers an older woman who lived here," Angelika said, interrupting my reverie, "who was a midwife. She had five children, and one of the daughters was named Laura."

"That's my great-grandmother Leah," I said. "Does she remember Leah's eldest daughter, Irenka?"

Angelika asked her and then told me, "She's not sure."

"Does she remember that they used to pump seltzer from the ground and sell it?"

"Yes. She said they had a little general store in the front room of the house."

Angelika turned to listen to something the old woman was saying.

"Also, she says she bought the house after the war from a man named Schwartz."

"That would be Laura's father," I said, "but that's impossible. He didn't survive the war. No one in my grandmother's family did." I motioned to Angelika not to translate that. I felt strangely sorry for the old woman, knowing that she had found it necessary to invent a story like that, to justify her life spent in this home.

"She wants to know if you would like to go inside and see it. She hasn't changed anything since she bought it, she says."

"She won't mind?" I asked, incredulous.

"Not at all. Go ahead."

I made my way gingerly down the path to the side door of the main building. Once inside, however, I immediately regretted my decision. The house was extremely dirty and reeked of human waste. I couldn't imagine my scrupulously tidy grandmother in a house like that. I emerged a moment later, trying to cling to some of the nicer details. There had been one large room in the front and one in the back. The ceilings were high and beamed; old, cumbersome chandeliers had dangled from between the shallow rafters, dusty crystals catching the faint rays of sunlight that weakly illuminated the darkened interior. I imagine they had all slept there, in one bedroom, the parents and their ten children. No wonder my grandmother had been sent to live in Nyíregyháza as an adolescent. There had been no room for her.

That was why she wasn't gassed, my grandmother had once told me. Because she had been deported separately from her family and hadn't been holding a younger sibling when she faced Dr. Mengele at selection. Anyone holding a child was automatically sent to their death. Her whole family had been murdered on the same day. She was the only one who made it past selection and was deemed qualified for labor. But she had never told me anything else, except that she had been liberated from Bergen-Belsen. The time in between her arrival at Auschwitz and her liberation from Bergen-Belsen was a question mark in my mind. How would I ever delve into the secret of her courage and endurance if I didn't know what had sustained her through that blank period? But I reminded myself that, after all, I was just at the beginning of my journey, and the answers, if they came, would be arrived at in time, if I was brave enough to keep going until then.

The mayor asked if I wanted to meet the only Jewish family that still lived in town, and we crossed the square to a house of similar stature. The mayor told the Roma woman working in the yard that we were looking for Orsi Neni. Zoltán whispered to me that the mayor and Orsi were quite close and had an excellent relationship. He seemed to be trying to say that race wasn't an issue here, especially not now. "She is one of the most beloved people in town," the mayor said eagerly, motioning for Angelika to translate.

Orsi Neni emerged from her home, a tiny old woman with very round eyes set in a deeply wrinkled face. Her voice was a crackly whisper. I asked her if she spoke any Yiddish. She shook her head no, explaining that her father had spoken it but she had never learned it. She didn't remember my grandmother, she said, but probably because she had been very young during the war.

"How is it that you were able to come back?" I asked.

"They hid in Levelek," Zoltán told me, referring to a larger town about fifteen minutes north. "The whole town helped, and they refused to give them to the Nazis."

"My grandmother said she was born in Levelek. Is there a hospital there or something?"

Angelika translated for the mayor, but he shook his head. "There's no hospital there that I know of." He couldn't say for sure why she would have been born there instead of in Kántor-jánosi, where she grew up.

"Levelek is our next stop," Zoltán said. "I know the registrar there."

Before we left, I asked whether Orsi Neni still lit candles on Friday night and baked challah.

"Of course!" was her answer.

"Do her children do so as well?" I asked.

"No, just her," Angelika said. "When she dies, no one will continue the tradition. She herself doesn't quite understand why she does it; she only remembers that her father told her to do so, before she was deported, and she follows his instructions as best as she can remember. But she can't obligate her children to do the same. After all, they've grown up like everyone else around them. They have no connection to this anymore."

How strange it was to find a Jewish woman here who had grown up in the same circumstances as my grandmother but who by some reverse twist of fate had never left home, and despite that, had become completely disconnected from her heritage. I recalled my thoughts from earlier that morning—how easily this could have been me; would that have meant I could have turned out like the children or grandchildren of this woman? How to qualify something like that? Certainly a blessing, but at such a high price!

As we left, the Roma woman, her brows knitted together in her dark and wrinkled forehead, gripped my hand tightly. "What does she want?" I whispered to Angelika.

"She said she just wanted to hold your hand."

I flipped over my palm to see if she wanted to read it. The woman dropped my hand suddenly, as if it had grown hot, and her cheeks turned red.

"She says she doesn't do that anymore," Angelika said. I tried to apologize, also embarrassed at my own assumptions. I had recalled when Roma women had tried to read Isaac's palm outside the mosque in Córdoba, which was ignorant of me.

The mayor had continued his conversation with Zoltán about the town. "There is no anti-Semitism here," he repeated. "Jews, Gypsies, and Hungarians have always lived well together here." It was as if he was presenting the town as a model for tolerance. "We never had this problem of racism," he said proudly. We said good-bye then, and I thanked him heartily, and he stood in the dirt road as we drove off, waving until we had rounded the bend that led out of town.

We continued on to Levelek, whose mayor appeared slightly more sophisticated. He was younger and well dressed and had bright blue eyes. He said that his family had come to Hungary during the Polish revolution. "That's why he's good-looking," Zoltán joked.

Ledgers were open on the mayor's table, and he invited me to peruse them. There was the marriage certificate of Laura Schwartz from Levelek to Jacob Fischer from Nyíregyháza, my grandmother's parents. Their names, places of origin, and occupations were all listed clearly. Jacob was a Talmud scholar, which confirmed my belief that his parents had been wealthy—only the wealthy could afford not to work. I saw the record of my grandmother's birth, on January 8, 1927, a few years after their marriage. They had come to report it five days later, on the thirteenth—the very same day my grandfather had been born.

"Perhaps they lived here in Levelek for the first few years, if that's where Laura was from originally. Then it makes sense that their first child would be born here, before they left to open a store in Kántorjánosi."

"The mayor says he can take us to the Jewish cemetery,"

Zoltán said. "Perhaps you'll find more information on your family there."

We drove to the cemetery in the mayor's car. He was decidedly more upbeat than the Kántorjánosi mayor and seemed very excited to talk to Zoltán and Angelika. It felt vaguely surreal to know that I, a twentysomething woman who easily blended into a crowd in New York City, was the cause of so much excitement and fuss in a small village thousands of miles from home.

A shirtless man met us at the entrance, the sweat glinting like dewdrops on his hairless chest. Angelika translated for me, explaining that the man and his wife had decided to voluntarily take care of the cemetery about ten years ago, as their home abutted the property. We followed him down a dirt path to a brick wall with a small gate in the middle and waited as he unlocked it.

My hopes deflated as soon as I was on the other side of the wall. All I saw was an empty field, the grass mostly yellow straw. Then I noticed stubs of hacked-off tombstones poking out from the brush.

"Most of the stones were stolen by Gypsies before he started taking care of it," Angelika said, listening closely as the caretaker explained sheepishly. "They are considered very valuable for the quality of the rock."

"So they're all gone?" I asked.

"Almost."

I had noticed two on the other end of the cemetery and one in the far western corner. I approached the single one first but noticed as I got closer that all of its writing had eroded. I trudged back.

"I can't read the writing anyway," I said. "It doesn't matter; they're probably not here."

"Don't you want to take a look at those other two before we leave?" Zoltán asked.

"All right," I said and began wading through the weeds.

Somewhere close to the stones I must have brushed against stinging nettle. I had never encountered the plant before, and didn't know what it looked like, but the painful feeling spread quickly around my ankles and up my calves—it felt like I was being bitten by a colony of ants.

"Ow!"

Angelika laughed. "She stepped on some *csalán!*" she said to Zoltán.

"Don't worry, Deborah," he said. "It will go away in ten minutes."

When I straightened up, I noticed I was standing in front of the stones. Perhaps it was my stinging legs that prevented me from grasping what I was looking at right away. The writing on the two stones was perfectly legible.

WOMAN OF VALOUR, FAIGA LEAH, read one. SAINTLY WOMAN, FAIGA PESSEL, read the other. The only two legible stones in the cemetery belonged to my great-grandmother and my great-great-grandmother.

"Oh my God!"

The others looked over, pausing their conversation briefly. Angelika looked up from her phone.

"It's them!" I shouted.

They hiked over. "That's Laura's grave," I said, pointing. "Of all the stones in the cemetery, these are the only ones here still in decent shape! There has to be an explanation, Angelika. Can you ask him if anyone ever came by and paid money to have these graves maintained?"

The caretaker insisted no one had ever visited this cemetery or interfered in its upkeep. "It's just a coincidence," he said. "These were the only ones left when I started taking care of the place."

It couldn't be a coincidence, I thought. Then I noticed the message on the bottom of the tombstones: DESCENDED FROM THE HOLY LEIBEL FROM OSHVARI. Reb Leibel, the hidden saint! His name inscribed upon the stone as if it was a magic ward! The stories from my childhood about this mysterious ancestor came rushing into my memory now like blood into a wound. No, it was too much. It couldn't be this real, right there, literally carved in stone.

I wondered now if, given what I understood to be a super-stitious stereotype attributed to the Roma, it was possible to suppose that they too might have stayed away from those stones, just like other Jews had learned to do, out of fear of that very same legend I had been told as a child, passed down among their own. But the caretaker claimed to know nothing about it, and I knew I would have to live with that uncertainty.

On the way out of the cemetery, we stopped to pick sour cherries from slender trees with dark green leaves that grew wild along the path. I watched as Angelika sucked a whole bunch of them effortlessly off their pits, stopping to grind them into the ground again with her shoe. For each cherry she consumed, a whole lot of them might grow in its place. How incredible, I thought, to have food growing wild on the street. I tasted a cherry, and it was perfectly ripe, emerging from its thin, still-delicate skin in one tart, juicy burst on my tongue. I closed my eyes and remembered the taste of my grandmother's cold sour cherry soup, the one she served on hot summer days like this one. I wondered if she missed picking the fruit from the tree or lamented the quality of store-bought or canned sour cherries. Had she missed her life here? Or had she in some way been grateful to have rebuilt her life in America, in a vastly more civilized and developed place than this hot, dusty village, where the saving graces were wild cherries and potted geraniums?

On the way back we stopped for lunch in a village called Napkor. I pounced eagerly on a cold pear soup, served with sweet strips of *palacsinta*, or Hungarian crepes, as noodles. The flavors were impossible to place, a hint of something like nutmeg, a kind of cream that was neither sour nor sweet but faintly tart, and a dash of zest that might have been from a kumquat. My spoon came up empty all too quickly, but this was soon forgotten, as our duck arrived in clearly identifiable parts, a crispy-skinned leg each for me and Angelika, a breast for Zoltán, and an assemblage of parts and organs for our driver. The duck was served on beds of caramel-colored mashed potatoes with generous sprinkles of sweet paprika and accompanied by shredded cabbage and prunes stained a deep purple. We dug in, and silence reigned at that table until the plates were cleared.

Afterward, I marveled at how it was possible to eat such meals, meals that easily outranked the ones I had been served at New York City's fanciest restaurants in those months when my celebrity status had allowed it, in such a far-flung setting and at such ridiculously cheap prices. Was it really as simple as recipes honed for generations, water drawn from deep springs and wells, fertile, unspoiled land that nourished crops and animals? I supposed, in such circumstances, even a Michelin-starred chef would be rendered superfluous. To this day I prefer the honest, nourishing food my grandmother had once cooked for me with so much love to the excessively ornamental dishes served in restaurants so overtly snobbish as to be offensive in their incongruence.

It was late afternoon when we arrived back in Nyíregyháza, just in time to visit the synagogue before it closed. The Jews had been rounded up for deportation right in front of it, and it was there that I had most wanted to stand, in the spot where my grand-mother's own exile had so horribly begun. The square was now paved over, with decaying apartment buildings serving as wary witnesses around its perimeter. Their shabby terraces with peel-ing blue paint strips seemed like so many eyes half-closed in fa-tigue. This was not the Nyíregyháza my grandmother had seen on that day, but it seemed somehow to retain the memory of that moment in its tired bones nonetheless, and the deserted square and heavy gray sky seemed in agreement with my assessment.

The synagogue was a stately building with small high win-dows and a secure gate. I tried to imagine the roundup that had taken place there, but these were events dramatized in movies or vividly evoked in books I'd read; they couldn't possibly have happened in such a quiet and ordinary place. Reality would have to split apart for a moment to allow something like that. Life as I understood it, the banal pursuit of food, salary, and entertainment, would have to completely collapse; it would have to be replaced with something alien and otherworldly.

The synagogue was painted pink with white trim. It looked nothing like the *shuls* I had grown up around, and more like the Reform temples I had glimpsed in Manhattan. Inside, the synagogue had a low, unenclosed women's gallery, and in such a small building, those women would have been clearly visible to the men below. The synagogues I had grown up with had women's sections that were fully separated from the main room by height and enclosure. This had been a very Modern Orthodox community, nothing like the one I remembered my grandmother being a part of.

I posed a question to the rabbi. "Were there any Hasidic Jews living here before the war?"

Angelika translated. The rabbi shook his head slowly.

"None that I know of. From what I heard, there was a small group of them over in Satu Mare, now in Romania, and perhaps another small community in the southern region, but there were no Hasids in this area back then. In the eighties, they came to Budapest, the Lubavitchers, and tried to convert everyone. They even tried to convert me. Like I wasn't a good-enough Jew for them." Here he scoffed, underlining the ridiculousness of the scenario. Converting a rabbi indeed. It was insulting, he exclaimed, when you considered the long line of rabbis he was descended from, that the Lubavitchers, themselves part of a fringe movement only two hundred years old, would dare to impugn the integrity of his own heritage.

There was an old *mikvah*, a ritual bathing place, in the synagogue that the rabbi still carefully maintained, although he himself did not use it. But the Satmars, he told me, came every so often to visit the grave sites of their rabbis, and when they did, they often used it for a fee that helped keep the synagogue going. He offered to show it to me. It was accessible only from the cellar, which we entered from a cement staircase that descended into the earth from the rear of the building. In the cellar we climbed down into a dank and musty space that had been hollowed out, at the bottom of which lay a pool of stagnant rainwater collected by a pump. The smell was overpowering.

"They actually go in there?" I asked incredulously.

"Yes," he answered, somewhat bemusedly. "I try to freshen the water before they come, but it is what it is, you know. And there's not even a shower in the building where they could rinse off after. But this is enough for them. As long as it's halachically sound, everything else doesn't matter."

I wrinkled my nose. The one time I had immersed in a men's *mikvah*, I had seen a giant water bug floating next to me, and forty-eight hours later I had fallen sick with an illness later diagnosed as shingles, which the doctor ascertained had been caught in those warm waters that I had shared with countless other men and women. What had happened to those stories we had been told, of Jews being spared from the plague because of their hygiene rituals?

The rabbi and his associate gave us a ride back to the college, as our chauffeur had left for the day. I heard the two of them talking in exuberant Hungarian in the front seat, and I could just about make out that the conversation was about me. I asked Angelika to listen in.

"He is saying," she said with a laugh, "that he doesn't understand how someone can talk so much and listen so well at the same time, that your brain works so fast. But he says you are very sweet."

"Ach, you are translating for her?" the rabbi said. "No, don't be offended. We just don't often get such intense visitors—we are accustomed to a slower pace here."

"It's okay," I said, smiling. "It's not the first time I've heard that."

Zoltán walked me to my room when we got back.

"I'm so thrilled that we were able to do this," he said. "This is what I want to show, that Hungarians can help! There is no anti-Semitism here. There never was."

When I left Nyíregyháza some days later, I looked out the window at the passing world, thinking that this planet was like a snow globe that received regular shakes. The war had been a particularly vigorous one, and because of that, my grandmother had drifted over to the other side of the world amid the chaos, forever changing our family's legacy. And here I was, drifting back, looking for the place where I could land, wondering if it existed at all.

We wanted to visit my grandfather's hometown as well. Újfehértó it was called, only twenty-five minutes from the town where my grandmother had been born. The bureaucrat who was being paid to print birth certificates and death certificates and other such documents for people in precisely my position made us come back three days in a row, and each time she had a different excuse. There we were on the third day, with our official stamps procured, all fees paid, and the front door to the town hall locked for an hour already with Angelika and I still in it, and still there was this tut-tutting, the opening and shutting of doors with ancient ledgers peering temptingly behind them, the meandering phone conversations in Hungarian that I couldn't understand, and still those certificates weren't printed.

My translator indicated that I might have to wait and receive the rest in the mail. We'd had no trouble procuring the birth and marriage records of my grandmother, great-grandmother, and great-great-grandmother in Levelek. Indeed, the registrar had produced them with a joyous smile. Here in Újfehértó, I felt the tears come and quickly left the room. My eyes began to swim as the cleaner painstakingly removed the padlock from the double doors so that I could exit the building, and outside the scene blurred into brown and gray as I collapsed onto a bench.

Zoltán came and sat next to me, inquiring what was wrong. "I don't understand," I heaved, wishing I could stop sobbing. "Why does she have to be that way?"

The translator explained briefly, "Some people are just like that. Bureaucrats. It's unfortunate but it happens all the time. Not everyone can be a lovely person."

I'm so thrilled that we were able to do this, Zoltán had said to me after dropping me off at the college. *Hungarians can help. There is no anti-Semitism here.* Poor Zoltán. I was sure there wasn't a shred of anti-Semitism in his heart, nor was there any in the lovely group of people he had assembled to assist me in my research, but I know that he would have felt terrible to realize that on the rest of my trip, I would learn something very different from what he wanted me to.

Perhaps the first dusting of bitterness set in once I arrived back in Budapest, when I met, for the first time, a Jew who was afraid. I had arranged to meet a friend named Ella, whom I had first connected with online. She took me on a tour of the Jewish quarter, an area of special expertise for her, although she wasn't Jewish. Here I saw a living Jewish community, a kosher butcher, a Belzer Hasid from Israel who had moved back here with his children and was able to converse with me in Yiddish, women in *sheitels* escorting young boys with messy side curls, Hebrew writing next to Hungarian, and synagogues and ritual baths and all the familiar paraphernalia. Cholent, a staple dish in Jewish communities worldwide, was listed on most restaurant menus.

After we toured the Orthodox synagogue together, Ella and I decided to drop by the Judaica shop next door. A young man was working there, sitting behind a desk piled with books. He had curly brown hair and a nice familiar face, very Jewish-looking. So I asked. I did not see Ella's face behind me go white. Peter—that was his name—drew inward and away from me, his shoulders scrunching up in defense.

"That's a very private issue," he said.

Oh. Where I came from, it wasn't private at all. A Jew, traveling, meets another Jew and says, "Shalom."

"I'm sorry," Ella apologized in a whisper. "She's from America."

"Ah." Peter relaxed a bit.

"What—you can't ask someone if they're Jewish in Hungary?"

Ella nodded. "It's a very offensive question here, almost never asked for a positive reason. You have to be very careful in this anti-Semitic environment."

"It's that bad?" I thought back to the handful of days I had spent in the east of Hungary, where I had seen quite a few cities and villages and towns, and met so many people, and only the dreadful bureaucrat stood out to me as someone who might have been, just maybe, a tad anti-Semitic. But she could also have been a generally rude and unhelpful person, no? Or an overworked and underpaid civil servant? Or a frustrated matron resentful of an entitled American who swooped into her town with chauffeur, translator, and esteemed university president in tow? "I heard about the Jobbik party, and Gÿongyösi's idea for a list of Jews as national security risks, but that was laughed out of parliament, right?" I said.

Ella's forehead was creased. "He's got eight percent now, but with next year's elections, he'll get twenty percent at least."

"What happened? Is everyone suddenly going crazy? Is anti-Semitism becoming acceptable again?"

"The problem is, in Hungary, it never left," Ella said darkly.

There was still flooding then, so Ella couldn't show me the sculpted shoes that lined the banks of the Danube. Instead, she led me to the larger Dohány Street Synagogue, with its stately courtyard, now a memorial, where the Jews of Budapest had been made to await deportation. In the last days of the war, she informed me—when the Nazis had retreated in anticipation of the Russian advance—the Hungarians had taken it upon themselves to drag the remaining Jews down to the river and shoot them into it. To save ammunition they had tied groups of five or six together and shot just one; the rest of the group would fall into the river and be drowned instead.

They had been made to take off their shoes first; big and small, old and new, they had lined the banks afterward. The sculptors had re-created the scene by placing replicas along both sides of the Danube. For weeks, Ella told me, the Danube had been red with blood. "They weren't under any orders," she said. "They just wanted to get rid of the Jews before the world came to its senses again and the opportunity was lost."

My observations of Jewish life in Budapest were especially absorbing because now I was able not only to imagine prewar Judaism but to actually see it, for the community that had remained had proceeded as if no time had passed. Did I want to see those ancient tenement buildings around echoing courtyards from which spectral tormentors drove their sobbing victims? There they were, still as shabby and rotting as they had been then, children's voices echoing through the courtyard like trapped spirits. Could I visualize the archetypal Jew, his head bent in humility, looking at the floor, all his movements restrained so as to draw the least amount of attention to himself? There he was, the man who stepped out of the kosher restaurant and put his kippah in his pocket, checking to see if he was being watched. What did I know of this life, where one's identity must be kept secret, where one must always look over a shoulder in search of a menacing pursuer? No, I never knew such privations. I had yearned to take off my Hasidic costume so that I could blend in and be normal, but I never experienced a desire to do so out of fear. It was fear that had kept us so separate in Europe, and that continued to do so in a place like Budapest, but could that threat still apply to me? Even I had eventually realized that those stories of hate and persecution, designed to teach me to keep my distance from gentiles, no longer applied in the New World, in the melting pot of Brooklyn where I had grown up. The question was, was this true anywhere else? Had Europe changed at all, or was it still the same place my grandmother had described?

5
REISE
רייזע
JOURNEY

The next stop on my journey was Sweden, the only place I had ever heard my grandmother speak of solely with fondness. She had spent most of her time there with her friend Edith, who had been with her in the camps. I had never been permitted to meet her nor was she allowed in our home, due to her status as a nonbeliever. My grandmother had kept those visits a secret from everyone else except for me; she had entrusted me with the story of their friendship, and I had learned that Edith was the other woman in that photo of my grandmother being carried out of Bergen-Belsen on a stretcher lifted by handsome, smiling, fair-haired men, squinting shyly and uncertainly into the camera, for it was she who had insisted that my grandmother was still alive, even as she lay intertwined among the gray corpses, her breathing so slow as to be barely noticeable. Edith had accompanied my grandmother during her rescue by the British Red Cross; they had obtained transport on the same ship to Sweden, where my grandmother was sent to recuperate from typhus in health resorts that had been temporarily refashioned into refugee camps. Now I realized that back then, it must not have mattered that Edith was on the verge of renouncing her faith while my grandmother was about to dive in headfirst. It seemed clear to me that faith must have been irrelevant in a world turned upside down by war; rather, it was something to grapple with when the ground steadied itself underneath one's feet.

Later my grandmother would explain to me that there were only two justifiable alternatives after the Holocaust: to renounce God completely, because the Shoah itself served as proof of either his nonexistence or his irrelevance, or to embrace the idea that God was a ball of fury and set out to appease him by sacrificing oneself on the altar of ritual worship. To her, Edith's choice was as grounded and rational as that of the survivors who had founded our community; that the two choices had so diverged from each other was a matter of arbitrary happenstance.

In Sweden, there would be a chance to fill in some of the gaps in my grandmother's history. I arrived there by flying to Copenhagen and crossing the bridge to Malmö by train, knowing that the city had been the first port of entry for the two women, as demonstrated by the stamps on my grandmother's travel papers. I took a bus to the outskirts in search of the local *Riksarkivet* division, and once I had an audience with the woman working at the archive, I opened the little shoebox I had been using to store the relevant photos and documents and they spilled out onto the counter in a haphazard pile. The archivist lifted a photo gingerly from the assemblage; there was my grandmother standing next to Edith in front of a grand house, with tall pine trees filling the background. "This looks like the lake region," she mused. "It's a collection of spa resorts in the center of the country."

My grandmother, she explained then, had been brought to Sweden as part of Operation *Vita Bussarna* (white buses), the Swedish relief effort that rescued hundreds of Holocaust victims directly from the camps. "But that wouldn't have been her," I said. "She was rescued by the Red Cross—look at this photo here! Was there another way she could have arrived in Sweden?"

"They painted red crosses on those white buses," she explained. "That's how they were able to get past the military."

"But why her? Why would they take her?"

"She had typhus, correct? At that time, Sweden had a special program to rehabilitate typhus victims, and because they were especially equipped to support sufferers, and the Allies were afraid of an epidemic, most of them were quarantined in the lake region."

But records of my grandmother were not in the archive. The clerk took another look at the copy of the Swedish alien's passport I had pointed to. Perhaps here, she said, pointing to the stamp from the Swedish Aliens Commission. The way the archives program in Sweden was organized, she explained, each city was home to a different archive. Nothing was digitized. The records of the Aliens Commission were located in the *Riksarkivet* in Stockholm, she said. I would have to take a train all the way across the country.

It took six hours; the train was old and made loud clacking sounds on the tracks and seemed to traverse painfully slowly through an unchanging landscape, and although the weather was moderate for summer, the beating sun warmed the cars past comfortable temperatures and the windows propped open did nothing to help. I arrived in the Swedish capital sweaty and exhausted from the trip.

In Stockholm I found a cheap hostel to sleep in, as the hotels were all extremely expensive, in comparison to not just Hungary but also New York, and I did not want to exceed my budget for the trip only one week in. I purchased a single room with a shared bathroom; it was so tiny it had room only for a ninety-centimeter bed and a small table that folded out from the wall, but the window overlooked Gamla Stan, the old town of Stockholm, and I could hear church bells ringing in the distance.

After I showered, I went out into the bright midsummer evening to find a bar in which to have a drink and something small to eat before going to sleep, and around the corner from the hostel, in a large square facing a canal, I met Erik. I was looking for a café I had located on a map, trying to orient myself according to its grid. Perhaps I looked quite obviously like a tired tourist in need of help, and he offered it in passing on his way home from work. I suppose I was my usual American self, in that I shared too much information and requested too much of it from him, but this time it did not seem to offend or unnerve him like I had become accustomed to expect from Europeans. First he offered to walk with me part of the way, then all the way, and by the time we had arrived at my destination, he turned to me and said shyly, "You know, I know a better café where we could have dinner. I would love to invite you for a meal, if you don't mind some company."

I was surprised but very flattered. Erik was very Swedish— tall and slender with fine, angular bone structure and very pale eyes. I found him handsome but also foreign, and I felt toward him the way, for example, I had felt upon having my first taste of lobster in Paris—attracted but also nervous and uncertain about what to expect.

I could have spared myself the anxiety. In Erik I found a deeply kind, gentle, and intelligent man, one who had wrested himself from the poorer rural provinces at a young age; at twenty-six he was already a junior associate at a prestigious law firm and he blushed self-consciously when he informed me that he had recently been awarded a Wallenberg scholarship to study international law at Stanford. He was to move there in August and was very excited, but also nervous. He didn't know any Americans, although he liked what he saw in movies, and, he told me, I confirmed all of his fantasies. I was friendly and open, he said, unlike other Swedish people he knew; he liked my directness. It seemed we both liked the foreign qualities in each other that would be taken for granted in our homelands.

After having drunk enough of the rosé he had ordered, I confessed to finding him handsome, and this seemed to surprise him so much he actually accused me of joking at his expense.

We walked back toward my hostel in the evening, which was still in a kind of early twilight phase as the midnight sun had peaked only ten days earlier, and upon seeing where I was staying Erik hesitated, then said, "This may seem wildly inappropriate, but I can't help but mention that I have a lovely spacious apartment not far from here that is probably way more comfortable, and definitely more safe, than this arrangement."

I laughed. "Are you asking me to go home with you?"

"No! Well, yes. But that's not what I meant!" And he was so charming in his stumbling that I couldn't help but kiss him.

It was not love, but something else, something sweet and light and above all palliative after the psychological tension that had been building since the beginning of this trip. I told him the real reason I was in Sweden, having feared, at first, that the seriousness of purpose and the mention of the Holocaust would turn him off. But he was sympathetic and curious and wanted to help, telling me where to go first thing on Monday morning and even drawing a route for me on the map.

On Monday, Erik went to work and I took a bus to the address he had written down for me, which was the main archive center. At the information desk I was informed that the division I was looking for was closeted away in a special room that only one expert had access to, and he needed to be called in. I waited impatiently for an hour until he arrived. A lanky, middle-aged man, gray-haired, bearded, with skin the ghastly white color of chalk, he took the ticket that had been wordlessly issued to me and disappeared for twenty minutes.

He came back with a slim white box, which he opened on the table in front of me.

"Sorry, but this was all I could find," he said haltingly, in heavily accented English, and removed from the box a thick folder containing sheaves of documents about my grandmother, all in Swedish. I was speechless with joy at this unexpected bounty. At best, I had hoped for a one-page record of her temporary presence in the country. I reached over to give the archivist a spontaneous hug, which almost made him jump out of his skin.

"You don't know how much this means to me," I said.

He backed away, his eyes widened in alarm. "You're welcome," he said, once he was at a safe distance, and he continued to walk backward until he was out of the room.

. . .

Later, Erik and I spread copies of the documents out on his kitchen table and he helped me with the initial translation. There were pages of testimony about her experiences during the war, which had been collected by international police. The translation was wooden, but I could almost hear my grand-mother saying those words out loud. The testimony had been taken in German, the documents said. Had she indeed spoken a rudimentary German, or was that Yiddish they were referring to? I had never heard her speak a word of German. Certainly she had not spoken that language, the language of those peo-ple. No, it must have been *Daytshmerish*, that dressed-up version of Yiddish that we had made fun of as children, what Rezzori had termed *yiddling* in his book *Memoirs of an Anti-Semite*, what I myself had made use of in Hungary to commu-nicate with Zoltán.

She had been one of two hundred Hungarian women chosen for their ability to perform skilled labor, culled from Auschwitz and taken to various munitions factories throughout Germany, where they were forced to fashion weapons for the Nazi army. They had to have known that they were aiding the war effort, I assumed. Later, I would learn from online research that a memorial had been erected for those two hundred women in the small town in Germany where they had worked, at the site of the former factory where the munitions had been produced. The memorial was erected out of sensitivity to those women who had been forced into the particular cruelty of man-ufacturing the agents of their own destruction. I tried to imag-ine my grandmother producing guns, bombs, or grenades. My grandmother, who could whip a meringue so fine that it hov-ered over the bowl. Had her fingers shaped cold metal? Had they been blackened with powder? Try as I might, I couldn't envision it.

It was so unreal, all of it. Tangible, on paper, incontrovertible evidence, and yet unreal. I couldn't build the mental bridge between everything I had experienced as a child raised in my grandmother's home and this chilling war story. For try as I might, I could not see the connection between this tale and the story of our community. She looked so modern in the photos, so independent. She had been so industrious in Sweden, after her recovery. Having been sent with other refugees to the south to pick fruit for a paltry wage, she had succeeded in quickly separating herself from the others by landing a post in Gothenburg as a couture seamstress—*sömmerska* was the word in Swedish. I thought of summer when I read it, which seemed fitting, for my memories of her are bound up among roses and sunshine and birdseed.

There was a long list of places and dates in her file; they were penciled on yellowing paper and difficult to decipher, but they comprised a detailed itinerary of her time in Sweden. I asked Erik to show me where the places were on a map. His finger swiped haphazardly from region to region, north, south, east, west, back and forth, as he scrolled down the list in chronological order.

"How could she have moved around this much?" I asked. Erik wondered if the refugees had been shipped according to how much room there was for them, and where.

I knew I didn't have time to make it to all the places on the list. Some of them were a day's ride away. But the next day, without so much as a discussion, Erik called in sick to work and rented a shiny gray Volvo and we drove to the lake region in central Sweden, where spas and resorts traditionally used by Sweden's upper class for restoration had been converted into temporary refugee camps after the war. These were the places my grandmother would have recovered in. Afterward, she worked in a small town, then in a big city, in the house of a local designer. There she had found the friends who had tried to help her emigrate.

Sweden's lake region consisted of deserted roads of pebble and dirt and an endless horizon of tall, spindly pines with raw trunks the color of cocoa powder. We drove past lake after lake after lake, each one shimmering a cold, clear blue under a comparatively pale sky. When we arrived at Loka Brunn, a famous old spa town now restored to its former architectural glory, the small settlement was deathly quiet. The doors to the cluster of houses there were all open, but the buildings were silent and still. Together they served as a kind of museum, designed to explain the town's role during World Wars I and II, but although it was officially open for visitors, there were neither any of these nor any employees in all of the rooms we peered into.

At the next address, we were able to walk around the enormous old castle in which the refugees had been housed, the grand house in that photo of my grandmother and Edith, with its elegant veranda, the wall of which Edith had perched on in the photo, her hand wrapped around the support beam and the rest of her body leaning out as if getting ready to swing off and jump to the lawn below. My grandmother had stood there with her back straight, her head tucked slightly to the side and her smile an obligatory pose for the camera—it made her look much older than I knew she had been, older in fact than anyone I knew, so old that I thought such a smile would look misplaced on any human being, for it was entirely otherworldly in its aching sadness.

Now the house where she had stood and smiled for the camera was shut down, in need of repair. The residents in that small town were all senior citizens. Erik approached a woman who was sitting on her porch in a rocking chair and tried to show her the photos we had; he asked her in Swedish if she knew anything about the role that the town had played after the war.

The woman was older than my grandmother, seemingly senile and hard of hearing, but after several painstaking attempts she seemed to understand Erik. She explained slowly, as if struggling to recall the words, that she had been a young newlywed when they had brought the refugees here, and she pointed to a wildly overgrown meadow that began where her street ended. "They fenced them in," she explained. "In the beginning, to make sure they weren't sick. There was a wire fence around the whole thing. I remember seeing them behind the mesh, but I never spoke to any of them, and they didn't speak to us. A year or so later, they were all gone, transported elsewhere."

So they had been confined here too, I realized, and this revelation had a bodily impact on me; it was as if stones had landed in my stomach. I wanted to cry, but I didn't want Erik to see me and feel burdened, so I turned and walked quickly toward that overgrown meadow, as if to inspect it. At the end of the street, buried under thorny bushes and fat vines, were the rusted remains of a wire fence, intertwined among the foliage. I touched one of the metal tentacles, twisted by time and weather, and thought of that moment years ago when a similar one had ripped itself into the skin of my hand, and for a brief moment I wanted to plunge this one into my ribs, if just for a second to feel something stronger than this overpowering grief.

The next morning Erik went back to work and I wandered aimlessly around his neighborhood, Södermalm. I walked up the bustling Hornsgatan, stopping at the window of Café Giffi after noticing in it many familiar pastries of my childhood set out in the glass display case. My grandmother had made those, but who had taught her how? They were certainly not traditional Hungarian confections and couldn't have been passed down from her mother, as she'd claimed. I went inside to order a coffee and one of those round lacy cookies I remembered. They were called *toscaflam* here, the owner explained. They were sandwiched together with pastry cream, not dipped in chocolate as she had done.

"Are you Jewish?" the white-haired Chinese man who owned the café asked as he brought me my coffee. I had this panicked thought that someone had informed him I might be coming, which I immediately dismissed as ridiculous.

"Yes," I answered in a cautious tone.

"Are you American?" he asked, with even more enthusiasm this time.

"Yes," I said again.

"I knew it! You look just like Woody Allen!"

I look like a cantankerous old man—great, I thought.

"You should meet Leon," he urged. "My best customer. Comes in every day. Also Jewish."

"Sure," I said, thinking that Jews must be a rare thing around here if he thought we needed to stick together.

Leon turned out to be a garrulous and somewhat raunchy old man, a childless bachelor who still behaved as if he was in his teens, nothing like the solemn and dignified elderly people

I had grown up around. He was eighty-six, exactly the same age as my grandmother. He had come to Sweden as a refugee from Berlin when he was eight years old, before the war. He'd never been married, he said, but he now regretted it. He didn't like feminists, he informed me, as if to give me advance notice.

"Do you remember the survivors?" I asked, trying to steer the conversation away from his obsolete political views. "When they came here after the war?"

"Of course I do. They were impossible to ignore, although they kept very much to themselves, although I think that was mostly because they scared everyone else. They had these swollen bellies, you know."

"Because of the shock of sudden nutrition?"

"I suppose. They ate a lot. They were hungry all the time. They were all trying to compulsively put on weight."

The photograph of my grandmother that I had found in her file at the *Riksarkivet*, taken only months after her liberation, had shocked me. I could barely recognize her in it, with her swollen face, her hollow, unseeing expression.

"Did they seem sad?" I asked.

"Sad? No!" he said with great certainty. "If anything, they seemed very strong."

I left the café after that, wanting that sentence to define my conversation with him. Of course my grandmother had seemed strong. It wasn't the depressives who survived the horrors of war; it was the stoic and valiant who made it through. Of course she wouldn't have spent much time lamenting her losses. She threw herself into skilled work, made plans for the future. She wanted to replace the family she had lost by marrying and having many children. I suppose it made sense that she would choose someone familiar for a husband, someone who spoke her native languages and came from her region, when she had lost everything else familiar in her life.

After all, it was I who struggled with this wasteful emotion, with this useless and burdensome grief, as if in her refusal to indulge it she had simply handed it off to me, and I bore the burden in her honor. The way she had lit those candles for her murdered siblings, I kept the memory of her grief alive. I was afraid to let go even for one moment.

I had pieced together from her file that the Hungarian government wouldn't give her an identity document after the war. She had appealed over and over to the embassy in Stockholm. It was only after her influential friends in Gothenburg interceded for her that Swedish diplomatic interference ensured she finally received a piece of paper stating she was born in Hungary but that did not constitute acknowledgment of her citizenship. This had proved enough to apply for an alien's passport, which had then allowed her application for U.S. citizenship to finally be approved, after three tries.

It provoked me deeply, seeing evidence of her travails in this arena. It was unimaginable that someone who had just survived hell should have to be consumed for three years with the maddening process of begging for a home in any country that would take her. She had even considered immigrating to Cuba under the condition that she would only perform agricultural labor. It was written into an agreement she signed with the Cuban government. She had also stated, over and over, her intention to immigrate to Palestine. She, who had ultimately married into a fervently anti-Zionist community!

"Everyone was a Zionist then," Leon had told me.

What I couldn't understand was, what happened to that

strength that she had so bravely displayed then, completely on her own, in a mad world still reeling from chaos? In the years in which I lived under her roof, I never knew her to speak her mind or advocate for her needs. This fortitude I now had evidence of had been left by the wayside in exchange for the complete self-sacrifice required by the Satmar rabbi. Was this what ultimately marked one as a survivor, then—the urge to subsume one's identity under the heavier mantle of martyrdom for the sake of the dead?

Once when I had briefly visited New Orleans on my book tour, a tall man with a T-shirt proclaiming his Native American heritage had approached me on the street in the French Quarter.

"You've got dead people all around you," he'd said to me, his face stern and serious.

"What?" I'd said, thinking he was joking.

"Dead people. Everywhere. They're following you. Probably your ancestors. That's what they're telling me."

"No, you're making a mistake," I told him, laughing nervously. "They can't be my ancestors. My family disowned me. I'm cut off from my community. I doubt my ancestors haven't caught on."

"You're the one who's mistaken," he said, glaring, the tone of his voice impatient. "They know it all. But they're still there, and they want you to know. Don't neglect them."

I had looked around then at the quiet street, darkening in the early evening. Which ancestors? What were they like? And why would they bother with someone like me?

In Hungary, I'd asked myself who I could hope to be if I didn't first know the person my grandmother had hoped to become.

Was this why her story seemed embedded in my own sense of self, why I felt compelled to know her dreams through mine? I had searched all my life for a magic of my own, an answer to my grandmother's inextinguishable essence. I had sought the location of my own unbending will, the source of my strength. In myself I had found only fallibility and fear, but what I now realized I had inherited from my grandmother was the knowledge that home is an internal space you could carry inside you, that it could never be violated, even if your whole world was turned upside down. My grandmother had unwittingly taught me that to be a whole person, you did not need the certainty of blood relations or confirmed origins; you needed only your convictions. She was showing me again now, through her own story of heroic survival, that I did not need family to survive. Even when ugliness abounded and it felt like the hate of the world was directed at her, she demonstrated that the integrity of the self could never be compromised.

Her memory modeled a true independence for me, the kind that renders you free even behind the tallest fences, because your mind is a series of doors that open outward.

Perhaps I could have returned home right then, satisfied with the results of my undertaking. Perhaps, if I had not booked my return flight from Berlin, I might have decided to skip that last step in my journey. But deep down I must have known that setting foot on German soil was an inevitable part of this unearthing process, and not simply to follow the trail of my grandmother's suffering, but to confront that black hole in my own consciousness, that enormous knot of pain and fear that was associated with all things emanating from the term "German."

Erik accompanied me to the airport. He nearly cried when we had to part, and suddenly I felt guilty for having taken advantage of his hospitality. I had failed to notice that he had developed an emotional attachment, one that I myself had not felt. Though perhaps this said less about Erik than about myself, as I hadn't allowed myself to develop attachment in any kind of romantic situation.

"I'm afraid I'll never see you again," Erik whispered.

"In a few months, you'll be in Stanford, where every girl will go crazy for your Scandinavian good looks," I responded jokingly, "and trust me, you'll be so distracted by the assortment on offer, you won't even want to see me again."

He looked hurt, and I chastised myself for not simply telling him the truth, which was that I couldn't even imagine myself deserving of such a pure man as himself, who had no baggage or trauma to hold him back, whose entire future was wide open, and in which I would only represent an unjust burden. I had a child, and I was stuck within my allotted radius, and to let Erik into my life would also mean enclosing him within my prison, both physical and psychological. So instead, I led him to believe that I wasn't interested in a long-term relationship with him. Truthfully, I said it with conviction, but looking back I do not believe I could have possibly known how I felt, for I had clamped down on my heart for so long that it was a suffocated and bloodless pulp.

Back then my romantic adventures had been dalliances in psychological power games, dances around barriers and taboos, an exploration of the dark, the forbidden, the shameful. I recalled, as the plane ascended, how only a year or so earlier I had gone on a date with a man named Otto who worked the cash register at my favorite bookstore. He was German American, very tall and broad-shouldered, with a strong nose and a jaw that broadened impossibly when he smiled. Our date ended at the foot of the Williamsburg Bridge, with us pretending it was 1939, and I was a Jewish girl he found on the street.

Afterward we were both embarrassed by what we had done— Otto for getting so carried away, and me for feeling as if it were real.

Otto and I never saw each other again. I avoided the bookstore after that. What had I been looking for that night? It would take me years to understand it.

I remembered that during my time at Sarah Lawrence, I had met a young woman who worked as a dominatrix in a Manhattan dungeon and who confided to me that she repeatedly had visits from "rabbis" from my community who wanted her to dress up as a Nazi and beat them.

"They're not all rabbis just because they have beards!" I said, but that anecdote stuck with me, and I mulled it over for a while. Were there really men from Williamsburg, raised by Holocaust survivors, who sought to put a face on their inherited persecutors and reexperience the pain their parents and grandparents endured? Was this simply survivor's guilt, or was there something darker, and more erotic, in that impulse? More important, did I suffer from the same affliction?

I had never articulated to myself a desire for pain, but I had noticed my attraction to a sense of power, both in myself and in others. Something in me was crying out for the stick, and for the chance to overpower the one who wielded it. Of course, there might have been a simpler answer—I was controlled and overpowered as a child, and here was my opportunity to relive the experience with a different ending. And yet, there was also something very seductive about the prospect of giving up my power, only to conquer it once more, tenfold. For with the return of my power came the lifeblood of the enemy that sought to rob me of it—simply by losing, he abdicated all of his own might to me.

I landed in Vienna and headed straight to the Hauptbahnhof, where I purchased a flexible ticket to Munich. I boarded a train going in that direction and found myself sitting across from a handsome young man named Martin, fair-haired and blue-eyed, who didn't realize that the German I was speaking to him was Yiddish. He assumed, when I used a word that he didn't understand, that I was speaking some strange mountain dialect. I explained to him that I was American, but that my grandparents still spoke this old dialect, and at one point I asked him, innocently and offhand, if there was any anti-Semitism in Austria. His eyes widened in disbelief. "Here? Of course not! We never had anti-Semitism here. You are confusing us with the Germans." The way he said it, with earnest conviction, made it clear he really believed that statement.

He lived in Salzburg, and recalling suddenly the vibrant tales Gregor von Rezzori had spun around that location in that stupendous novel *Memoirs of an Anti-Semite*, which had impacted me like nothing so much as a wheeling blow to the head, I decided to get off there as well, and spend just the one night. On that particular evening the city was a blur of drunks and live music. There was some kind of festival going on; all the streets were closed to traffic and rowdy men in lederhosen crowded around bar tables set up in the street while waitresses in dirndls sloshed tray after tray of beer in front of them. The people seemed red-cheeked and lively; they danced in public squares and laughed boisterously and slapped each other's backs. I moved like a morose shadow through their crowds, feeling an inexplicable weight on my back. Their happiness made me sad.

I recalled the unforgettable voice of von Rezzori's protagonist:

> Salzburg in the summer of 1937 was just awful. It was overrun with Jews. The worst of them had come from Germany as refugees and in spite of their luggage-laden Mercedes cars, behaved as if they were the victims of a cruel persecution and therefore had the right to hang around in hundreds at the Café Mozart, criticize everything, and get whatever they wanted faster and cheaper— if not for nothing—than anybody else. They spoke with that particular Berlin snottiness that so got on the nerves of anyone brought up in Austria, and my sharp ears could all too easily detect the background of Jewish slang. . . . I could have slaughtered them all.

Of course you can be happy now, I thought sullenly as I tried to squeeze through a rowdy group in lederhosen. *All the Jews are gone.* It was as if every face could have been the character in *Memoirs of an Anti-Semite,* for if there was anything I had learned from that book, it was that anti-Semitism was a parasite that lurked even in the finest of human specimens—the question was always not if but to what extent it had wormed its way through, leaving a trail of rot in its wake.

On a conscious level I knew that the voice in my head was being dramatic, was trying to engage not with the world around it but with the world it imagined existed simultaneously on another plane. Yet was it all those books I had recently read that had convinced me that this plane was more real, more concrete, than any banal and tangible society I might be immersed in?

In my brief tour of Salzburg I would not find one memorial to the Jewish community that had once thrived here. Salzburg was the first city invaded by the Germans to have its Jews deported by Austrians who were only too happy to collaborate. The city is famed for conducting an enormous public book burning in its main square. Yet this site was now a banal tourist attraction with an ornamental fountain and horse-drawn carriages eager to ferry visitors around town. The old synagogue, now a chintzy hotel, did not even boast a small commemorative plaque. In Google searches, I discovered that Austria's reasoning for failing to erect memorials to the Holocaust was fear of reprisal through anti-Semitic vandalism and attacks. Their answer to anti-Semitism seemed to be to appease it instead of uprooting it.

What remained instead, Google informed me, was something called *Stolpersteine*, or stumbling stones. These were small memorial stones embedded in the streets of Salzburg and other cities, in apparently random places. Yet after a comprehensive tour of the small city, I had not come across even one. When I stopped to ask two young girls who were DJing in a public square to help me find them, they looked at me with extreme confusion and said they had never heard of such a thing. I explained myself more clearly in German, insisting that the stones had to exist. Perhaps they might know where I could get a map of them? Now they were annoyed. "They are here, but hard to find. Maybe in that street up there to the right. But we don't know."

There were no stones to be found in that street up to the right, even though I scoured the narrow alley at least five times, eyes glued to the cobblestones. In another square, young men and women in white garb were performing a traditional Austrian folk dance, and a crowd had gathered. I retreated to my cheap hotel on the outskirts of the old quarter to grab my suitcase, and as I arrived at the eerily silent triangular intersection, I paused suddenly before crossing the street to my hotel, for I had been held up by something that resembled a flashback.

Only it wasn't my memory. It couldn't be, because the image of myself I had in my mind now, in a frilly pinafore, with two long braids tied with ribbons, being swept up a street just like this one by a middle-aged woman wearing long skirts and a tilted hat, her waist cinched by some invisible contraption, to visit an old woman on her deathbed—this wasn't even of my time. It was as if I was remembering something a hundred years past, in a city I had never visited, among architecture I had never glimpsed before, seeing the faces of family members I did not recognize. I stood transfixed at that street corner, staring at the building in question that had conjured this strange vision, an old apartment house painted the palest shade of lilac with white trim, its windows darkened and motionless. Why was I being assaulted with these strange, otherworldly déjà vu moments now? Was this a memory that I had inherited, or had I invented it, patched together an amalgam of my grandmother's stories? Had they fermented in me all these years? Did they now rise to the surface as if to be expurgated, the way I had watched my grandmother skim the fat off the chicken soup? I shook now on this warm summer day as if from a deep chill, and I hurried all the way to the train station, even though I was in no rush, because I felt as if there were specters in this town I needed to shake off. If I stayed a moment longer, I thought, they would attach themselves to me like *dybbuks*.

I got on an ÖBB train heading west, but I couldn't figure out if Munich was the train's last stop or if the train continued beyond my destination. Because the stops were not announced in advance, I had to be ready to disembark at any moment, as the doors remained open for only a minute or two before the train moved on. As we pulled into each station I would check the monitor screen and look at the platform signs to gauge where I was. At one point, I looked up to see the words "München Hauptbahnhof" on the screen and raced to the door before it closed. The conductor, a thin, older man with a fluffy white mustache that obscured his mouth, was just about to lock up.

"Munich?" I asked.

"*Ja*, Munich," he said and urged me off through the half-open door.

Only when I had descended did I realize that the platform sign read ROSENHEIM. I quickly turned back, trying to reboard the train, exclaiming to the conductor that this was the wrong stop, but he simply shrugged as he looked me in the eye and slammed the train door in my face.

It was as if I had just witnessed an act of unspeakable cruelty. My chest contracted, my lungs burst; my breath came out with a fit of tears, and I collapsed onto my little pile of luggage on the platform. In the distance I could vaguely glimpse, through the grayish film, a line of people at the other end of the station, watching me silently.

When I finally arrived at Munich Central Station, having found a local train at the other end of the Rosenheim station, it was pouring rain outside, and I went to the station bar, where I ordered a coffee in German. The bartender asked where I was from; she said my accent was *süß*, sweet. And because I was only just beginning to navigate this strange language that was both comfortingly familiar and threateningly distorted at the same time, because I heard the German word *süß* as the Yiddish *ziß*, I didn't know if I should take it as a compliment or condescension, but I was at the very least glad to see my origins were not quite clear.

"Why don't you guess?" I asked.

"I don't have the faintest idea," she said. "Usually, I can tell right away, but your accent is a mixture of many places. Czech? Polish? Swiss? Maybe the Netherlands?"

I smiled into my cup. She was fixating on my strong *ch* sound in *ich*. "A mixture," I answered.

Two very drunk men proposed marriage to me as I ate at three o'clock in the afternoon. They stood too close to me, their beers sloshing in their glasses.

Onlookers told me not to be concerned, that this was Bavarian culture. "We are very friendly," one guy said while gripping my hand tightly. I extricated my hand and tried to excuse myself from the bar.

It was Markus who rescued me then, interceding among the drunks and settling himself protectively on the bar stool next to mine. Tall, broad, German-looking in all respects, but with a crooked slant to his nose that made him more personable, and a perpetual half smile of amusement that alleviated the severity of his angular features, he loomed suddenly on the horizon of my vision, blocking everything else out, and it was as if someone had passed a cooling hand over my brow—now I had only to concentrate on this focal point directly in front of me, and all the foreign and frightening layers that lay in wait behind him could recede into irrelevance for the time being. We exchanged pleasantries and I could see he was sober and decent. He complimented my thick-framed glasses and told me, in an almost wondrous tone, that I looked as if I had fallen out of a Woody Allen movie. I forgave him the cliché this once in light of the circumstances, and soon the conversation migrated to more interesting topics. I told him about how I had planned to retrace my grandmother's steps through Europe, and that Germany was the inevitable last stop on my route. I waited for him to get defensive or turned off by the topic, but he responded with serene curiosity. He told me, with a face as straight as was possible despite that implacable half smile, that he was descended from Mennonites on one side but Nazis on the other. His grandmother had even boasted about kissing Hitler's hand, he said, as if daring me to be shocked.

I paused, looking at him searchingly. The moment felt like a portentous opportunity; the first conversation I had ever had with a German-speaking man who did not retreat into denials or talk about a grandfather in the resistance. It seemed to me that Markus felt removed enough from the past to experience little pain as a result of addressing it, and I was immediately aflame with curiosity as to why.

"It's not so much about what your grandparents did," I said to him thoughtfully, "or about what any of our grandparents did, but about what you yourself would have done if you had lived back then. Can I feel sure that you wouldn't have gotten swept up in that craziness and killed someone like me?"

"Can you be sure that you wouldn't have killed me, if you had been the German and I had been the Jew? Can you ever really be sure of anyone until you see them in those circumstances?"

"I'm not capable of that kind of hatred or violence."

"What if you had been raised by avowed anti-Semites? Who, then, is really in full possession of themselves?" His eyes sparkled. It was clear it was all theoretical for him; he was enjoying the philosophical aspect of our conversation. I marveled at his detachment.

"Did you know that Judaism actually believes in the precept of visiting the sins of the father upon the son?" I responded. "I grew up knowing that our suffering was an atonement for the *Haskalah*, the Jewish Enlightenment. But in the same way, I was taught that the Germans will always be judged as evil for what their ancestors did. We would have to hate them forever."

"But you're not your upbringing anymore. You're you." His smile was still there, patient and tranquil.

"What if I'm both? What if I can't decide?"

None of my brief romantic encounters until that moment had been characterized by this intense, raw intimacy. When Markus offered to join me for the next leg of my journey, it seemed like the most natural thing in the world.

"Are you sure that's a good idea?" I asked him, out of a sense of duty. "We may end up hating each other."

"I'll take that chance," he said.

He went out into the rain to get his car, and I waited for him by the entrance. Across the stairs, a group of youths dressed in black, with tattoos on their necks, smoked cigarettes with idle, dismissive expressions. How is it that you tell apart a Nazi and a punk again? What did a skinhead look like anyway? Every face seemed menacing, and I felt more and more skittish as the minutes ticked by. A random set of eyes met mine coolly, and I cringed and looked at the floor. A tall man smoked a cigarette a little too close to me, and I felt my heart rate speed up. Was I imagining his leer?

Finally, my phone vibrated. "Come around the corner," Markus texted. "I'm parked outside of the Starbucks."

I didn't want to go back into the crowd. "Can you meet me at the exit?" I asked. "I'm feeling a bit overwhelmed."

He did. I looked up and there he was, massive without being threatening, his impish smile never once subsiding. I still don't know how to explain the feeling I had then, which I had never experienced before, of looking into a completely new face with the conviction that it was somehow supremely familiar to me. I looked at him and felt instantly as if I had known him always.

We argued over who would carry my suitcase in the rain.

"I'm a feminist. Let me do it myself!"

"*Genau*," he said, "exactly. Be a good feminist and hold your tongue."

We bantered like that all the way to his car, on the drive to the hotel I had booked, and in the supermarket we visited to buy groceries. We teased and argued and laughed, stopping only for necessary conversations with the cashier and the hotel receptionist. We couldn't look away from each other's eyes.

We ate hastily in the room, stuffing slabs of dark brown bread with creamy goat cheese into our mouths. We had been sitting on the edge of the bed, and inevitably we fell into it after the last crumb had been brushed off our laps. I remember not being able to contemplate doing anything else. I felt like I had conjured a golem of sorts, a lightning rod for my projections and complexes.

That story I had grown up with, the one I had believed for so long, that there was an entire nation of people on the other side of the Atlantic who still burned with hatred for me because I was Jewish . . . well, here was a pin in that balloon. The heat of his skin on mine, the smile in his eyes, his shy movements— these made him human in a way I never could have grasped intellectually. In those moments, no lines existed between us, racial, cultural, or emotional.

I had this sensation of a very old wound starting to close. Nerves tingled and came alive, muscles twitched and shuddered, and my whole body throbbed—it was as if two cliffsides struggled to move toward each other to bury the gap between them, but I feared that monumental quake would only serve to bring on an avalanche.

My original plan had been to trace the route my grandmother had taken from camp to camp after she had been selected at Auschwitz for forced labor, the first one, just north of Munich, then on to Saxony and Lower Saxony, until she was dumped at Bergen-Belsen when the enemy was getting too close. But now, in the presence of this man, a man who made me want to check into a hotel and not leave for two weeks, I realized I was tired of being sad, of being trapped in the past while everyone else got to live in the here and now, tired of this heavy allegiance that demanded every ounce of psychic energy I possessed, and I wanted nothing more than to just be human for a little while, to be just one person, divorced from all the baggage of my ancestors that I insisted on carrying with me. Perhaps there was a way to maintain my allegiance to this original goal simply by being here in any way at all, by confronting not what had been wiped out, but what had continued. And so I said to Markus, "Let's not do any Holocaust stuff just yet," and he smiled at me and said *"Zum Befehl!"* in that way that he had of employing irony with a straight face, so I never quite knew where he stood.

The next morning, I placed my bags in the trunk of his hatchback and instead of heading north we drove into the heart of Upper Bavaria. About an hour south of Munich, the Alps loomed into view, and we climbed the foothills in search of a place to stay. I knew nothing about the region except that it had been home to the Blue Rider movement, which Richard had educated me about, and I knew there would be many museums dedicated to the era that I could explore. We settled on a small bed-and-breakfast in the sleepy town of Murnau am Staffelsee, perched just at the foot of the mountains, with a sweeping view on all sides.

The owners of the bed-and-breakfast were a couple named Gina and Frederic; she was a painter and he was a cook, and together they had created something of an unusual retreat in homage to the history of the area, an inn filled with paintings and sculptures that also served sumptuous meals at the attached cantina. The property had numerous nooks and crannies to hide in, with an abundance of plants, trickling fountains, and cozy seats and hammocks suspended at various angles. A plump British shorthair cat was sunning himself in the driveway as we dragged our suitcases across the pebbles.

Markus went to pet him, crooning and cuddling the now

purring cat with almost childlike enthusiasm. I watched with amusement as this large man bent over the tiny animal.

"Look," Markus called to me where I stood with my case. "He's rolling on his back to show his tummy, look how happy he is. Isn't he the cutest?"

"That's Max," Gina called from the entrance. "He lives here. Let me show you to your room. I hope we'll see you at dinner later?"

I nodded. I had read excellent reviews of the restaurant online on the way there. "We're really looking forward to it."

Our room was a charming alcove suite on the second floor, with a porch that faced west, where the sun was already setting behind the sloping tiled roof. Amber light striped across the bed and on the floor. It was as if we had found a place where time stopped and held its breath, just so we could discover each other in that sacred space between inhale and exhale, before we had a chance to think about how this would work when the moment inevitably came to an end and breathing resumed.

But first, we took a walk around the picturesque town. Outside the church, I saw an enormous memorial, cast from granite, with fresh roses and daisies laid at its base. It was titled *Unsern Helden—To Our Heroes*. It consisted of the names of local citizens who had died fighting for Nazi Germany.

"Can they do that? Can they turn them into heroes now?" I said.

"Not everyone wanted to fight in the army," Markus said. "A lot of them were forced."

"Don't you think a more appropriate title for this memorial

would be 'Our Victims,' or perhaps 'Our Martyrs'? *Heroes*—don't you see what that implies?"

He shrugged. Out of the corner of my eye I noticed a young teenager with a blond buzz cut glance over at me surreptitiously. Had he understood what I had said? Was he a skinhead? I pointed him out to Markus.

"Don't talk so loud, yeah?"

"But that's the point! I should be nervous about talking about it, here, where it happened? Where supposedly there is the best Holocaust education in the world? Do you see any memorials here for the Jewish heroes who died?"

But there were none, not in that town, and not in any of the other small Bavarian towns we visited in the area. I did not bring it up again, but I decided that the absence of memory was a kind of denial. To avoid the issue was to pretend it had never happened, and in that sense Bavaria was similar to Austria—it had become convenient to forget, or rather to revise. It wasn't fair to hold Markus responsible for that, but even though there were no lines drawn between us when we were alone in a room, outside it became easier to see him as on the other side of some great gulf.

At dinnertime we wandered over to the cantina, a lovely whitewashed grotto carved out of the property's east side. Inside, it was already lively with the sounds of beer glasses clinking, dishes and cutlery being sorted in the back, and the vibrant chatter of diners. Every table was full, as the restaurant was open to the general public as well, but Gina spotted us. She approached us looking regal in a floor-length robe, her hair wrapped in a silk turban.

"Come outside," she said. "I always keep a special table for the guests."

We followed her out the back door into an enclosed yard full of rustling ferns, illuminated only by Christmas lights strung between the trees. Under a broad umbrella sat a lone table, its slatted wooden top draped in a white mantilla. Red roses floated in a bowl at its center. Three men already sat around the table drinking red wine from stemless glasses.

"A table for friends," Gina said, smiling and nodding at the others. "Away from the noise. Here we can actually talk."

The men each introduced themselves; they weren't all local but they seemed to be good friends of Gina's. An academic, a mechanic, and a biker—it was hard to understand what made them a group. After Frederic poured us some of that deep red wine and brought out small plates of crispy octopus and pork croquettes, I relaxed a bit, and it was then that I must have switched to German without realizing it.

"Deborah! You didn't tell us that you speak German!" Gina said. "What a shame, I would have spoken to you in German as soon as you arrived."

"Oh no, I don't really speak it," I said, "or at least, I speak it very poorly."

"Not at all," Gina said. "You speak it quite well. In fact, you should speak it more often. It would be a shame to waste it."

"You'll see," I said. "It's not really German. If I speak it long enough, you'll understand."

The biker smiled and emptied his glass. "This is a country of many dialects. You should hear me when I speak Bavarian."

"It's true." The academic nodded. "I can barely understand him."

"What is your dialect?" the mechanic asked. He hadn't talked much since we had arrived and was still nursing the same glass of wine.

"It's really old," I said, reluctant to explain. Instead, I invented. "My family is of Franco-German ancestry, and my grandparents spoke this dialect, which they must have inherited from their parents and grandparents. I don't think it's spoken in present-day Germany anymore." Markus looked over at me then, a curious expression in his eyes. He had been busily consuming tapas as I had carried the conversation, in his typical reserved style. Now he sat with his arms folded and lips pursed in amusement, saying nothing.

"Why didn't you tell them it was Yiddish?" he asked me later, as we stumbled back to our room in the dark.

"I guess I was afraid of their reactions," I said.

"I was wondering if that was it."

"There are no Jews here, Markus. Not one. I can actually feel it, like it's something in the air that's missing. And this scares me for some reason."

It rained then, for three days straight. On the third day, we gave up trying to go out. We were lying in bed, and we had the windows open for air, so we could hear the drops pinging off the metal drainpipe and bouncing off the clay-pot roof. They plopped onto ferns and broad-leafed trees and splattered into the muddy driveway.

"I'll sing you something, okay?" I said to Markus, who was lying next to me with his eyes closed. "Tell me if you understand it. It's a lullaby from my childhood."

"Mmm." He nodded, relaxed.

I began to sing in Yiddish.

Sleep my child
Rest my soul

Close your eyes
In her arms
A mother is holding you
Do not fear
Do not worry
That the sun goes down
A new morning will come
Full of joy and happiness.

"*Sehr schön*," he said. "It's a nice little song."
"Wait," I said. "It's not finished."
I continued:

My child, you had a mother
You barely knew her
In the flames of Auschwitz
They burned her.
An evil wind blew then
A cold, wet rain
When I found you my child,
In the wet forest.
Both of us ran off together
In search of a safe place
We came upon some partisans
and stayed with them. . . .
Don't worry my child,
sleep well. . . .
One day you will yet meet God
And then you can ask him
to avenge your mother's blood.

"That's my lullaby," I said, and turned to look at him. "That's what they sang to children in my community."

His eyes were open now, and he raised his eyebrows. "*Ja,* that's quite intense."

"I feel like that song sums up my whole childhood." It was a kind of apology, and something of a warning at the same time. I wanted him to understand that I couldn't help all these feelings that were whirling to the surface now, like a typhoon I feared would lash at him as they emerged from the depths in all their uncontrollable fury. Perhaps I was trying to tell him to retreat, to protect himself.

Finally, the sun came out. When we opened our eyes in the morning, we jumped out of bed and scarfed down a quick breakfast. We were anxious to take advantage of the weather and do as much as possible, as the forecast was predicting more rain later in the week.

"Where shall we go?" Markus asked once we were in the car.

"To the mountains, of course!" I'd never seen the Alps up close, or any mountain range that could compare. I was thrilled at the prospect. It was a beautiful drive, the slopes a steady wall in front of us, never seeming to recede or shrink as we came closer the way I expected them to. We stopped at Mittenwald, the last town before the Austrian border, to catch a glimpse of the Isar River, a glacial runoff with waters the color of mint-chip ice cream, frothing around rocks and boulders, in a hurry to get somewhere. We stopped to take pictures at the riverbank, the Alps a splendid but still distant backdrop. Then came the sheer drops and sharp turns over the border, and finally, somewhat carsick, we arrived in Innsbruck, Austria. We walked

through the old town, which was packed with tourists, and purchased a picnic lunch at a supermarket. Then we headed back
out toward the less populated area, to a park with ancient
willows and birches on the banks of the river Inn. Across its
sparkling green rush, the brightly colored homes ascended the
hills, and the snowcapped mountains soared breathtakingly
above them. Spires and cupolas peeked playfully out onto the
scene. We finished our lunch and climbed down some makeshift steps to the riverbank. Markus took off his shoes and socks
and ventured in, and I rolled up my jeans and did the same.
The water was ice-cold and sped furiously around my feet.

"Would you swim in this?" I asked Markus. "It's probably
dangerous because of that strong current."

"I've been watching that big branch out there in the middle,
and it keeps coming back in circles. It's like there's a circular
current out there, or two separate currents going in opposite
directions." I followed his gaze, and sure enough, a large branch
was whipping back and forth in the middle of the river, seemingly tossed between two opposing forces. I stared at it fixedly
now, wondering if it was a sign. Was I that branch, doomed to
whip forever back and forth between the forces of my own instincts and the inculcated beliefs of my past? Would I remain
essentially trapped in that state for the rest of my life?

"So," Markus said, once we had our shoes back on. "Where
would my Jewish princess like to go next?"

I was looking at the map. "Did you know we were so close
to Italy?"

"You want to cross another border?"

"Since we are already here, it feels like such a shame not to.
Who knows if I'll ever be in this part of the world again!"

"How far is the drive?"

"An hour, maybe an hour and ten," I fudged. Most likely he knew that I was lying, but he didn't say anything.

In Bolzano, I noticed that the signs were printed in both German and Italian. We parked in front of a big church and walked across the street, where Markus ordered some pizza from a street vendor in German. We stood at a tall table under an umbrella to eat. Sparrows began to crowd around us hoping for crumbs. After eating his fill, Markus started to feed them.

"Look at this," he said, making the sparrows fly to his fingertips to eat the bits of bread he held out. I watched as they approached him tentatively, batting their wings as they hovered near his hand, trying to take some bread back with them. Most of the piece would crumble to the ground, and they would be left with only the crumb in their beak.

I threw some of my crust at the sparrows perched on the hedge near us.

"Don't do that," Markus scolded. "Make them come to you."

"I'd rather not. It feels wrong to make them do that just for my entertainment."

He scoffed. I watched as he continued to coax the birds to his outstretched hand, grinning triumphantly each time a sparrow flew awkwardly out to meet it. He had mentioned to me many times how much he loved animals, and I'd seen him stop for every cat and dog on the street, but this struck me as a peculiar way to express that love.

A pigeon approached and I tossed some crumbs its way, remembering how my grandmother had always left food out for the city birds on our porch.

"Ach, don't feed the pigeons!" Markus said. "They're just stupid."

"Does that mean they're less deserving of a meal?"

A crowd of pigeons descended then, and the scene quickly turned to chaos. Markus had been right in a way. I watched the pigeons stumble blindly in circles, seemingly unable to see the food in front of them. Then a sparrow flew into their midst so quickly I almost didn't see it. It left in a blur with the food in its mouth.

"See?" Markus crowed. "They're too stupid to even eat what you throw at them."

We walked around the city for a bit, stopping at every gelato stand until we had stuffed ourselves silly. Then we embarked on the long drive back, stopping at Hall in Tirol for an aperitif and then Seefeld in Tirol for a very late dinner. On the way home, I brought it up, trying to couch my own insecurity in dark humor.

"You know, you may not have realized it, but that story with the birds was kind of a metaphor for the whole idea of survival of the fittest," I said. "You singled out the intelligent birds as the ones deserving of being fed, and then made them dance for their crumbs. Kind of fits with your whole Übermensch thing, doesn't it?"

He shook his head impatiently. "We already agreed on this, no? That's why I'm with you, for some *Wiedergutmachung*, right?"

"I don't even feel that that's funny anymore."

"I should stop joking about it?"

"I remember reading about Katrin Himmler, who married an Israeli Jew, the son of Holocaust survivors, and she used to say that everything was great until they argued, and then she was a Nazi and he was a Jew who couldn't get over it."

Markus's face showed no expression. His hands remained on the wheel as we sped down dark roads.

"Of course I don't see you like that, as Himmler's descendant. I know you're not like that; it's just that sometimes the voice in my head that screams *All Germans are evil*, that voice I grew up with, it just kind of takes over."

"*Genau.* Understandable."

I leaned over and kissed him and stroked his neck. He had the most beautiful face. How could I be so horrified by my relationship with him in these odd, random moments when my whole body seemed to thrill in his presence?

The next day I felt a bit off. It was raining again. We decided to nap after lunch. I fell asleep for thirty minutes and awoke in the midst of what felt like the peak throes of a panic attack. I had never woken up in such a state. Before I even opened my eyes, I could feel my heart racing, my body trembling from the force.

I lay paralyzed with fear and shock for a few minutes before I was able to whisper to Markus, who was lying next to me reading a book. He had not noticed I was awake.

"Markus."

"Yes, my dear?"

"Can you feel my pulse?" I asked. I didn't want to seem crazy. I assumed that I must look ordinary on the surface, as I was lying still on the bed. One couldn't see a racing heart.

"*Ja, natürlich,*" he said and took my hand, looking at his watch.

After a minute, he looked over. "Quite fast, *ja*, especially since you're lying in bed, no?"

"Markus, I, I—" I faltered. "I feel really sick."

He looked at me with concern, and immediately my anxiety let loose like a racehorse at the sound of a pistol shot. My heart was pounding even harder, and now I could feel my hands and legs getting numb. I started to hyperventilate.

He got up and came over to my side of the bed.

"I'm scared, I'm so scared," I cried as I thrashed under the sheets, trying to shake off the sensation.

"Calm down," he said, holding my arm and looking into my eyes. "What are you feeling?"

"Everything's numb. What's happening to me?"

"Just breathe," he said.

I followed his breathing, deep and slow, even though it didn't feel like it was helping. After about ten minutes, I started to feel a bit more like myself, although still woozy. I sat up.

"You're okay?"

"Yes, I think so. I need some air."

He went back to his side of the bed and resumed his reading as if nothing had happened.

Outside on the patio, I reflected that no one had ever looked at me when I felt my craziest and made me feel that normal. Although I had been diagnosed with anxiety shortly after my arranged marriage at the age of eighteen, this had been my first panic attack in years, and it had happened, also for the first time, during sleep. What was my body saying? Was I betraying my grandmother by neglecting her journey and replacing it with a tryst with the enemy?

And what was it that frightened me so much about this place? I wondered. I knew only that it was time to leave. No matter how many beautiful visions I had encountered here, I was too uneasy to really enjoy them. Perhaps the fact that it was so lovely was the very thing that was disturbing me—did it have any right to be such a picturesque, fairy-tale-like region when it had been the birthplace of one of the greatest horrors in the world? As if I were looking through the lens of a Grimm brothers' tale, I wanted the forests to turn dark and gnarled, the sky to be an angry purple. This place, I thought, should reflect what happened. To appear so innocent and calm was a wrongdoing on its part, an unforgivable betrayal.

We checked out the next morning and drove to Frankfurt, stopping only for lunch in a tiny town in Hessen. I had to move on to Berlin very soon, from which I had booked my return flight, but I decided to stay in Frankfurt for a day or two because Markus had arranged for me to meet his mother. I was curious to meet her because she had been raised by real Nazis. Although Markus had told me that she had always had a very troubled relationship with her family and their beliefs, I still wondered if I might detect any trace of her background imprinted on her character, the way mine was no doubt imprinted on me.

Ada had recently been widowed and was now living in the small apartment she had used as her private sanctuary throughout her marriage. It had a lovely garden out front and another in back with a little terrace, and that's where we sat. Young pink climbing roses were carefully tied to the terrace railing; the plants were immaculately tended in attractive ceramic pots. Ada had pure white hair, large pale blue eyes, and very fair skin. My eyes swept over the garden, and for an instant it was as if I was looking at that garden in my memory, so similarly was this one constructed; it was as if I had come to visit my own grandmother. As we made small talk on the porch, I realized for the first time just how much I missed having an older person in my life, the way I used to.

"I wanted to ask you about your parents," I said eventually, after we had licked clean a bowl of strawberries and cream. "I'm really curious what it was like being raised by them, and how you were able to turn out so differently and raise a son like Markus."

"My parents hated everyone who wasn't German, not just Jews. Even on his deathbed my father expressed no remorse. My mother could never stop talking about the time she kissed the Führer's hand. Come, I'll show you a picture of them."

We walked into her little office, and there was an old sepia photograph taped to the side of a curio, showing a surprisingly diminutive couple walking their German shepherd in the rain, smiling from underneath their shared umbrella. His face seemed to disappear under his squashy hat and large, thick-rimmed glasses, but I could detect a decidedly prominent nose. He looked like the average middle-aged Jewish man buying a bagel on the Upper West Side. She was no different, with a narrow forehead and thick, dark eyebrows.

"They look more Jewish than most Jews I know!" I said.

"Right?" Ada laughed. "And with their German shepherd, so proud of themselves. They looked nothing like the ideal Germans they had in their fantasies."

"But you do," I said before I could help myself. "You're so fair and blue-eyed. It's interesting—Markus looks nothing like that."

"Markus looks like his father." Indeed, he had a tall, broad forehead but a large nose and dark hair. His eyes were hazel, but his smile was distinctly German to me, the upper lip coming out slightly over the lower, which lent him a look of perpetual haughty bemusement.

"My generation was different. Back then, everyone was rebelling against their parents, against what they had done. We didn't want to be anything like them. It didn't help that my parents were brutal to me as well. My mother used to stick my finger in the electric sockets as a way of disciplining me. I tried to accuse her of it when I was an adult, and she wouldn't even discuss it with me. It was clear she knew it was sick."

I remembered seeing all those photos of Hitler cavorting with children, reading how Nazis would go home and hug their wives. It never occurred to me that some of them might have been as cruel to their own offspring as they were on the job.

Markus drove me around Frankfurt for a short tour of the city. I asked him if any of his siblings had turned out anti-Semitic, wondering if these patterns were in any way genetic, like Ada claimed, skipping generations and then popping up again out of context.

"My younger brother went through a phase when he was a teenager, but I think he's mostly grown out of it."

"What do you mean by 'mostly'?"

"It's how young people do their rebellion here. You know it's against the law, and it's considered politically incorrect, so of course that's the issue that young people will pick as a way of showing they are going against the grain. It makes them cool. But it's abstract for them; it's not like they actually know any Jews. My brother is not an anti-Semite; he just makes an offensive joke once in a while."

"I would say that's an anti-Semite, Markus."

"Every teenager in Germany is an anti-Semite, then, because that's what they do now, to be cool. They make politically incorrect statements, to show they don't give a fuck, and since Jews are a sore topic here, they like to pick at the wound."

"Would your brother disapprove of you being with me?"

"I don't think so," Markus said. "But it wouldn't matter anyway."

"It would matter to me," I replied.

We slept together on our last night in his narrow bed, neither of us moving from the position we fell asleep in, with his arms wrapped around me and the humid summer air cooking us like chickens on a rotisserie. My head swam when I awoke. Markus needed to return to work, and I had a train to catch to Berlin, where I would spend the remaining week before my return flight. He kissed me on the forehead. "Call me when you arrive," he said. I nodded and watched him lumber off the platform from my window seat on the train, never looking back once. Whether or not either of us harbored the intention, it would become clear very soon that our relationship had already acquired a life of its own, and neither of us would prove capable of arresting its natural course.

———

When I arrived in Berlin, I immediately felt as if I had lost that magical sense of orientation that had guided me through most of Europe. Berlin's sights lay sprawled in every direction, and I felt dwarfed by the scope of the city, beleaguered by its complicated maps, its chaotic layout. The streets were filled with scaffolds and trenches; there was construction happening everywhere. What had become of those orderly arrondissements and neatly delineated quarters that I had encountered in other European cities? Here the river was not something to skirt around via a pedestrian bridge; it was not even a body of water you could easily view in its entirety, the way you could see down the Seine in Paris. Elevated tracks crisscrossed on top of it, and buildings squatted over its narrower parts.

In my first few days there, I was oddly afraid to leave my hotel room. Markus was no longer at my side, and it was suddenly strange to navigate my life without him. I was staying on the edge of the old Jewish quarter, but it was only when I finally ventured out that I realized that. The old synagogue was a two-minute walk away. It had been perfectly preserved in its mostly disheveled state, with bits of still-intact marble and mosaic cordoned off. I had to go through an extensive security check and a metal detector just to get inside. On the exterior of the building was a plaque that described how the synagogue had been violated and ultimately destroyed. Underneath the description was a line in bold, enlarged letters: NEVER FORGET. I snapped a photo, and the security guard standing alongside it smiled as if to pose. I wanted to tell him that a smile was inappropriate, but I stared straight ahead instead, pretending I didn't notice.

After that I descended into the subway and headed in the direction of the Holocaust memorial, for after all I was in Berlin, the capital of Germany, the main stop on the Holocaust trail, so where else should I have gone? It was a gray weekday morning, the stations were empty and quiet, and aboveground the wide city blocks with their cold contemporary buildings seemed forbidding. Until now I had stayed away from Holocaust exhibits, perhaps not consciously, but I needn't have worried—the memorials here were brief and succinct. I descended into the underground chamber below the memorial, where the Holocaust was summed up for tourists and school-children. I joined the procession of visitors that passed slowly along its corridors.

"It happened, therefore it can happen again; this is the core of what we have to say," read a quote by Primo Levi emblazoned on the wall behind the entrance. Levi had only recently entered my library, but upon doing so had immediately seemed to be the voices of my grandparents speaking to me about the experiences they had never been able to put into words.

I shuffled in line past the high-definition photograph of the *Einsatzgruppen* moving among a writhing pile of naked moon-white women, rifles cocked as they shot each one individually, and followed the crowd into a darkened room, the floor of which had a small collection of backlit testimonials from various victims of the Holocaust, collected from postcards or journals.

Here was a poem by Radnóti Miklós, the Hungarian Jewish poet of whom I now recalled Zoltán had spoken so fondly. It was translated into German and English. I whispered it out loud to myself.

I fell beside him and his corpse turned over, tight already as a snapping string. Shot in the neck—And that's how you'll end too—I whispered to myself; lie still, no moving.

Now patience flowers in death. Then I could hear Der springt noch auf—*above, and very near. Blood mixed with mud was drying on my ear*
　　　　　　　　—Szentkirályszabadja, October 31, 1944

I choked on the sound that burst suddenly from my throat. I had to sit down, and the one tissue I had on hand wasn't enough to mop up the mess of mascara and snot on my face.

How vivid and powerful those words were that I felt as if I was lying right there beside him as he died, and it was unbearable.

Der springt noch auf. My German was good enough at that point to make sense of that easy phrase, "he still leaps up," and also to recognize it from Imre Kertész's *Kaddish for an Unborn Child*: "*I leapt up and so to say concealed again after all*, ich sprang doch auf, *indeed I'm still here, though I don't know why, unless it was pure chance, the way I was born, I'm just as much an accomplice to my sticking around as I was to my coming into this world—*"

I recognized in Kertész's words my own inherited inability to reconcile my existence with the annihilation of so many others. There was that old warning from my childhood, the one that asked: Had I paid the debt of my grandmother's survival that had been transferred to me?

The other visitors stepped cautiously around me, but I was blind and did not care. I sat in front of the poem until my chest stopped hurting so much. I recalled the intense rage and sorrow I had experienced the first time I had seen those images in the U.S. Holocaust Memorial Museum as a teenager. It felt just as fresh. Would this feeling ever dissipate or dilute itself?

In another room, the names of the victims were being read, with descriptions of how they had lived and died. In the next room was an explanation of the death camps. A little boy around the age of seven sat in one of the audio booths with earphones pressed to his head, listening to information about how Auschwitz was operated. I looked at him in shock: he could have been my own son, and he looked somberly into my red, swollen eyes. You shouldn't be here, I wanted to say; you're too young. Was there really such a thing as a seven-year-old boy who needed to be educated about death camps?

Isaac did not yet know about the Holocaust, and this made me realize that I could not recall a consciousness that did not include it. Did my awareness of my grandparents immediately coincide with my awareness of them as survivors of genocide? Was there ever a moment in which I did not align my identity so neatly and perfectly with theirs, knowing with certainty that I too would have been a target, and still could be if the world lost its mind again before I died?

In a room off to the side, a group of German schoolchildren clapped loudly but perfunctorily as a Holocaust survivor finished her lecture. As the students filed out of the room, their faces seemed to say, *Yeah, another one.*

I remembered seeing my son's head when he was born, his wet curls still gleaming blond, and thinking, Thank God, he'll pass for non-Jewish, before I collapsed back onto the pillow.

I wrote something in the guest book then, underneath a message from a young Ukrainian student that read, "We must always remember."

> *How can I describe this feeling of being at once alive and wiped out? To be descended from the living and the dead? A part of my soul has been erased. How will I ever heal this wound in my family? How will I tell my son about this?*

I signed my name underneath.

. . .

At the exit, I found myself in front of a life-size photograph of Bergen-Belsen at liberation. This was the scene that first greeted the dumbfounded British troops when they arrived. They had proceeded to document everything. Here was an image of skeletal women sitting up among piles of corpses as if rising from the dead. It was an unimaginable horror: as far as one could see, a vision of a postapocalyptic wasteland. I stood transfixed before it. My grandmother had witnessed this. She had been there that day, lying in that filth and ugliness and inhuman horror. It would never be erased from her memory. I felt that rage from earlier return like bile in my throat. I left the exhibit and raced up the stairs to disappear into those concrete pillars. Walking down the aisles in between them was spooky; here and there I'd catch the ghostly shadow of some other visitor passing fleetingly between the aisles. They were there, and then they weren't.

I stopped in between two pillars and leaned against one of them and let myself cry with the intention of drying up my tears for this trip. *Just this once, get it out, and then you'll be through. There's nothing left to cry about. None of this is new for you. Someday you're going to have to stop crying about all of this.*

That night I woke up in my pitch-dark hotel room at three a.m. after a bad dream. I lay awake remembering the photograph of the *Einsatzgruppen*. What was it about those men that made them capable of this?

I called Markus. He was awake.

"I can't sleep. Bad dreams." I told him about the photograph.

"Can you find it on Google and send it to me?"

I did.

"That's a pretty bad picture."

"I feel, for the first time in my life, that I really could murder someone. I am filled with anger, which scares me, because maybe somehow that explains what they did, and I don't want it to. It can't. I just remembered something a good friend of mine once told me," I interjected suddenly. "She's Jewish too, with a grandmother who survived the camps. She's from California, very liberal, a lesbian who married a non-Jewish woman. She said she could confront her family with anything—they were so open-minded—but that the one thing she could never do was bring home a German. It's like this line we know not to cross."

I wondered if, in the act of crossing every line that had ever been drawn in front of me, I had somehow failed to draw any of my own.

The next day I signed up for a tour of Sachsenhausen, the model concentration camp just outside Berlin. On the trip there, I met a Jewish couple from Park Slope in Brooklyn. The woman was a daughter of Ukrainian survivors. She told me about how she and her mother had gone back to their little Ukrainian village and had been chased out by an angry, drunken mob.

"How could you let them do that to you, in this day and age? How could you bear to let them get away with it?" I asked.

"What was there to do? It's Ukraine."

"I would have done something. I wouldn't have let them treat me that way. The world isn't like that anymore. They can't do that to us."

She fell silent, her head bowed toward her lap.

"Do you think there is anyplace in the world where we can go and not experience anti-Semitism?" I wondered out loud. I told her about the conductor slamming the door on me in Rosenheim.

"You've got to be careful of what you speak about in front of the Germans," she whispered, nodding toward the other passengers. "They're very sensitive about these things."

"They goddamn well should be."

"You're a guest in their country," she said. "You can't just go around talking like that."

"Like my grandmother was a guest in their concentration camps?"

"Why are you here?" she asked.

"I'm trying to deal with this part of my identity, to put it behind me."

"That's impossible," she said. "You'll never put it behind you. I've tried my whole life."

"I think I'm doing okay," I said. "I believe I can achieve some measure of closure. Most of why I feel so bound up in it is all the secrecy I grew up with. I knew about the Holocaust, but no one ever discussed the details of their experiences. It was as if life before America had been a collective experience, summed up by one word. I need to feel like I know the individual stories; I think that will bring me some peace. I don't want my grandmother's story to be diminished by a broad category."

There was a beautiful blond man in our tour group. He was Swiss-German, very tall, with a chiseled jawline and hollows under his cheeks. His eyes were cool blue marbles under a golden brow. He didn't talk much. I invited him out for a drink later; we were staying in the same neighborhood.

"Why did you decide to visit a concentration camp while in Berlin?" I asked, wondering what someone so clearly non-

Jewish and so young and normal-looking would be doing on a tour like that.

"Don't you think it's important," he asked, "to learn about those things?"

"It happened to my family. What's your relationship to it?"

He cleared his throat and pushed his drink away. "It's obvious to you, no?"

"Was your family involved somehow?"

"No, they were not, but in some way, I think we all feel connected to this event, from both sides. We all participated in a way, even just by being bystanders."

I remembered meeting a German man in my coffee shop back home. Peter was his name; he had been born shortly after the war. "Every German has a story," he had told me, "of being refused service, or of a door slamming in their face, or of a hand left dangling during an introduction. We take it for granted. But when I was a child in school, history stopped at the First World War. The education about the Holocaust didn't start until recently, until people felt they could sufficiently separate themselves from the actions of the Nazis."

I walked back through the streets of the Scheunenviertel, the old Jewish neighborhood, in the late afternoon. There were some lovely, quiet side streets, with neat rows of beautifully restored homes once occupied by working-class Jewish families, now gentrified by skinny-jeans-wearing residents. I approached a beautiful gated park and then noticed the haunting sculpture at the entrance. This was once the Jewish cemetery, I read. Since the stones had been completely destroyed by the Nazis, it was now a public park. I saw a young mother and her toddler in there, and the little girl was running down the garden path on chubby legs, squealing happily. My heart skipped a beat at the sight. Did that mother know her daughter was running over the desecrated graves of Jews? What kind of reality is this, to raise children on the very streets on which so much blood was spilled and so much havoc wrought?

I burned with the desire to ask them this but remained silent, watching. It was difficult to admit that I had come here wanting the satisfaction of knowing that this earth was somehow permanently scorched, that it couldn't sustain a replete life anymore. But here were children frolicking among the ghosts, as if none of it had occurred. To my right, a group of artists were working on a colorful mosaic on the wall of the apartment building next to the cemetery. It was a happy mosaic of dolphins and butterflies. The banner beside it read THE PEACE WALL PROJECT.

Finally, on the way back, I saw my first *Stolpersteine*, those stumbling stones I had searched for so fervently in Salzburg. I noticed it by accident, embedded in front of an elegant home, four of them grouped together, a name on each one. They were for a family that had lived there. The stones gave the date of their deportation as well as of their death. Yet from above they seemed so innocent, a part of the touristy decor. How chilling it was to think of the people who walked over these stones nonchalantly every day. Even more haunting to think of the people who now built their lives in the apartments that had been systematically freed up for "true" Germans. How could one stand to be around all these reminders? I could never live in Germany, I thought, not when I risked running into memorials around every corner.

At the airport, I called Markus. We had not spoken in a while. I had been distracted.

"I was wondering if you'd call," he said. "I thought that with our not being together, maybe you felt your passions ease up a bit."

"Is that the case with you?"

"If anything, my passions have increased."

"Then why assume that it's different for me?"

"I guess we are always afraid."

"Do you remember that part in *Pride and Prejudice* where Darcy tells Elizabeth he loves her against his better judgment, despite the inferiority of her connections, and she's so insulted?"

"Mmm," he said.

"I guess I love you against my better judgment. Against the part of me that says you live too far away and you're descended from Nazis, against it's too damn hard to make this work. I can't believe I let this happen."

"I guess you could say that I love you too, against the odds. I believe I do, yes," he said, as if he was checking internally to make sure.

I felt my stomach sinking. "What are we going to do? This can't possibly work out."

"I'm coming to visit you in September," he said. "Let's see how it goes."

"Okay," I whispered. "I have to get on the plane now."

"Call me when you get home."

"I will."

I settled into my seat and peered out the window, wondering at my ability to stir up so much movement every time I was abroad, and how it would feel to return to the life in America that awaited me, with its contrasting energy of waiting and watching.

. . .

But first Isaac and I flew to California to spend the rest of our summer vacation in milder climates, and to celebrate the identical birthday Justine and I shared. I was turning twenty-seven years old. I spent the day scared and anxious. Twenty-seven! It had been five years since I'd left, since the first birthday when I had started the ritual of measuring my progress. I had acknowledged that the transition years would be difficult. I had allowed myself a few miserable years; I had not been naïve about what to expect. And I found myself at my birthday each year thereafter assessing how far I'd come, internally and externally, from the last. As my external world had shaped itself so exquisitely from year to year, I lamented my slow-to-catch-up internal self, which still felt displaced and depersonalized.

I was twenty-seven. Only a few years ago I had met Justine for the first time and pondered a distant future; now I had built the life that I thought would have brought me security and peace of mind. Yet if there was something I had to face about this birthday in order to move on, it was this: there was nothing I could point to, externally, that would ever bring this transition period to a close and propel me into the future, which I had sacrificed everything to achieve. What had to happen on this birthday was an end to the ritual of measuring, of being hard on myself, of giving myself a time frame in which to achieve the impossible. I was right, then, when I thought I needed to build a home, but I had found the wrong place to build it: outside myself.

I knew then that I would not be charting my path anymore. It wasn't a race or a contest. I would need to learn to be okay with a little uncertainty in my life, a few blurry edges around my personality.

Justine, Isaac, and I drove down into the wilderness of the peninsula en route to Santa Cruz to take Isaac to the beach. On the way there, we stopped on a cliff to take a closer look at a slender strip of fog that remained out on the ocean, the rest having burned away. Bent at one end, like a refracted beam of light, it was reflected in the water as a silvery slash amid the brilliant blue. Two enormous red-tailed hawks cried out above us, and I looked up to see them flying in a circle around a nearly full moon. My phone rang. It was Isaac's dad.

"Yes?"

"Are you okay? Is Isaac okay?"

"Yes, of course. Why do you ask?"

"Someone started a rumor that you committed suicide. I freaked out."

"That's ridiculous. No, we're fine. We're on our way to the beach."

It wasn't until I ended the call that I noticed all the messages on my phone. I checked in on social media and saw that indeed the rumor was thriving. On Facebook, my friends were tagging me in posts that read "Homicide or suicide?" or "Is it really that hard to leave?"

I tweeted a photo of Isaac and myself. "We're having fun at the beach! Sorry to dispel the rumors."

As I put my phone away and took a last look at the splendid, glittering ocean, I reflected on the irony. Why would anyone believe I could be at the moment of despair now, when I had put those dreadful years of wandering behind me, when my life had just started to feel real? I had left, and it had been worth it; that much was clear just by watching Isaac frolic on the beach. But something else had happened to me this summer, some great progress toward a self. I had been imbued with a story; I was no longer a ghost, threatened with obliteration.

———

In September, Markus and his mother came to visit. Isaac had already started second grade, and the leaves had started to curl by the time they arrived. The weather was glorious, with clear blue skies that showcased clean, clear sunsets, like a ball dropping on New Year's Eve. We rowed across the deserted lake in the evening, the summer crowds having returned to the city after Labor Day, and crunched leaves underfoot as we explored picturesque New England towns.

I drove them into Manhattan one day, just to show Markus's mother the city. It was her first visit to the United States, and her first time traveling without her husband.

We walked through Central Park, tasted gelato in the shadow of the Flatiron Building, and narrowly avoided a collision with a truck driver in the East Village. We drove over the Williamsburg Bridge and I offered to drive them through my old community. It was Sukkoth, so the streets would be dead, but the Hasids would be out in full regalia. I pointed out the little wooden huts in people's front yards, on their porches and fire escapes; the holiday was based on the ancient biblical celebration of the harvest, when people slept outside in makeshift huts to watch their crops.

Ada gazed out the window, transfixed. I drove past the double brownstone I had grown up in. It looked silent and implacable, its window blinds tightly drawn, its heavy metal doors indifferent. In the next house, an old woman sat under the shade of her doorway and stared at me as I drove by. I bent my head to avoid being recognized. At the red light, we paused, and across the street a family of Hasidic Jews crowded on the corner, young girls cooing at their nieces and nephews in strollers, a young couple standing shyly, removed from each other by the mandatory four feet.

"It's impossible for me to imagine you here," Markus said. "I look at you, and I look at them, and I just can't make the connection."

I thought, *I can't either at this point. It doesn't feel like my past, not when I look at it up close. My life is too different now to accommodate that story. But if this isn't my past, then what is?*

I drove down Kent Avenue and we parked at the waterfront. We walked down toward the little beach, from which you could see the entire Manhattan skyline.

We posed for a picture against the splendid, glittering backdrop. Ada held the bulky camera awkwardly, trying to figure out how to use it, and I froze my smile in patient expectation. But as the flash finally went off, Markus leaned in suddenly to kiss me on the mouth. Later, over a seafood dinner in an outdoor beer garden, I looked at the photo on the camera's small screen and thought it odd that the surprise and unease I had felt in that moment weren't at all apparent in the image.

At night we rolled toward the center of the bed, latching on to each other as if to avoid falling. He, who had never been able to sleep in the same bed with someone, and I, who had lain awake on those nights I spent with Erik, the weight of his arm heavy on my chest.

"It's crazy how well we fit together," he whispered. Indeed, I felt like an oddly shaped key that had finally found the right lock.

I took them to the local farmers' market on Saturday.

"How can this be?" he said as we drove past the exquisite

views I had already become accustomed to. "It's exactly like the postcards! They don't even have to Photoshop the images."

His mother was positively gleeful when we arrived at the market. A bluegrass band strummed in the gazebo, and shoppers milled about in the autumn sunshine. "Just like in the movies," she whispered, enthralled.

We ran into various people I knew around town, and so I introduced them. There were my friends Dan and Debbie, Jewish lawyers, and Anita and Harvey, more Jewish lawyers from New York City. When we returned to the car, loaded up with fresh tomatoes and cheese and jam, Ada's face had suddenly gone white, and she appeared tired and withdrawn.

"What's wrong?" I asked her in German, but I couldn't quite make out her mumbled reply. I nudged Markus. "Ask her what's going on," I whispered.

He turned to his mother. They had a rapid exchange in German.

"Ah, she's never met any Jews in real life before," he said to me. "She's feeling a bit overwhelmed—actually she feels guilty." His tone was, as usual, neutral, almost amused.

"Guilty? Why would she feel guilty?" I asked, incredulous.

"Because of what her father did. It's her first time encountering the actual people who were persecuted by him. I think it just hit her."

"But I'm Jewish! She wasn't traumatized when she met me."

"True. But I think she's just starting to process what it means, you know. She never dealt with it before because it didn't come up."

Later, in my living room, she told us about her memories of her father, about how he had beaten her older brother when he came home talking of a Holocaust film his teacher had shown him. Ada's father had then visited the teacher in his home and threatened him with violence if he ever showed such filth in his classroom.

"I don't care about what your parents did," I said. "I want to live in the present. I want my life to be filled with love and understanding and forgiveness. I don't want to get stuck with those old grudges and prejudices like the way I grew up. I want to get past it."

"Yes, but it's easier for you, perhaps," she said. "Only the forgiving can speak this way. The guilty cannot simply say that they want to get past it."

I drove them both back to the airport that evening, feeling numb. I couldn't imagine how I'd feel once Markus was gone. At the drop-off point, Markus looked at me and said, "It's like going skydiving. You know you have a parachute strapped to your back, but it still feels like falling to your death. That's what it feels like to be leaving you right now." He laughed weakly, his eyes tired. I saw in his face the same exhaustion I had felt earlier. The feeling was too strong, too intense—there was no way he wasn't feeling knocked off his balance like I was.

"We'll be fine," I said briskly. "The parachute will open. We'll go back to our routines."

"I don't know," he said. "Maybe." He watched me drive off from the curb, holding his backpack with both hands. In the rearview mirror, I glanced back at his forlorn face, just once.

I thought about distance then, about my pattern of forming attachments to people who lived farther and farther away, which had formed itself over the last few years. I wondered if it was as simple as perpetuating my own alienation, or if somehow I understood that by moving the goalpost ever farther, I was somehow galvanizing myself to travel as far from my roots as possible.

In my life, I had expended so much effort to put distance between myself and the place I had come from, and yet there still seemed to be this chasm lying ahead of me, reminding me how far I truly had to go.

These people that had come from far away to breathe newness into my life, they moved me. It was as if I was a playing piece on some enormous chessboard, inching along to victory in the grip of some shrewd mastermind intent on taking the long view. The strategy had seemed unfathomable at times, but I could not deny that I was still on the board, advancing in the direction of some end goal. Though what awaited me on the other side I could not guess, what a marvelous thrill it was, at times—contemplating that unknown shore toward which my inner compass invariably strained.

Perhaps in search of this forward movement, I saw Markus again in November. This time I flew to Frankfurt during my free portion of the Thanksgiving break, and he picked me up from the airport. This time I put aside the pressures we had imposed upon ourselves during the summer and its aftermath; my journey was on pause and I was leaning into the day-to-day of life. We decided to drive to Paris for the weekend, falling back into the rhythm of road trips that had defined our relationship from the beginning. As we approached the German-French border, we saw a large white van on the side of the road, with a dark-skinned family piled outside it. Police were going through the inside of the vehicle. We slowed as we approached the officer guarding the road; Markus rolled down his window and the officer bent down to look inside the car, his gaze sweeping over myself and Markus. "Where to?" he asked.

"Paris," Markus said with a smile.

The officer looked over at me again and smirked. *"Well then, have fun, you two lovers,"* he said in colloquial German, and rapped the palm of his hand on the top of our car to signal that we could go. We cruised by the family at the side of the road, and I turned around to look at them as Markus sped up, incredulous that because of my skin color I was no longer the suspicious one in this climate, that times had changed and the baton had passed to other scapegoats.

In Paris I took Markus to Richard's gallery to show him the work that I had been talking about and to introduce him to the owner, Yann, who had, in the meantime, become a good friend of mine, and the many patrons, such as Bruno the banker and François the industry heir, who regularly visited, whose boisterous and idiosyncratic company I found highly entertaining. I was not sure who was showing off to whom; Markus, my handsome, enigmatic boyfriend to this arty and eccentric coterie, or my thoroughly fancy French friends to my very German love interest. Yann invited us to dinner in the evening, and although the conversation flowed, it seemed to flow around Markus; he was a silent island amid the good humor and overlapping chatter, cutting into his steak in rhythmic motions, that ever-present smirk playing at the corners of his lips, which I now saw as a betrayal of weakness instead of charm. After dinner, Yann pulled me aside.

"Deborah," he said. "Why are you with this man? He is nothing like you! He doesn't talk!"

Before I could protest or defend Markus, he interrupted

hastily: "Don't get me wrong, I have nothing against him, but you know, he is so *German*. Look at him—he is all angles and corners." This wasn't Yann being traditionally French and discriminatory; in fact, Yann spoke German nearly fluently and was very fond of the country and its people. So I listened to him then, as he continued, "Are you sure you are interested in this person, Deborah? Or are you just interested in the place he comes from?"

That question burned itself into my mind, for I had known this was true for a while now, perhaps from the very beginning, that this man had been a door for me, a door to a world I didn't know how to go about entering; I had hoped to find in him the guide that would carry me over the threshold unscathed.

Probably I knew, even before I got on the plane, that the relationship, or at least its romantic element, was over, and when I informed Markus of that a few days later, I can't say he sounded surprised. Years later, I would explain to him how we sometimes fall in love not with people themselves, but with the prospect of accelerated personal development they promise, the way they can transform you into something that feels closer to the person you are convinced you can end up becoming. He would take some time to understand what I was trying to communicate but would eventually come to the conclusion that his experience had mirrored mine, that he too had propelled himself toward a new character phase as a result of the encounter. In truth, each connection, be it brief or extensive, adds new facets to our selves, but this process feels more urgent when one's self seems to be a blank surface with no facets at all.

In regard to all the relationships I formed during those years of transition, the memories they have left behind are tinged with a strange guilt, for I cannot separate the affection I felt for the person from the very real and primal act of using them to propel my own personal metamorphosis, as if I were playing both sides of the chessboard. Perhaps that also served as the primary clue that heralded the realization that I had arrived at the other side, for my relationships suddenly ceased to be conduits to some far-away destination and became the destination itself.

I know that this process, of hitching on to people as if they were vehicles bearing my freight in the chosen direction, was integral to my original goal, that subconscious one I had set for myself many years ago upon leaving, to free myself from the intense, irrational fears and judgments that had been branded into me during my childhood, and that Markus had been essential in the journey toward that freedom. I knew I was one step farther along my route, although I could not pinpoint how, or how many steps I had left. But I sensed it, as surely as I could look back at the progress of the last few years, of the intense changes I had undergone. I knew that this roller-coaster pattern would continue for some time, that in a few years from now I would be as different a version of myself from now as I was in comparison to five years earlier, and how satisfying it was and would be to look back and know that my instincts were worthy of trust. I try to forgive myself for this way of being in the world, the only way I knew in those years, because at the time it felt that I had no other tools at my disposal and that it was a question of survival, of looking down at the abyss underneath me and grasping the only rope I could find.

The winter that set in that year was marked by thick, heavy snows that seemed to muffle all sound like an oppressive blanket. The icy temperatures were unrelenting and put a muzzle on our usual activities; there were many days when the roads were deemed too treacherous and school was canceled as a result. We often lost electricity as a result of a frozen or snow-overloaded tree falling onto the old cables, and it was rare that Richard and I managed to see each other. I therefore spent that winter remarkably exiled, feeling the full force of the isolation inherent in the lifestyle I had chosen. The only bright spots were the books I had stocked up on; the fire we kept roaring full time in the enormous brick contraption that had been erected more than two centuries ago and somehow still functioned, around which the spacious kitchen had been built as if in homage to the tradition of hearth; and the large bay windows on both sides, which afforded us a view of the bird feeders I had erected.

Those books I now dove into indiscriminately, veering wildly from one to the other and back again. Now their voices began to compete with one another in this new and isolated mental space that was my mind in winter. I sometimes read without really understanding the effect the words were having on me, only to have the stories and images come to life again in disturbing contortions in my dreams. I knew deep down that I was experiencing more than just a winter crisis, and although this became clearer with time, I could not find a solution to this conundrum, for I still felt as trapped in this world I was at odds with as before.

In the meantime, Eli had begun to change his lifestyle drastically as well, perhaps as a result of the woman he was now dating, who was from a nonreligious background. Suddenly Isaac began to deliver reports of his dad eating non-kosher or violating the Sabbath. By the end of the year, Eli's beard and *payos* had completely disappeared, and he had moved away from the Orthodox community. Now we did not fight over Jewish holidays anymore, or that Isaac celebrated Christmas, and I did not have to worry about the gap in our lifestyles and the emotional effect it might have on our son. As so often happens, Eli's new love interest was a distraction that meant visitations were now far fewer, and I began to nurse the hope that someday this arbitrary limit around our lives would be lifted, simply by his willingness to free us given his own contented state.

———

Eventually the winter in New England came to an end. It passed the way it always had, seeming incredibly slow moving in its day-to-day progress, but then suddenly gone, replaced by a riotous spring. Then it was Easter, and with it came its Jewish equivalent, Passover. Though I participated in the egg hunts with Isaac and ate lamb at a table in the sunshine with other parents at Isaac's school, I did not make plans to celebrate the Jewish holiday on my own.

I believed now that Passover was about liberation, and I was not feeling the spirit of liberation at the moment. When my divorce judgment had arrived on the eve of Passover in 2012, I had reflected on the irony of celebrating my freedom from an arranged marriage while celebrating the deliverance of the Jewish people. I had thought Passover would always be a time when I could look back at how far I had come since I left my ill-fitting life behind. But the halo of this triumph had faded with time.

As a child I had viewed Passover itself as an ordeal. I was required to stay awake until the very end, which often coincided with the sunrise, and it was rare that food was served before midnight. Like the other women and children at the table, I was expected to mutely follow the progress of the men as they conducted one painstaking ritual after another, up until the moment when my grandfather paused to catch the attention of the children nodding into their empty plates. We watched as he made a show of folding pieces of homemade matzoh into a white damask napkin, tying the ends together before throwing the bundle over his shoulder, at which point all of us children rose sleepily from our chairs to hold hands and follow him in a slow shuffle around the dining room. This reenactment of the exodus was an annual tradition, and the only time I ever witnessed my grandfather taking the time to interact with small children. The central tenet of Passover is to relate the story of the exodus to the young, and so not even the sleeping newborns were exempt; they followed him in the arms of their mothers.

After my grandfather finished his march, he resumed his place at the head of the table, looking resplendent in his white kittel, and held the matzoh in his hand. He spoke of the thin potato gruel that had sustained him during his stint of forced labor in the Hungarian army. But although he repeated this story each year, in my fatigue and hunger I must have missed the point. I thought he was drawing a comparison between the story of Passover and his own liberation from enslavement, but rather, he was reflecting on those early years, when he had struggled to rebuild his life from ruins, when God had led him, through the miracles of stolen passports and false credentials, across the Atlantic Ocean to the new world waiting on the other side. It was here, after years of uncertainty, where he also found a sense of consolation and promise in the words of the Satmar rebbe and joined in the effort to build a new home for the surviving Jews of Hungary. My grandfather insisted that because of his experiences, he could especially identify with the Jewish slaves who made it to the Promised Land, and that through our connection to him we could do the same. He conceded that the God who had liberated our ancestors with great showmanship had not ushered them via express route to Canaan, but though he dragged them through the desert for fifty years, he performed miracles to sustain them along the way, in the hope that their faith in him would strengthen over time and their new identity would inform a consciousness still heavily influenced by an oppressive past. And he did deliver on his promise, my grandfather told us; while we might never understand the reason for the delay, all that mattered was the happy ending. The wandering, he was implying, was more important than the arrival.

I had not expected to wander for too long after leaving the world I grew up in; I had been determined to emerge as quickly as possible from those feelings of loss and homelessness as if from an obsolete cocoon, discarding the useless sheath and stretching my new, unblemished self as if reborn. Now it seemed clear that the life I had dreamed of was, if not unattainable, then still very far away.

On the first night of Passover I found myself once again at a table in Paris with Richard and his many patrons, digging into plates of "le cheeseburger" and red wine. Bruno, the patron of Richard whose mop of white hair now hung loosely over his eyes as if released by his inebriation, leaned in to share with me an observation that I found somewhat unnerving at first.

"You know, Deborah, I've always felt that the religious laws of kosher and halal are a form of violence," he said, "however passive they may seem, for there is a basic violence inherent in separating people from your table. *La table*," he insisted, as most Frenchmen will, "is the common ground for all humans. To bar others from it is to violate your own humanity."

I was surprised by how comfortable Bruno felt about expressing such a brazen, not to mention politically incorrect, opinion, but I couldn't offer an easy response. Instead, I looked around at the vibrant, epicurean group seated at the table, and although there was no ritual to mark the occasion, I felt suddenly that there was a ceremonial significance in the meal we shared. It was Passover, and I was here, and perhaps my grandfather had had a point, that the holiday was not so much about the moment in which we break our bonds, but about what follows: the long, slow haul toward a new future.

I had glimpsed that future in my son, who had told the Passover story to his classmates at the point at which African American slavery had been taught in his second-grade history class. His teacher told me that he seemed so proud to share his own perspective; it was the first time some of his peers had heard about the holiday. When the children were asked to talk about people in their families who had exhibited bravery under difficult circumstances, my son told the story I've told him so many times, of how my grandparents survived the war, and how their grief trickled down through two generations. "I think my mom is brave because she learned how to be happy," he said. "Even when everyone around her was sad all the time."

Did he really believe that? Had I succeeded in pretending? To me the miracle of Passover lay in my son's joyous disposition, in his fearless curiosity and uncomplicated affections. It amazed me that I was the link between him and my past, for the two were irreconcilable in my mind.

It was my fifth Passover outside of the Hasidic community. I thought about the Haggadah, the text we had read aloud from each Passover in my community, and remembered the section containing instructions on how to educate four potentially different sons on the story of the exodus. They are respectively referred to as the wise, the simple, the ignorant, and the wicked sons. The wicked son is quoted as phrasing his question to his father using the pronoun "you." This is interpreted as meaning he excludes himself from the question; he assumes the answer does not apply to him. It is his self-selected exclusion that is equated with wickedness here. It denies a basic principle of Judaism, which is conformity and joining; that is, we are redeemed through enduring unity—with individuality comes the threat of breakage, of fragmentation. What is the only acceptable answer to this wicked son? The Haggadah says to knock out his teeth, implying that to reason with him is hopeless, since individuality, once it takes root, cannot be excised, and the only way to defeat it is to disable its means of expression. If the wicked son had been in Egypt, the father is supposed to say, then he would not have been redeemed.

I too am a wicked son—or rather, daughter—I realized now, looking around the table as the others talked and laughed as if they hadn't a care in the world. (Interestingly, the Haggadah wastes no time instructing fathers how to answer their daughters.)

I was first and foremost the wicked daughter because I had left the Hasidic Jewish community and had written a memoir about what life was like in that world, an act of self-selected exclusion in that it violated the unspoken rule of speaking publicly about the problem of fundamentalism within the Jewish community. I was most viciously attacked because I dared to discuss the laws of marital purity—which is the very foundation of the patriarchal oppression of women that plagues Jewish history. Then, in an attempt at rebuilding my life from scratch once outside the Hasidic world, I had embarked on a journey to discover my own version of Jewishness that felt honest, compassionate, and real. But this form of Jewishness that I had been in search of didn't comfortably fit into any mainstream or acceptable idea, and so my critics could now claim my Jewishness wasn't real. The possibility that authentic Jewishness can exist outside of their narrow spectrum is anathema to them, as it was to the authorities who expelled Spinoza from their midst so many centuries ago. And yet, I am nothing else if not a Jew; a banned Jew is still a Jew, alone within his own sphere, counted only to be rejected. The double exclusion marks them like a lesion.

———

But the truth I had to acknowledge now, if ever I was to liberate myself not only from tangible bonds, but from the shackles we are often programmed to place on ourselves, was that I was running from Jewishness itself. I resented having a group identity and the politics that came with it imposed upon me like some burdensome inheritance; I was fighting an impossible battle to be released from the ranks I had been born into and to embrace the simultaneous singularity and absolutism of being nothing more than human.

The old hope that remained was the possibility to at the very least live among people who would accept this about me as something natural and conclusive, instead of imposing a modern-day *cherem*, or ban of excommunication. Would I ever find myself among my veritable peers, in a world whose emotional language I understood, a place where I would not be brought to buckle under the pressure to conform to fashion and dictates? Did this world even exist? I sensed it was out there, but I knew I would have to research its cartography, for even if I had to wait until my son was an adult, it was undeniable that I would one day claim my place in that realm.

6

ENTDECKUNG

אנטדעקונג

DISCOVERY

I had emerged from the doldrums of winter and all its existential questioning to face a season so bright and blinding it threatened to erase all meaning completely. I had always been flabbergasted by the strange and artificial pace of summer and the way time seemed to be freewheeling in every direction for those months, and this summer was no exception. Eli had become engaged to his new girlfriend and was busily planning their wedding, and we agreed that Isaac's visitation would be postponed to the end of the summer vacation that year, when the celebration was to take place. So from the start of June it was just Isaac and me for ten long, lazy summer weeks.

You could say I was not surprised when the opportunity fell into my lap to travel once more for those last two weeks of summer 2014—to participate in a film project I had casually signed up for more than a year earlier, one that I had not expected to get financed—and now that it had suddenly been cleared for takeoff, I felt as if I myself had conjured this event in advance to save me from a future I had sensed approaching. It was as if there were many selves operating within me simultaneously, with no linear relationship to one another, with no fixed point in time. There was the past, constantly flickering at my haunches, and here was this sort of future self, which I felt had reached back in time to pluck me from my referenceless state.

I would be traveling again to Europe, the only continent I had any real interest in at that time, and this time there would be another first visit, to Holland, both its countryside and its capital. But Berlin was also on the list of film locations. This time I did not go to Berlin as a classic tourist, staying in a generic hotel in the city center. This time I stayed with a crew in an apartment in a barely renovated residential neighborhood in the old eastern part. My days were spent researching and working and interacting with others as a consequence, but I am convinced this is not enough to explain why this time it was as if Berlin was a completely new and different city than the one I had passed through exactly a year earlier. Part of this effect had to be attributed to the changes I had gone through in the time between the two visits; most assuredly it was not Berlin that had changed, but the person now disembarking once more into its irrepressible urban wilderness.

During this trip, when I was not working I sat in cafés on busy streets and observed the wildlife, so to speak. I began to notice certain identifying characteristics about the city's denizens, which I had not had the opportunity to do last time among the tourists milling about the landmarks. What I noticed over and over was that Berlin was not a city like New York, Paris, or Rome—it did not seem to participate in the endless race toward money or status, or at least this was not evident in the way people dressed or behaved toward one another.

I walked around the city in overlapping circles and zigzag routes, this time daring to decipher the complicated map, struggling to understand how Berlin could be divided up into so many disparate sections that seemed to relate very little to one another and were poorly connected by public transport. Every tram I boarded stopped at the old Berlin border; to go farther I had to find another route. Yet during my walks through leafy Charlottenburg and graffiti-splashed Friedrichshain and all those neighborhoods in between with their unique atmospheres and encapsulated communities, which I learned were called *Kiez*, I began to notice one delightful common factor in all of them: bookstores. It felt as if there was one on every corner; everywhere I turned I came across shop windows packed with books, carts outside advertising used volumes for less, some stores even specializing in a specific genre, others in a foreign language. Even the coffee shop where the crew ate breakfast in the morning sold used books for one euro each in an adjoining room.

Berlin emerged as some kind of secret paradise to me for these two principal factors: money did not seem to be a primary driving force but books were a flagrantly shared passion, and in light of this, it was easy for a moment to forget about my last trip, to imagine one could set aside the history that had overshadowed every prior moment I had spent in Germany. There were so many languages spoken all around me, and so many different-looking people, that I surmised that Berlin was after all like no other place in this country. And sure, I knew then and know now that it is impossible to know a city in a week, or a month, or a year, or perhaps even a decade. Since then I have continued to make surprising discoveries about Berlin, as if peeling away its surface layer by layer. Quite possibly I will continue to do so for some time, but it is important to explain that these two revelations, should they be accurate or not, first roused in me the recognition that there might be a place in the world with a value system that could indeed attract even someone like me, who had always expected to feel lost and rootless all over the world, just as I had been warned. This theory I was developing would soon be confirmed by the people I would meet during filming, who one after another seemed to have their own individual stories of flight and reinvention; it soon became clear that these people I saw as Berliners were in truth always from somewhere else, and most often with no option of return to that place of origin. I met people fleeing oppression both political and religious, but also people who had overcome the smaller-scale hardship of judgmental small towns, toxic relationships, controlling families. Persecution, discrimination, poverty, war, dictatorships, sects—in fact, anything any human being ever deemed worth escaping—in Berlin you could find multiple persons who had broken away from each category. This created a kind of unique solidarity among people of very diverse backgrounds. Without having to field questions about yourself or provide any additional information whatsoever, you were simply accepted into the society as a fellow "runner." Here, for the first time, no one made me feel like a freak for my background; like everything else, it was simply something I had abandoned, and what mattered was the here and now. In America, I had felt like the only person with my problem; here, I met people who saw it as the most natural and commonplace thing in the world.

But I was still trapped in America after all, at least until Isaac reached adulthood. As my trip progressed and the date of my return drew nearer, I was filled with increasing wistfulness and sorrow. I told myself I would begin visiting Berlin more often, that it would be my place of escape that would give me something to look forward to and plan for the long term. But truthfully, the more I fell in love with the city, the more frightened I became of the inevitable letdown back home, for I knew that by stoking this passion I was only making it more difficult to go on living without it.

On my last night, attending a dinner party, I expressed this to a new acquaintance of mine, a young man named Benyamin who had also left a Hasidic community in Israel and had fled to Berlin to reinvent himself five years earlier. He seemed happy and content in a way I could never imagine myself to be. He said to me, "Why don't you get your German passport? Every Jewish person I know in Berlin has gotten one, because of their ancestors. Don't you have someone German in your family history? At least get the passport back, and for your son. You never know, one day this could be very useful." The words flowed into my mind like a stream of light that spread into my body with tantalizing warmth. Indeed, it was as if an old nerve was tickled just then, for I remembered that old family tree and the letter from my uncle, which I had opened and perused and then set aside, for German ancestry had not appealed to my fourteen-year-old self in search of acceptance and belonging in a world that made impossible demands in exchange for it. It was not as if I thought then, I will get my German passport and move abroad; no, I thought simply: a project; a project that would give me some sense of purpose and groundedness.

The plane ride home was the worst I had experienced. It was as if every fiber of my being was screaming in protest against this movement in the wrong direction. Little did I know it would be my very last journey westward.

———

In September we continued work on the film in New York, but in my free time I began to study with a German tutor I had spontaneously hired off Craigslist, a young jazz musician from the Bavarian countryside named Michael, with a shock of white-blond hair and a boyish face. We met two or three times a week, sometimes in Brooklyn, where he lived, and sometimes he took the train up north and we studied in the garden, which was now slowly, gently mellowing into a golden autumn. Michael helped me configure some German radio channels; in those days *B5 Aktuell*, Michael's local radio station from back home, was running constantly in the background, and I got to know the names of highways, intersections, and towns in that region by heart as I listened to traffic and weather on repeat while I performed housework. But I was most fascinated by the literature programs. Now I could listen to books being read out loud as *Hörspiele*, a kind of audio theater, and endless interviews with authors and live readings and heated discussions between literary critics. My ideas about what it meant to be German were slowly becoming more complex. First it had been Markus and his mother; now it was my teacher, Michael, a shy, sensitive, and intelligent young man who struggled to help me turn my Yiddish into *Hochdeutsch*, even though he had never quite been prepared for this challenge. I remembered the advice of that acquaintance Benyamin on my last night in Berlin, and I found that old envelope that I had been so eager to set aside more than a decade ago. I perused its contents carefully, as if for the first time. For to embark on this project was about much more than a passport. It was a betrayal of my community, of my family, of my grandmother—not only physically but spiritually as well.

But I could not resist, not with all the photos and documents in front of me for the first time in many years, the information hitting me in a totally new way. What had my uncle written about this mysterious great-grandfather of mine? His birth certificate stated he was from Munich, but nothing else, which was strange in comparison to the birth certificate of the woman he had later married, upon which even the occupations of her parents and their origins could be read. But there was only his name, Gustav, and of course that was not his real name, just the one his mother must have chosen for him to use among non-Jews, just like my grandmother's Irenka, or my own recently acquired Deborah.

With a birth certificate like this, in gothic script and with the official stamps of the local offices in Munich, it should not prove too difficult to obtain German citizenship, I assumed. I had little else in the way of official documentation, but I decided to visit the consulate in New York and open a case. A polite young man there took my papers and explained to me that while it was an interesting place to start, in Germany birth certificates weren't proof of nationality the way they were in America, and therefore it most likely wasn't enough to qualify.

"But what else am I expected to submit?" I asked. "It's not like I would have his passport, since it was confiscated."

"Yes, I understand. But unfortunately this is how the law is written. Nationality in Germany is a matter of blood, not place of birth." He looked at me inquiringly. "Why do you want a German passport? You know, as an American you can live in Germany without one. You can apply for a student visa, or an artist visa, as you are a writer. There are many other ways to go there. You don't necessarily need to become a German citizen."

"Yes, well, citizenship or no, I have a custody agreement that keeps me here."

"Ah, I see. So why is this necessary to you?"

I hadn't articulated it until that moment, but now it was suddenly clear. "It's a part of my inheritance. I want to claim it before it disappears completely."

He had advised me to continue my search for documents that would help prove nationality, which, he explained, could only be acquired through the patrilineal side in this case, and he suggested that finding the official asylum documents issued in England for my great-grandfather might be a good beginning. He told me to apply for the birth certificates of all the people in between myself and Gustav in order to prove our connection as well. I commenced upon the search with a surge of energy that could not really be explained by my desire for a European passport, because it quickly went above and beyond archive requests and notary stamps. It did not take long to discover that Gustav had completed a doctorate at the Ludwig Maximilian University in Munich, the thesis for which he had submitted in 1934, only a year after the laws had been passed preventing him from attending the classes he had shared with Josef Mengele. The thesis was titled "Verdingungspolitik in München und Nürnberg 1905–1930" (Indenture Policy in Munich and Nuremberg 1905–1930). He had studied federal economics; his special interests had been the impact of war on economic policies in the Bavarian state. A copy of this thesis had arrived at most of the Ivy League universities in 1935, which seemed miraculous. How had a Jew managed to complete a doctorate after 1933? How had his thesis made it to libraries worldwide while it was burned in his home country?

I called the library at Yale University, which was closest to me, to inquire if the copy that had arrived then was still there. It was, the librarian said, but it could not be loaned out. If I wanted to see it, I would have to show up personally, hand over my ID as collateral, and sit in a special supervised area to view it. I did not hesitate, as it was only a little more than an hour's drive from where I lived. I showed up on the storied campus on a gusty October morning, weaving through gaggles of students loaded down with books and papers.

The library looked almost like a great cathedral, a place of worship for the written word. The reception desk I needed was located under a drafty stone arch. The young man at the desk seemed unfazed by my request; he took my passport and gave me some forms to sign while he disappeared into some hidden storage stacks to retrieve the work. He emerged shortly after holding a small paperbound book, yellowed and crumbling at the edges. It was the only copy, he explained. No one had ever checked it out, most likely because it was written in an old-fashioned and difficult German, he surmised.

For a moment I froze. All I could do was hold the fragile sheaf of papers reverently, overcome by the significance. If not for me, would anyone have ever sought this out? I felt for a moment that the responsibility I had been shouldering for so long was more real, for if I didn't tend to the past, who would? Certainly not my mother, who believed that it was better left buried.

I sat down at a heavy wooden desk, switched on the Tiffany-style desk lamp, and began to peruse the book, but I was left bewildered by most of it. I made quick sense of the dedication,

though, and I kept looking back at it. "An meiner unvergesslichen Mutter gewidmet!" (Dedicated to my unforgettable
mother!) he had written, with an exclamation point. That
would be the Regina on his birth certificate. I knew nothing
about her. My uncle had named her Rochel. On a photo of
Gustav's grave I had read his Hebrew name, Naftali, and what
I assumed to be the Hebrew name of his father, Avraham. Why
wasn't he in the dedication? Where were the proofs of his existence? If I was to make my case for citizenship successfully, I
needed to know more about him.

A few days later, the documents I had requested from the
British archives arrived. The asylum seemed to have been officially granted only in 1948 and had been granted to Gustav;
his wife, Jetta; and his three children simultaneously. But their
collective nationality was listed as Polish, I noted with sharp
disappointment. How could that be? I had seen no proof nor
heard any rumor of Polish ancestry in our family.

I wondered if the new borders after the war might have had
an impact on how Gustav and his family would be perceived by
the British government. Perhaps his parents had come from Sile-
sia, and by the time official asylum was offered, this had become
Poland? It was a weak theory but it was the only one I had. I
decided to submit the documents at the consulate anyway, because I had been assured that once the *Bundesverwaltungsamt*
(Federal Office of Administration) initiated its own investigation, any internal documents attesting to nationality would show
up. I just needed a case strong enough to provoke such a step.

Now Isaac took note of my sudden fervor, my frequent trips
into Manhattan, and my discussions with archivists on the
phone, and naturally he asked me what I was doing. I told him

about my trip to Berlin. When I had returned then to pick him up from his father at the end of summer, he had only said to me, "Mom, promise you will never get married?"

"Why would you want me to promise you that?" I asked, surprised.

"Because I am afraid you will get married and forget about me," he said. I immediately responded with conviction, "Yes, I promise never to get married, and I promise never to forget about you."

Now I asked him, only half-serious, what he would think about going to live abroad for some time, as an experiment, explaining that I had been so impressed with Berlin as a city. He looked at me and smiled and said, "Mom, I think we are about ready for our next adventure."

Surprised, I could only mumble, "Well, we will have to see what your dad thinks about that." I could not have predicted it, not then and certainly not a couple of years earlier, but Eli would soon hear of this conversation from Isaac, and relate it back to me.

"You want to go abroad?" he would ask casually.

"Well, yes, I would. I think it would be a great opportunity for Isaac as well. But of course it's up to you." What happened next was in a sense completely out of my hands, for somehow the idea took root in Isaac's brain, and he must have told his father about the prospect over and over and over, until at some point Eli simply said to me, "Why don't you just go, then?"

Of course, it wasn't that simple, as sheaves of papers would have to be signed. I suspected that somewhere along the way Eli would lose heart, and I admit I didn't really take the idea all that seriously, or at least I didn't let myself hope until that last custodial permission form bore his signature. Then suddenly it hit me, square in the gut: I was free. This time, really and truly so. After all these years, all those battles, Eli had given me my freedom.

Now that the dream was an actual possibility, would I have the guts to go through with it? After all, it was still Germany. I remembered that all it had taken was a couple of glasses of red wine to get Richard and me started on the many German jokes we had in our repertoire, what with my travels and his experiences at art fairs. For years I had been thinking of Germany in clichéd terms, as much a result of the culture I was surrounded by as my own innate tendency to reduce the frightening to the comical. But I had learned, in general, to push past the superficial layers of my own fear, and now I tried to put my preconceived notions aside and see Berlin for what it might be. The city had many advantages, after all, which even Richard had to concede; it was cheap, vibrant, and international. It was also, apparently, full of liberal Americans, especially New Yorkers. Like everyone else we knew with vaguely creative inclinations, Richard and I romanticized the Paris of the twenties and the role it had played in the art and literature of the era. Now there was the dawning acknowledgment that Berlin had become that kind of city, or had perhaps always been one; a perpetual panacea, that magical realm in which no boundaries have been set, where everything and everyone can thrive. The historical legacy of the city seemed to fit well into the pattern of my own destiny, and I believed, perhaps irrationally, that this was something I would actually be able to feel when I lived there, like a vibration in my body, that it would soothe my anxiety like some kind of final karmic reconciliation.

. . .

I had struck up enough friendships in Berlin during my last visit to feel like it could be a manageable transfer. I sent around emails with pertinent questions about the practical details of adjustment; based on the responses that came in, I made lists of what had to be shipped, what would have to be acquired, and what had to be registered or applied for and in what order. What I feared most was the bureaucracy, but naturally there was another question in the back of my mind that I knew I would have to grapple with. I asked some Jewish acquaintances in Berlin to give me advice about that delicate and uncomfortable matter, namely, how did one go about being Jewish in Berlin? The impression I got from those carefully worded replies was that if one had an American passport and didn't act Jewish, it wasn't really an issue. Sure, Jews were attacked on the streets or in the metro, I was informed, but mostly only if they were overheard speaking Hebrew or wearing a kippah, and surely I would do neither of these things. As long as I could avoid sounding or looking Jewish, they told me, in a manner that conveyed a tinge of uneasy shame, I would be fine, and so would my son. I had a conversation with Isaac in which I tactfully explained to him that we were heading to an environment that might have more pockets of intolerance than he was accustomed to, but that was okay; the world was a complicated place, but that didn't mean we had to live in fear; we just had to have strategies in place to deal with complications, by which I meant it would probably be best if he didn't talk about his Jewishness with people he didn't already know and trust. Not that anything would happen to him, but it was better to be safe, I said. Coming from a school where he had been proud to share Jewish customs and stories with his classmates, that was a bigger change than one might realize. He wasn't old enough to register the snarky remarks that I had heard around town about Jews and their money; anti-Semitism in New England was more subtle. I felt somewhat guilty imposing this new fear onto him. I couldn't help but remember the terrible tales I had been told as a child, about the people who lurked just outside the invisible boundaries of our community, who would not hesitate to chop me into pieces if I so much as strayed by one city block. In a sense, it was crazy to be volunteering to relocate to a world where just being who we were could be dangerous, when right now our situation was relatively comfortable in that regard. After all, snarky comments rankled, but they were no threat to our physical well-being. Yet today I wonder if it isn't the open anti-Semitism I prefer to the more cleverly concealed versions; after all, it's difficult to grapple with something if it isn't even acknowledged.

A few weeks before we were scheduled to leave, I ran into my gay Jewish friend Jonathan, another New York City transplant to rural New England, at the local bakery and announced that I was moving. He was more shocked than I expected.

"How can you go live there, as a Jew? I just don't get it. . . . Do you really think you can be happy there?"

"Well, what were you thinking when you came up here ten years ago with your husband? That you'd be embraced as local color by all these uptight WASPs?" I responded.

"Touché," he said. "I guess people like you and me thrive on a challenge."

I watched him head into his car, loaded with coffee and doughnuts. It had been absolute hell to earn the acceptance of the local community when he had first arrived, I knew. And although he had slowly managed to integrate himself here, I wondered if he knew the limits to that integration, and if he cared. Perhaps not knowing, or at least being able to block it out, was a gift. For me, I had decided, it would be the exact opposite. It would be to embrace the very essence of what it meant to be an outsider, to go to a place full of outsiders and live out the experience of marginalization to its full extent.

It was more difficult to find an apartment in Berlin than I expected, especially from so far away with only the internet at my disposal, so when a 3,5 *Zimmer Altbau mit Balkon* became available on Craigslist, I signed a contract immediately, with promise of cash upon key exchange, hoping against hope that it wasn't a scam. I had talked to the subletter on the phone, and he had seemed genuine, and although the apartment was located in Neukölln, a neighborhood I had not yet glimpsed, when I asked him about it he simply responded, "You're from New York, right? Well, Neukölln is like New York." This would turn out to be true, if one's understanding of New York was formed by its outermost boroughs . . .

I sold off most of my furniture, and what I could not sell I gave to Richard, who I knew would make good use of it. I can't deny the fear that began to accumulate as I rid myself rapidly of the possessions I had worked so hard to acquire in the last five years, as concrete proof of the new life that I had built for myself on the outside. Who would do something as crazy as starting over from scratch twice in one lifetime, let alone twice in one decade? Nonetheless, I arranged it with Markus that the few possessions I would have shipped through the postal service would be addressed to him; he would pick them up from customs and drive the boxes from Frankfurt to Berlin. We had settled into a pleasant friendship, and I was happy that I would get to see him again when he delivered my things.

———

We left New York in the midst of a freak blizzard and arrived in Berlin on November 30, 2014, early on a gray Sunday morning. As the taxi pulled up in front of the entrance to the apartment complex, I was surprised to see that the street I lived on had Arabic writing on every shop window. I had planted us smack in the middle of the most Muslim neighborhood in the city; our new home overlooked the raucous, multicultural *Sonnenallee*. In my entire apartment complex, I soon learned, I was one of very few non-Muslim residents. As Markus and I unloaded my boxes in the hallway one day shortly after my arrival, my neighbors inquired about my origins. When I said I was from New York, their guard suddenly dropped. "New York, you said?" one of them replied. "Well, in that case, welcome! We own the Turkish grocery store next door. Come by if you need anything." Being American seemed the least of many possible evils. I knew enough not to share any other clues. As I started settling in, I found myself in intimate dealings with my neighbors; the man who ran the print shop on my corner where I would compile my documents for the *Behörden*, the authorities; the vendors in the markets; the shops where one could get a falafel for lunch on the cheap. I rested on the safety of my Americanness, on the international image of New York as a melting pot where it was often hard to isolate ethnic identities from one another. Perhaps they looked at me, assumed that at some point I had had a Middle Eastern ancestor, and satisfied themselves with that.

Like all newcomers, I lined up at the *Bezirksamt*, the district office, in order to "report myself." I had learned that in Germany one was constantly required to do this—everything required an *Anmeldung*, a registration. Although circumstances are obviously very changed since then, it felt vaguely disturbing to me that the language used for this was the same that was used back then, when the government was keeping tabs on undesirables instead of merely distributing tax ID numbers. For I had heard the German word *Anmeldung* as a child, and for me it would forever be associated with the Gestapo, the way the word *Achtung* spoken by the recorded voice on the metro would only remind me of the *Appellplatz* in Primo Levi's invocations of Auschwitz. Luckily, in time this negative association would fade, for as I would delve deeper into this new yet familiar language in the process of making it my own, my total perception of this vocabulary would encompass the role it had played not just in the Holocaust, but in the whole history of the German language, its inseparability from the language of my childhood and the history of my own origins. I would begin to see the relationship between the two vocabularies as some kind of macabre yet beautiful dance, my one opportunity to find a connecting bridge to a familiar world. After all, I would not be the first: most notably it had been Paul Celan who had remodeled the language and made it his own, and as a result it seemed to me that the rending of the German language that had occurred as a result of the *Shoah* had broken it down into elementary particles that could be shifted into new and radical permutations. In a sense, the German of today was a new language for everyone speaking it.

At the *Bezirksamt*, no one spoke a word of English, and I was glad I had taken the time to fully convert my native Yiddish into a somewhat fluent German before I had left the States. I handed the woman on the other side of the desk all the necessary documents and she entered my information into her computer. She glanced over to me and asked, "What's your religion?"

"Excuse me?" I said, wondering if I'd misheard.

"Your religion. You have to divulge it to the state."

"Um, okay. Well, I'm Jewish."

She pursed her lips. "Hmm, sorry, that's not an option you can choose."

"What?" I asked, thinking it was a joke.

"It's not on the list." She turned the computer screen toward me. On it was a long list of different religions, including various sects of Christianity, Islam, Buddhism, and even Zoroastrianism. But nowhere on that list was there any kind of Jewish option.

I giggled uncomfortably. "Um, it's kind of ironic that this is happening, do you realize that? I'm one hundred percent Jewish; this is the only option I have, sorry." As the words emerged I couldn't help but be reminded of my grandmother's argument all those years ago. She must have convinced me after all.

"Well, I'll just put in atheist, then," the woman said, her fingers already clacking away on the keyboard.

I opened my mouth to protest, then shut it. I wanted my confirmation of registration even more than I wanted to give her a lecture. When she handed me my stamped certificate a moment later, I was relieved to put the process behind me but was left wondering at the fact that the woman behind the desk was so clearly unequipped to handle the matter of a "Jewish" resident; I would have thought that the workers in the office would have at least had some sensitivity training.

. . .

A huge chunk of my childhood education had consisted of teachings on anti-Semitism. World history as it was taught in the Satmar community put Jewish suffering in sharp relief: the developments of human industry and exploration faded to the background, and the saga of humanity came to sound like one long crusade against Jesus killers.

Although the Manhattan Jewish day school my son attended during his preschool years had rigorous security procedures, I never felt I was endangering him by making him a target, as I would if I sent him to a Jewish school in Berlin or took him to synagogue for services.

The local authorities were quick to demand that Isaac attend the local district school as soon as he arrived, but the one in question, Rütli, had an entire page in Wikipedia that was enough to warn me against it. Isaac would have a hard enough time adjusting to the new language. I would not drop his sheltered mind into the fire.

I toured the various Europa schools in Berlin but was most smitten with one in particular, which struck me as diverse in the way that I was used to, not in the way diverse had come to mean here, as a euphemism for a large Arabic population. In this school, there were children of every religion, color, and national origin, but of course I was informed that the waitlist for applications was two years long, and there was no chance of a midyear acceptance. But the assistant principal who tried to dismiss me did not know who she was talking to after all, for I showed up there every day and waited outside the office until they took my application. Then I called every day for three weeks to check on its progress, at which point the principal himself sighed into the phone and capitulated. "Fine," he said, "you can bring your son on Monday and have him enrolled."

Once Isaac had started school, where he seemed to settle in remarkably quickly, my practical obligations subsided somewhat. I had been consumed in the first few weeks after arrival by the basic tasks involved in starting somewhere new, the opening of a bank account, the unpacking, the enrolling, and so on, but now that most of that had been accomplished, I was left reeling, wondering what was to follow. Sure, in two months I would have to show up at the *Ausländerbehörde* (immigration office) to extend my automatic ninety-day visa, but that still seemed far off, and already on the day of my arrival I had received official confirmation from the *Bundesverwaltungsamt* that my citizenship reclamation case had been accepted. I was not so much worried about the tangible challenges involved in integrating myself emotionally into this city. Around this time I chose a place that would become a kind of early garrison for me, a place through which I would come to know this city and it would come to know me, and that place was a café.

Café life in Europe has always been and still remains vastly different from its counterpart in the States, in my view. This is primarily visible in the way Europeans insist on drinking their coffee and eating their meals outdoors at all hours of the day, in all seasons, regardless of the weather. I had been flabbergasted in Paris by the way people had huddled outside under plastic tents when it rained, warming themselves poorly under the heat of braziers. In Berlin, people rarely rushed in and out for their morning coffee or a quick sandwich the way they did in New York. Instead they lingered, often for hours, nursing a cigarette or leafing through a newspaper; some sat in a corner with a book and a cold, empty coffee cup for what seemed like an entire day; others congregated in huddles outside, chatting or watching people walk by. The café a few doors away from me that now became my fortress within the urban jungle of Neu-kölln was called Espera, Spanish for "wait," a tongue-in-cheek reference to its location at a bus stop. Often one could combine one's wait for the bus with a coffee and a cigarette or a crois-sant on one of its fruit-box stools under a burgundy awning.

I began to use the perch of Espera to view the world around me, to bring it into a more familiar and comfortable focus. It was there that I would build my first friendships in the city, with people who, like me, came to the café for their daily dose of caffeine and socializing, artists with unusual work schedules, students and interns subsisting on minimal incomes, and older intellectuals who discussed politics and the changing face of the neighborhood, the city, the world. The café became for me a miniature universe, a kind of multidirectional crossroads for the many varieties of residents who would spend a small part of their day there before continuing on. Even though in those months you could say I sat perfectly still, I felt as if each day my sense of the city was deepening. I was doing once again what I had done in Manhattan. I was simply and quietly observing, letting it all wash over me, waiting for the city to tell me its story.

———

Two days after the *Charlie Hebdo* terrorists in Paris were caught and killed, I sat at the rain-splattered window in Espera, read-ing the reports in the newspaper, and an Israeli man asked if the seat next to me was taken. "Shalom!" I said. "Sure, you can sit here. I'm Jewish too."

"My condolences," he responded dryly.

"I guess you mean that in light of recent events." He grimaced in response as he set down his coffee next to me. I asked him how long he had been living in Berlin and what it was like for him.

"I'm going back to Israel soon," he said. "I'm not like you guys, you know," he added with a smirk, only half-kidding. "I'm the new breed of Jew. You're the exile Jew. Just that difference in perspective radically alters the way you see yourself in the context of surroundings like these."

We joked about the Jewish tendency to create a hierarchy even within our own relatively small sphere. But after he left, I pondered that phrase "exile Jew." He was saying people like me were still stuck in the diaspora, unable to make the conscious choice to liberate ourselves. It was like a form of Stockholm syndrome; we stuck purposefully to our displaced origins, probably more for the comfort of familiarity than for any other reason. I had heard that the Israelis in Berlin, of which there were many, didn't often mix with us so-called exile Jews precisely because of this distinction. To them, Jews like us were a mystery: our entire worldview was so distant from their own as to be not only incomprehensible but also of a nature that fated us to be permanently divided. The truth is that the non-Israeli Jews I know in this city do behave differently: they struggle to make their Jewishness inconspicuous in public, only embracing their identity during the moments they spend among their own. Israelis, on the other hand, wear their Jewishness like casual dress; they act completely comfortable and unselfconscious about their poor, Hebrew-accented German and the various other details that betray their origins at first glance. Was it all because they had a home to go back to? I had always felt the need to dispense with the identifying markers of Jewishness, and now more than ever I wanted to overcome these signifiers and blend in. I liked it when people couldn't trace my accent or deduce from my looks where I came from, and therefore what kind of person I might be. But perhaps I had assessed my own drives incorrectly—perhaps the man was right, and it was just an extreme form of Stockholm syndrome that had drawn me to this city, my desire to embrace my status as an outsider exactly how I had been programmed to.

After the terrorist attacks in Paris, I saw my move to Berlin in a whole new light. My sense of anxiety heightened, but the knowledge that I was on the front lines of a new wave of anti-Semitism, and the corresponding one of European nationalism, tore into my previous convictions that the move had been the right decision for us. I couldn't tear my eyes away from the news. When I was invited by friends to attend Shabbat services in a liberal synagogue, I declined. It seemed obvious that one did not ask for trouble by showing up at synagogues and kosher supermarkets.

Choosing to live here at a time like this might be crazy, I thought, but I was here for many reasons, some more complicated or irrational than others. And I would heartily defend my right to be here, both politically and spiritually. In the wake of the attacks, I was reminded of the question Claude Lanzmann posed to Benjamin Murmelstein in his film *The Last of the Unjust*. He pointed out that Murmelstein had a clear way out of the Nazi sphere of power, yet chose more than once to return instead of becoming a refugee like so many others. "Why would you want to stay?" Lanzmann asks him. At first, Murmel-stein denies that he had real options, but eventually he admits to a desire to see all of it through to the end, and to do what he could as the only world he had ever known went down in flames. I thought of the Israeli I had met at Espera, who had been smug with the knowledge that he would be going home soon. Perhaps I would be safer elsewhere, but a part of me wanted to be here for last farewells, as it were.

A large part of the chaos and confusion that marked my early months as a Berlin resident can be attributed to my own inner turmoil and self-doubt. It was as if my fear of having made the wrong decision in coming here was reflected back to me in the actions and statements of others I came in contact with. Perhaps I was even unconsciously searching for confirmation of this suspicion, wanting Berlin itself to prove to me that the old voice in my head, now raging like an infuriated drunk, was right after all. For if I regarded my move honestly, it was an illogical and unfounded step, on paper a move in a back-ward direction toward the past and its problems, which the people who raised me had struggled to escape. Perhaps the only factor that kept me within the frame of sanity in that first year was the quiet assurance in the pit of my stomach that stood firm and unwavering despite the onslaught, an assurance as insuper-able as it was irrational, which insisted that if I simply waited patiently, all would be revealed to me in time.

This "gut voice," as one might call it, was not new. It was the same voice that had guided me through the often senseless and arbitrarily imposed restrictions, both physical and psychologi-cal, of my childhood and adolescence, and it had traveled with me through those five years of transition in the States. In the process, it had grown stronger, firmer, and even more implacable. Now it seemed to freeze me in place. It was the only reason I did not flee, but I also did not venture too far past my neighborhood.

Had you been walking down Sonnenallee in those days it is highly likely you might have glimpsed me at the window of Café Espera, or huddled on a bench outside with my *New Yorker* magazine, the subscription to which I had transferred to my new address and which consequently arrived three weeks delayed. Perhaps you would have spotted me in conversation with some of the neighboring residents I had struck up tentative friendships with: a student from the former East Germany who spoke fluent English, a poet and musician who was so anti-capitalist as to refuse to participate in the society he was now forced to live in, a young psychotherapist and part-time DJ who had sorrowfully abandoned the radical left-wing views of his youth in the kind of slow resignation that is often forced upon us by adulthood, and a former editor who was now running his own independent publishing house and who could often be found smoking while reading the reviews of his authors that appeared in the national newspapers. Interestingly, this group of people was interconnected: the poet was published by the editor, the editor was the next-door neighbor and friend of the psychotherapist, who in turn had applied for the position of roommate at the home of the student, thereby striking up a friendship. We could often be found in a group formation in front of the café, and occasionally other friends of friends would be pulled into the circle, writers and translators of the publishing house, colleagues or associates of the others, and my own paltry circle of acquaintances in Berlin as well. Benyamin, who had now become a fixture in my world, a kind of stalwart of solace because of his intimate knowledge of my past and his ability to understand what I was going through, became one of them. After school, Isaac would often join us for a hot chocolate and a snack, and when the café inevitably closed, we more often than not simply changed locations. My apartment was outfitted with an enormous formal dining room, which I regarded as a shame not to use. We cooked large dinners in the underequipped kitchen and served them up on the giant oak table against the backdrop of raucous Sonnenallee evenings, the flashing lights of shop signs and sirens streaking across the darkness pressing up against the enormous windows. In the evenings as I put Isaac to bed, there would be people congregated in my living room drinking beer and speaking in hushed tones or smoking cigarettes on my balcony, and this was a form of benefaction; this was the feeling of being constantly surrounded by people I cared about, who seemed to care about me too, regardless of my probably obvious discombobulation. Slowly, without me realizing it, this began to create an emotional buffer, a cushion of security that allowed me to relax.

My days began to fill with more and more warm moments, fits of laughter, stirrings of happiness. As these moments accumulated, the strange and threatening aspects of life in this new world began to fade in comparison, the people around me came into crystalline and tender focus, and I felt, for the first time in my life, loving and optimistic toward the society I was surrounded by.

———

Around this time I began to run into some trouble with the pile of bureaucracy that the application for an *Aufenthaltstitel*, or residence permit, consisted of, something I would be occupied with for the majority of that first year. Each time I showed up in that waiting room in House C, Floor 2, I felt as if I was begging for permission to stay, and when I did so it was as if the angry ghost of my grandmother rose within me like some outraged poltergeist. I felt humiliated and disgusted as I subjugated myself in a country that had once perpetrated the ultimate subjugation against my ancestors. It was the unflappable support of my new friends that gave me the strength I needed to see the process through to the end. Eventually, the publisher would enlist the help of his partner to intimidate the clerk in charge of my case—all it would take was his suit and his aristocratic surname to make all the obstacles to my receiving an *Aufenthaltstitel* magically disappear. But that would happen nine months after my arrival, and until then, there were many painful visits.

Of course, I was humbled when I lined up at the biweekly market at the Landwehr Canal to get my falafel with all the toppings for 1.75 euros and chatted with the affable seller, whose origins were in Ramallah but who had been born and raised in a refugee camp in Lebanon. I was struck with sadness upon learning that although his grandparents had been the ones to lose their homes, he still experienced the world as a refugee two generations later. He was hoping to get permanent residence in Germany; having long since given up on building a life in familiar territory, he would settle for any place willing to accept him. His circumstances stood in sharp contrast to my own.

For someone like me, raised by Holocaust survivors and deeply aware of the unique agony that comes with displacement, I felt a compassion tangled up with guilt, unease, and self-consciousness. On the other hand, this man who served me my falafel was trying to see me as a human being and not the enemy. At least that's the way it felt when he went out of his way to smile and joke with me as he rolled up the *laffa* bread. This dynamic that existed between "us" and "them" is one that only "we" were fully aware of, and I was suddenly and perpetually conscious of it in Europe. Neither of us, not me the Jew nor him the Palestinian, had ever been perceived as our simple and individual selves outside of our charged bubble—for among the rest of the world, the conversation about how we related to each other was firmly mired in our political identities and all their associated implications. It struck me as the height of irony that we could only be human to each other. Indeed, the most surprising of my experiences as an American Jew in Berlin were my interactions with Palestinians, a segment of the population that I had not previously encountered in real life. A taxi driver who overheard my son speaking about a Jewish holiday told me his family were also Palestinian refugees who had ended up in Germany. Upon seeing my nervousness he assured me, "Eighty percent of Palestinians just want peace. They don't hate Jews. It's Hamas that betrays us."

In early April, during the Easter break, I traveled with Isaac and the film crew to Israel for two weeks, as we were planning on shooting some scenes there. It was my very first time in Israel, and after the experiences of the last few years, I approached the trip with a mixture of excitement and trepidation. I had not forgotten what that Israeli Jew had said to me two months earlier, about how Jews like me were relics of the diaspora, a dying breed destined to be overtaken by a new kind of Jew, empowered, self-satisfied, and best of all, freed from the psychological complexes imposed by an inheritance of oppression and victimization. I wondered if my experience in Israel would reflect these stinging accusations tenfold, if I would be made to feel like some pitiable and pitiful specimen of inferior breeding. Even in the small and closeted society I had grown up in, I had seen how judgmental and hierarchical Jews could be to one another. Now I was filled with vague unease at the prospect of immersing myself in a magnified version of such a society.

After extensive questioning at the airport, we exited into the golden afternoon light of Tel Aviv, and it was at first delightful to walk among the stone edifices, burnished by age, and to glimpse the blue waves of the Mediterranean, with a sun that hovered directly above it like I had first glimpsed in California. My first impression of this port city was not all that different from my impressions of port cities I had visited before on the islands of Greece and Italy. There is something about metropolitan life on a waterfront that seems to resemble nothing so much as itself.

On our first morning, as we headed to the café across the square to get coffee and breakfast, I could see a change in Isaac, for he was relaxed and forward in his interactions with café personnel, spontaneous and friendly with strangers at the next table, and I realized that for him, being surrounded by Jews clearly did mean something, even though we had never discussed it after that first and last conversation before moving to Berlin. Now he seemed to relax and take it for granted that he was in a country where everyone was just like him, where he could behave accordingly. Seeing his new carefree spirit, I felt a sudden, sharp pain that in my life choices I was depriving him of the one thing I had ceased to value, which I had extrapolated to be universally valueless.

. . .

Those first few days were very lovely ones; we sought out pretty beaches and narrow streets bursting with flowers; we ate familiar food and laughed loudly and no one looked around to see what the fuss was about. Even I started to feel a little different. It was having an effect on me, this homogeneity, this new and strange feeling of being, for the very first time in a long while, exactly the same.

The moment that feeling went from being pleasant to being discomfiting was on the first day of Passover. I had already seen how in the grocery stores they had covered the aisles of forbidden foods with thick brown paper, as the law dictated, but it's difficult for me to describe my outsize shock and outrage when I sat in a non-kosher restaurant with other secular Jews and was told I could not order anything with bread. It was as if I had landed within those old and familiar walls that I had struggled to scale; I felt as if I had fallen backward in time. How patronizing was the state in its assumption that basic Orthodox precepts applied to all Jews no matter their individual perspectives or choices; how invasive its unwillingness to tolerate dissent. The waiter seemed surprised and uncertain in the face of my indignation and apologized profusely, explaining that serving me bread meant risking a large fine for the restaurant, and that it had nothing to do with his personal beliefs. I explained that I was American and that it was simply a shock for me to be in a secular and non-kosher environment and still somehow be subject to regulations I viewed as obsolete and ludicrous. It wasn't about the bread. It was about the theocracy, I told him.

By the time my first week in Israel had come to an end, it had become clear to me not only that the authorities I had struggled to free myself from enjoyed, as a result of sharp shifts in demographic proportions, ever-increasing power in this country, but also that despite the exemptions still enjoyed by the comparatively diminishing secular population, there was something not only relieving but also dreadfully confining about being surrounded solely by people with the same ethnic identity. How could I cultivate *harchavos hada'as*—the broadening of perspective my grandfather had termed the key to personal bliss—in such a narrow, limiting environment?

I no longer felt intimidated by that Israeli who had derided my status as an exile Jew; now I pitied him instead, trapped within the small frame of a shallow social pool, prevented from realizing and cultivating a connection to the world that was conducive to growth and development. I wasn't an exile Jew, I realized, as I made my way to the Kotel (the Western Wall) and was relegated to the women's section in the back, as I was spit on in the streets of Jerusalem even though I was modestly dressed. If anything, it was Israel where I felt most exiled, exiled from my true self, exiled from the courage and enlightenment of the diaspora heritage, alienated from the diversity of the Jewish experience.

I realized that I missed Berlin in a way I had never missed a place before. I wanted to go home, and I say this deliberately because I had never before felt that burning desire to go back from whence I had come. Never, not once. Not when I had left my community, not when I had left Manhattan, and not when I had left New England. But now I felt this new and foreign yearning: to return.

When I landed in Berlin, I dropped my suitcase in my apartment, and moments later I was sitting on the bench in front of Café Espera, face turned up to the sun, sipping a lemonade.

And who should walk by but the poet, whose gentle manner I had been missing those last two weeks. A short while later, the brown-haired student with an elated smile and a spring in her step joined us, and by early evening we had all been reunited again, sitting there in our magical circle under the streaky golden sun. Before night had fallen I knew, with stunning certainty, that I would never leave Berlin.

———

They say that Berlin has two faces, to coincide with the two seasons: the long, gray, gloomy, all-encompassing winter and the gorgeous, delicate, tender weeks of a truncated and precious summer. During my visits to Berlin prior to the move, I had only encountered Berlin's *Schokoladenseite*; I had formed impressions of life there as it existed through the tonal filters of long, light-filled days, of lazy, violet-hued evenings and cool, invigorating nights. I had seen everything in full bloom; I had witnessed the collective good mood of a people freed to celebrate, connect, and relax in public spaces and on green fields; I had watched enviously the carefree faces of young people riding bikes into a strong breeze, the short sleeves of their T-shirts fluttering in the wind.

I had not been adequately prepared for winter in Berlin, which was the season that marked my arrival as a resident. I had lived through winters before, naturally—after all, I was well acquainted with the balanced four-season year that marks life on the northeast coast of the United States—but I had experienced them very differently there. Winters as I recall them in America were dramatic, with big, open skies, crisp, cold winds, and pale golden sunlight that seemed almost brighter than summer light despite imparting a fraction of its heat. I have memories of repeated snowfalls, the new piling up on the old, the air often filled with thick and robust white flakes that retained their crystalline shape even as they landed on the wool of my coat or rested on my hair. I remember the way the sounds of life were muffled by this temporary mantle, the otherworldly pink-toned light that set in just after the snows stopped, and the inevitable high and clear blue sky that followed the next morning, the sun reflecting brilliantly off the white-blanketed ground. I had never experienced winter as a particularly dark or dreary time; like the other seasons, it had its pros and cons, but it was no more lacking in color and spectacle than any other. Never did winter envelop me in permanent, lifeless gray the way Berlin would in its notoriously rude welcome.

In Berlin, I had to reconcile myself to an apathetic and non-committal winter that I would learn could begin as early as October and last until May. Yet the majority of that time was not marked by invigoratingly clear, cold days but by damp chill and dim light, by an atmosphere that spanned a narrow spectrum between needlelike rains and stinging mists that seemed to hover almost perpetually in the air; it was marked by the ever-present thick, dense cloud cover, which seemed to hug the roofs of the buildings, giving me the impression that we were all trapped under some giant, suffocating tent. Worst of all were the moods of the people, the way they squabbled with one another on public transport or heckled one another in the streets, the way civil servants and public office employees grumbled and waitresses rolled their eyes.

So it is natural that my early months in Berlin were filled with suppressed panic: partly because of my fear of having made an uninformed and possibly regrettable decision combined with my auxiliary fear of having to admit that such might be true, and partly because of the culture shock that came into play on so many levels. Then, right around the time that I had started to relax into the buffer of my new and small community, the sun came out. First for only a little at a time: I remember five brilliantly sunny days in February, which, although it was still cold, we spent sitting outside. The awning of Espera was pulled back, and we huddled under jackets and blankets, practically drunk with joy at the bright light, so much so that I can't even remember feeling the cold. But it wasn't until my return from Israel in mid-April that the spring began in earnest. When the trees lining the island strip in the middle of the teeming Sonnenallee began to unfurl their leaves, and the shops selling plants and flowers lined up their wares on the street, and balconies were bedecked in bloom-filled pots, and the building facades suddenly exploded with grapevines and trailing ivy, then it became clear to me just what a transformation this city performed each year in its procession toward summer, almost like the changing of costumes between scenes of a play.

In those months, as the city came to life around me, something new came to life within me as well. I cannot attribute this process to any one specific thing; rather, it was an accumulation of factors: I purchased a used bike for cheap on *Kleinanzeigen* (the classifieds) and began to venture out of my *Kiez* via its pedals. I explored various neighborhoods, parks, and lakes with friends. In July, when Isaac flew to visit his father as we had originally agreed in the terms of our new arrangement, my priorities shifted temporarily from the everyday responsibilities of a young single mother, and I became, for a moment, like the others around me, young and carefree in Berlin, with the intoxicating and delusional conviction that the summer would last forever. In the evenings, we clustered around tables on the pavement of Sonnenallee, in front of an ancient and accordingly shabby but cozy pub called Kindl Stuben, cigarette smoke from the nicotine-dependent among us converging into streams above our heads. We drank and talked until the early hours of the next morning, at which point I pedaled the few blocks home and fell into a deep, dreamless sleep that I would emerge from, suddenly and quickly, at around noon, when the sun pierced through the thick curtains and warmed the room past comfortable temperatures.

Now we spent the early afternoon hours in front of Espera recovering from the night before. When the sun became too intense, we moved to the shade of the massive trees at Treptower Park with a book or two and some apples. In the early evening, when my apartment was cooler and dimmer, I sat for a few hours at my big dining room table, which belonged, like everything else in my should-have-been-temporary apartment, to the subletter, and I wrote. Not for a deadline, not something I had contractually promised or that someone was expecting, but just for me. It was as if I was experimenting again with my inner voice, seeing if it felt brave enough to emerge once more in this new space.

———

On the third of August I fell in love. Just like that, by accident; there isn't really more to tell, because in the end, every love story is the same, ordinary, universal. We say that love is about being your best self with the other, but before I had had no real self to put forth; I had performed one that was appropriate to the person and the situation instead, hoping that through the other person I would be given the gift, however ephemeral, of a projected self. But now it was as if not only could I be myself with this new person, but I actually had a self to be.

It was the first time I embarked on a love affair with someone who lived in the same city, and for me this was a clear sign that I had finally ceased my endless striving in the direction of "away," that I had found my *menuchas hanefesh*, my bodily peace. Bit by bit, Berlin became hallowed by the conventional acts of passion; every street corner at which we kissed, each café where we shared a cigarette and a glass of wine, every small location in which we conspired together, became branded, as if forever, by the memory of the experience. Even in the moments when we were apart, I would bike through my neighborhood and its adjoining ones, and the immediacy of each shared moment, of each caress and tender gaze, jumped out at me like some marvelous decoupage, like a mille-feuille of accumulated short-term memories stacked upon one another like layers of semitransparent film. As if it hadn't been enough to encounter Berlin in its sublime summer attire, now I saw it through the supplemental lens of romantic euphoria, and I fell in love with the city precisely for being the place where I had, for the first time in my life, experienced such a simple human happiness.

In that *Spätsommer*, that late summer, while I was falling in love with a person but also with a city, a life, and a possible future, I finally found an apartment of my own, a potential permanent address in Berlin, with my name on the contract and empty rooms to be filled with my own furniture and books and artwork. This felt like a very meaningful step in the right direction; in fact, only then did it become clear how unsettling it had been to practically squat, outside the realms of the law (of which I was only later informed), in an apartment under someone else's name filled with someone else's things, and so the move heralded a euphoric joy. I packed my few possessions back into the boxes I had used to ship them and transported them in shifts with a borrowed car. Friends came by to help me paint over the sickly green walls in the front bedroom, and when the work was finished, the fresh white coat gleamed in the sunlight streaming in from the enormous double-paned windows; the room itself felt fresh and clean and light, exactly how I felt in my own heart. A few days later, I woke up for the first time in that empty white room, and my eyes opened into the soft morning light and I glimpsed the many sturdy branches of the old plane tree growing right before my windows, the lush green leaves swaying to and fro in the breeze. For a brief moment I was in my childhood bedroom, nestled under the Hungarian comforter, sun illuminating the high white ceiling, listening to the creaking limbs of the enormous sycamore towering over our brownstone. And then I glimpsed the ornate facades of the pre-war buildings behind the branches of the plane tree and I oriented myself back into time and space. Even then, just watching the bobbing branches, I knew it was a sign. It was what I had longed for five years ago as I had stood at the window of my small, dark apartment in Manhattan, looking down into the courtyard at the locust tree, knowing in the core of myself that everything was wrong and would have to be corrected. Now here was this great and bounteous tree, its rustling laugh trailing into my open window—for how else could I explain the journey of the last five years and where it had led me if it wasn't some kind of supernatural guidance? It was the first indication of a phenomenon that would reveal itself to me over the coming year, that of the closed circle, of the parts made whole, of the narrative structure achieving perfect completion.

7
VERSÖHNUNG
איבערבעטן
RECONCILIATION

In the seventh year after my departure, I lost my language. I had commenced a relationship in a foreign tongue that I did not yet speak especially well. Nevertheless, it became the language in which I conducted most of my communications, and as a result, whenever I occasionally fell back into English it became clear that the near-native-level grasp I had struggled for so many years to achieve had now been meaningfully diminished. I was floating in between the two languages, and this state of being had an impact on my thoughts and feelings, on the way they were processed and perceived, how long this took, and how much effort it required. During this brief period of linguistic transition, I sometimes had difficulty understanding *myself*. I struggled to make sense of the confused vocabulary in my own head, of the mishmash of locutionary influences.

Like many Germans, my boyfriend, Jan, spoke two versions of his native language, a regional-accented High German as well as a dialect local to the small area he had grown up in. He explained to me that where he came from, the difference in dialect could be quite marked even from village to neighboring village; he was able to tell, based on word choice, pronunciation, or intonation, not only the region someone hailed from, but sometimes the particular town as well. He gave me examples of words that were said one way in his hometown and a completely different way only five kilometers away, to a point where I had to wonder how the locals could possibly understand one another. Although he had moved to Berlin almost two decades earlier, he still had many opportunities to use this rarified dialect, for he had formed a circle of friends over the years who also came from the same area, and they regularly met with one another, dissolving into indistinct and rapid mumbles each time they did so. Except it wasn't nearly as difficult for me to make sense of as it might have been for others, because the great irony was that this particular dialect had originated at the same time and in a similar region as Yiddish and therefore resembled it more than I had expected. Although I couldn't speak what sounded like an odd, distorted version of my own first language, I could, to my surprise, understand everything that was being said. It was as if my brain, in the process of converting Yiddish to German, had constructed a kind of Rosetta stone for all related dialects, a way of understanding the relationship between the main language and its many illegitimate children. I had unique access to a universal cipher for Germanic languages; in my mind I could deconstruct words into associative parts and their respective images, and I could run a list of permutations as to the many possible pronunciations and constructions and still draw the connections between all of the versions as if by instinct.

And yet I would soon discover, to my great surprise, that somewhere along the way my first language had slipped from my voluntary grasp. I could no longer isolate Yiddish at will. This was partly, I surmised, because I had gone so many years without speaking it and partly because I had, in a sense, traded in the language of my childhood for the language of my future. I did not desire to lose my first language per se, and the reason for this certainly had something to do with feelings of guilt and cultural obligation, but another more basic reason was the fear of somehow losing an integral part of myself in that process. Had I been at this time surrounded by other Yiddish speakers, the situation might have turned out differently; as it was, however, while my fluency and comfort level in German increased, I began to feel as if Yiddish was sinking deeper and deeper through the levels of my consciousness into the quicksand of my unconscious memory, permanently removed from my express dominion. Most of the time I was unable to control the recall process at all; instead it occurred independently of my efforts, at odd moments, in unpredictable flashes. Watching a film in Yiddish, or hearing a song, could often bring back individual words in stunning clarity, with all the memories and powerful emotions associated with them, but often those were painful experiences, and I drew back as if from a flame.

Meanwhile, the new words I was learning in this strange process of replacement began to attract their own aureoles of associations, memories, and feelings, much in the way the acquisition of new words in any language is bound to do. But for me there was an additional layer to this process, because with each new word acquired that shared a relationship with a word from my past, I merged old associations with new ones, and each term became a layered emotional experience, for underneath that instinct to avoid the past and its pitfalls, I began to realize that a part of me had been yearning for just such a reconciliation all along.

I remember during this time that Jan and I occasionally made a game of comparing unique words in our various native languages; he would put forth an old, forgotten term that no longer existed in German and I would offer the Yiddish equivalent, and vice versa. Often they were the same; sometimes in Yiddish the word would have been replaced by an Eastern European, Hebrew, or Aramaic term; but more likely there would be a harmonious counterpart. I would ask him how a certain word was pronounced and was surprised to hear the similarity; he would use whole phrases that I would suddenly recall from my childhood. While I was lying next to him one lazy morning, I thought of this magical link between us that this fusion of language represented, and I asked him if he recognized the Yiddish word *iberbetn*, which would be equivalent to the High German *Überbitten*. He wrinkled his forehead at this one, trying to draw the connections from memory.

As I told him, I remembered the word now with its full weight, and it struck me that it really was a marvelous concept for which an equivalent did not exist in any other language that I knew of. Originally, a few hundred years ago, the word *iberbetn* had simply meant to beg someone's forgiveness—in an Old German dictionary from the early nineteenth century you can find the definition *jemanden mit Bitten zu überwinden*, a rough translation meaning "to overcome someone with beseechment," which is quite similar—but over time it had evolved into a very important ritual, central to everyday life in our community. I remembered as a child being told by my teachers to resolve a squabble with a fellow classmate: "*Betet euch jetzt iber,*" she admonished us, and we were immediately compelled to make our peace. We had learned at a very young age that there were two forms of sin, that of *ben adam le'chavero*, and that of *ben adam l'Hashem*, literally between man and his peers and between man and God, and the only way for us to convince God to judge us mercifully for our sins against him was to judge our peers mercifully for their sins against us. So if one suspected one had sinned against one's fellow man, one simply approached this person and expressed one's intention *sich iber-zubeten*, at which point the basic obligation to forgive had already been imposed on the one approached. This was the case because the Talmud said that God was so merciful to his subjects as to be moved to compassion not at the point at which a prayer was issued, but at the moment when the lips were parted in the intention of doing so—meaning the compassion was issued in advance. Now, if God behaved so to man, then man must emulate God and do the same, and this meant to forgive the other even before the apology had been expressed. Over time, this came to mean that no apologies had to be made at all, and it was enough to simply express the intention, to say the magic word, and immediately there would be the swift and effusive insistence that it was hardly necessary, that no, in fact, the other was the one with the obligation, and before any regret or mercy had been articulated, a true, warm, and authentic reconciliation between the two had already been established.

By the time I was growing up in late-twentieth-century Williamsburg, the ritual had become something of a safety button, a mantra we repeated daily as if to protect ourselves from any overlooked sin. We performed it obsessively, as if perhaps tomorrow we would no longer have the opportunity and the accounting between us would be left unresolved; we made the rounds on fast days and before important holidays, asking our friends and neighbors if we had in some way, without our knowledge, hurt or disappointed them. And each time, regardless of whether this offense had been registered on behalf of the offender or not, an absolute pardon was offered generously and quickly, for each of us wanted to merit exactly the same treatment from God in regard to our sins against him. We were only too happy to pay this price of letting go of old grudges, relinquishing accounts, dissipating corrosive resentments. Perhaps those resentments did occasionally return—at the very least certain grudges proved more stubborn than we would have liked—but the consistent practice of this ritual would eventually prove more potent, and as we offered verbal absolution over and over, the repetitiveness would eventually render its impact more effectively, and we would not just perform but actually feel the forgiveness that we so dutifully expressed.

Now, lying in bed next to this man, who was probably no more or less German than the rest of his countrymen, whose family history and cultural legacy were both thoroughly average and perfectly exemplary, I reflected on the fact that there was something *unausgesprochen*, unspoken, as well in our own coming together, for unlike in my last relationship, I had not put us through the ringer of that revenge/penance dynamic; I had not forced him to assuage my guilt or satisfy my primitive lust for revenge. I had not compelled him to perform atonement for the history of his country or for the choices and actions of his ancestors. The intentions had been made clear when we had accepted each other's whole selves; it was as if we had leapt over the whole complex process in a single moment, and now we had landed at the other side of mercy.

The concept of *iberbetn* was so pronounced in my community that it became a general term for any form of unlikely concord, a way to describe conflicts and contradictions that were resolved not by reason but by faith. Was it not some kind of mysterious miracle that I was beginning to sense my own self taking form, here in this most unlikely of places, in the most improbable of circumstances? All along I had thought I was seeking forgiveness from my grandmother; now I realized I had been only trying to forgive myself. I had been trying to find a way to be happy despite the shame and the guilt and the grief, and now it was as if I had sewn them all into one cloth, and in their harmonious proximity to one another, the emotions took on different attributes.

Life in a foreign country takes on a new light when one acquires easy use of the language and has formed meaningful relationships with the locals. My new partner and I traveled together frequently and undertook many trips with our children, and having him as a companion and guide meant developing a more intimate and true understanding of what everyday life as a Berliner was like. Everything was going wonderfully, to the point where I had begun to forget about all my prior prejudices and disappointments, and I began to believe that from now on my life here would always be this idyllic. Everything felt so simple; I was in love with a good man and the world was ours to conquer together. I was finally living in the present instead of the past, and I must have convinced myself that I had exorcised all my demons, or at least was heading in that direction.

It was a rainy Sunday morning, and we had arrived early at the *Spaßbad*, a popular indoor/outdoor pool complex in Oranienburg. I was there with my son and with Jan and his two children. We headed straight for the slides, which Jan had warned would be choked with long lines later in the afternoon. After we had all had our share of shrieking fun, we retreated to the lounge chairs we had laid claim to upon our arrival. The children splashed before us in the wave pool. At one point Jan got up to issue a safety warning to one of them; upon his return, he mentioned casually to me as he settled back into his chair, "There's a Nazi in the swimming pool."

There was some context for that casual mention. I'd told him at an earlier point in our relationship that I still did not quite know how to recognize a Nazi myself. I was looking for skinheads but kept confusing them with punks. Nazis looked different today, he'd informed me then, pointing one out while we strolled through his bourgeois-bohemian neighborhood in the former East Berlin one sunny afternoon. I had turned around to see a young couple in combat boots, ripped biker clothing, piercings, and tattoos. The kind of kids I'd seen before on the street in San Francisco or New Orleans. Not the association I would have made. Rockers, maybe street kids, but not Nazis. "How'd you know for sure?" I'd asked. But he just did.

The Nazi Jan spotted in the pool was Marcel Zech, whose name would pop up in news reports all over the world soon after. But on that day, he was just a guy enjoying the weekend with his kid and some friends. I would notice those friends later on by their identifying characteristics, because on that day, I finally did learn how to tell a Nazi from a punk, a rocker, or a street kid. "How do you know?" I'd asked Jan, peering in the direction of the pool, and he'd answered clearly this time: "Iron cross on his ankle, black sun on his arm, Reich eagle on his chest, *und so weiter* . . ."

My jaw dropped, but Jan just shrugged. "At least he didn't

put a swastika underneath the wings; he just left that spot empty, framing his belly button." I got up and tried to walk casually to the edge of the pool, waving to my son as he splashed happily. I looked for the man with the tattoos Jan had mentioned. Many of the people there were heavily tattooed, so it was initially difficult to pinpoint the person Jan had been referring to, but then, so suddenly I thought my heart had stopped, there was a torso right in front of me, thick and spilling over the edge of a pair of too-tight bathing trunks. I saw the quote first. *Jedem das Seine,* "to each his own." I had seen it before, on an entrance to a concentration camp. But then, like a second blow, I saw the detailed sketch of the entrance to Auschwitz right on top, sprawling across a meaty lower back. I blinked, looked again. There it was, the barbed wire, the distinctive entry gate, even the brick detail.

I rushed back to my chair. "He's got a concentration camp! On his back!" I said breathlessly. "And the quote! Oh my God! Did you see that too?" Jan hadn't seen it. He looked over in the man's direction, squinting with effort. I was horrified, indignant, boiling with humiliation, anger, and fear. I looked around me, trying to see if others had noticed what I had noticed, if they too were talking among themselves in shocked and horrified tones. But the people around me appeared serene and relaxed.

"I can't just sit here and do nothing, I can't!" I argued heatedly. "I need to do something!"

When I realized that a man like that could frolic undisturbed while the tattoo on his back expressed support for the genocidal campaign that had eliminated all of my grandmother's relatives, I felt quite possibly the smallest and most powerless I have ever felt.

I think I scared Jan that day. I think the depth of my emotions scared him. I think he assumed they would make me capable of deeply irrational actions. We had a fight then. He yelled, he said some things he would later regret, and I saw the fear (fear of me!) in his eyes. We sat down to lunch with our children only two tables away from this man and his group of thugs, all similarly decorated with eagles and crosses and suns, and when my son asked me what was wrong, I told him simply that there were some bad people there that believed Hitler was right.

"Well, Mom, you should just ignore them!" he said, giving me the same advice he'd heard me dispense about schoolyard bullies. I looked at him and wondered painfully what kind of lesson I was teaching him that day, about confronting evil instead of looking the other way. I sighed and nodded and pushed my food around my plate.

"Is this him?" Jan later asked skeptically, showing me a photograph of a soft-faced man smiling angelically against a background of timber roofs and spires. We had just learned that the neo-Nazi with the Auschwitz tattoo whom we had encountered in a swimming pool the week before was a member of parliament for the National Democratic Party, which was the deceptively innocent appellation for the Nazi party of postwar Germany; and Jan was trying to find out, by way of searching through the party list for the region, the name and identity of the man in question. There he certainly was in that photograph Jan was proffering, looking harmless, sweet even.

I'd calmed down by then. We could almost joke about it. Pretty soon the photo was in all the newspapers, because there was another Berliner at the pool who must have felt as infuriated as I did, and he had the guts and presence of mind to take a photo and post it on Facebook, with the caption "Such people are allowed to move about unmolested in Oranienburg . . ." This photo came to the attention of several journalists, who proceeded to investigate. The story hit the headlines shortly after. Jan sent me the first link, in which it was reported that multiple members of the pool staff had been notified about the man's presence but had chosen to actively ignore the issue until finally one of the managers had agreed to kick the man out. This happened shortly after I left the pool, apparently. I'm sure Zech enjoyed those five or six hours he spent there until then regardless.

I found many other articles about Zech. First he was in all the German papers; then he made the international ones. It was discovered that the tattoo had been noticed before, at a lake outside Berlin last summer, and had been discussed on the radio. But no one had ever taken a photo of it. Now it was out there, in all its chilling ugliness, and could not be ignored. A few days later it was reported that the owner of the tattoo had been identified as member of the German parliament. Since the laws pertaining to privacy and personality rights in Germany don't apply to individuals serving the public interest, the case was now considered worthy of TV news.

I thought about something else then, about how ever since I'd arrived in Germany I'd been on the receiving end of the same message: that it was about time people like me got over the Nazis, because everyone else already had. Only four weeks ago, I had sat down to get a haircut, and my hairdresser, after ascertaining that my name was indeed Jewish as she'd suspected, asked me pushily if I didn't agree with her that it was time Germany put away the Nazi conversation for good. "I don't get this obsession with Hitler," she said crankily as she ran a comb through my wet hair. "It's gotten to the point where I'll vomit if I see one more advertisement for a book or film about the Holocaust." I don't think she liked the total silence I offered her as a response. I remembered her now as I toyed with the idea of putting my thoughts down on paper. It isn't Marcel Zech who is the problem, not really, but the people who want to pretend he doesn't exist. The ones who would make themselves small for him and his ilk; they've shown me that Nazis still have a kind of real power here. People think twice before confronting one, afraid of the physical consequences, but they're even inclined to refrain from expressing their opinion from a distance, because who can guarantee their safety? Evil still rules via terror, just like it did all those years ago, and the rest of us are still duly enslaved, even though it's difficult to admit it. We retreat to our bubble and rant and rave, but in the end no one I know, and maybe not even I, will have the courage to show these people that they can't get away with their message of murderous hate. Or would I? Would I simply remain silent in the background, because it was safer?

Seeing that tattoo took my breath away. It shattered the illusion that I had begun living under, namely, that Germany was a country in which the majority of people condemn right-wing extremism and have wrestled with their past and learned from it. I was understandably relieved, then, to discover that an investigation had led to charges. I followed the news avidly. Others were pessimistic—they warned me that an *Anzeige*, a criminal charge, was not an indictment. Therefore it was a surprise when the indictment was indeed announced, along with an accelerated trial.

Having witnessed this story from its beginning, I felt compelled to attend the trial proceedings. I asked a Jewish newspaper in Germany to provide me with press accreditation so that I could obtain a seat in the courtroom on December 22, exactly one month after Marcel had displayed his *brauner Speck* (brown bacon), as the headlines were calling it. On the morning of the trial, Jan walked me to the S-Bahn. "Try not to freak out," he said. He knew about the dreams that had haunted me these past few weeks.

As a child I had dreamed that recurring dream, the one where I was standing in line with my grandmother at Auschwitz. As we moved slowly toward the front, my fear would increase in proportion, as the moment of separation I knew was coming drew ever closer. When we finally reached the front of the queue, the faceless man waiting there invariably pointed my grandmother with a white-gloved hand to the right while directing me to the left, and I watched my grandmother disappear into her future while I remained paralyzed. It was clear she had been chosen to live, while I had been deemed unworthy. Each time, my death coincided with wakefulness, and I emerged into a dark night, sweaty and disoriented.

If I had been in Auschwitz, I had always imagined, then I would not have survived. After all, I wasn't strong; I wasn't disciplined; I didn't do well in moments of deprivation and humiliation. What my grandmother had in her, that iron fortitude I imagined, was not to be found in me. Therefore, even now, I thought, it must follow that I did not deserve life. I watched myself get sentenced to death in my dreams, and when I was awake, it seemed similarly inevitable that I would not survive whatever trials life might throw at me.

They had told us in school that the Holocaust was part of a pattern of violence that had repeated itself throughout history and would do so again, like the unstoppable momentum of a wheel on a slope, gathering energy as it moved along. Not only would things not get better for us, but they would likely get worse.

I waved off Jan's concern, yet when I arrived at the courthouse in the small town of Oranienburg, the street was empty except for a tight circle of sketchy-looking characters out front. I recognized Zech's profile immediately. He exchanged hugs and laughs with his neo-Nazi pals, all sporting similar chin beards and rat tails, tattoos creeping out of cuffs and collars. I had to walk around them to get into the courthouse, and suddenly my heart started pounding so hard it was almost like a drumbeat I could hear. My own fear disgusted me. I wanted to be cool, like the other press people already gathered in the courtroom, joking with their colleagues. I found a seat in the front row, next to a kindly older journalist from the *Süddeutsche Zeitung*.

Zech was cheerful at his trial. He laughed; he leaned back in his comfy office chair; he draped an arm lazily around the chair next to him. He exchanged smiles with his many fans and friends in the courtroom. He understood, just like my friends had, that the trial would have no consequences for him. His lawyer was Wolfram Nahrath, another right-wing extremist descended from a long line of Nazis, eager to jump to the cause.

The journalist seated next to me, having ascertained that I was American and unfamiliar with German court proceedings, explained that in his view, this trial wasn't about Zech, but about showing the public how important it was to stand up to people like him. The proceedings had been accelerated at the cost of punishment, actually; the regular maximum was five years in prison, which was reduced to one year in a fast-tracked trial. But in the eyes of the state's attorney, a quick reaction was more necessary and effective than a harsher punishment. This case was for show, the journalist explained, and pointed out how patient the judge was being with the press, giving the camera crews plenty of time to get their shots just right. After ten minutes of flashes from all angles, the cameras left the room and the trial began.

It started in a straightforward manner: Zech was asked to confirm his identity and personal information, the prosecution stated the charge, and the witness who had identified and documented the public tattoo display was called forward to deliver his testimony. Alexander M. was the only witness to show; others had been summoned, namely staff at the pool, but had failed to show up. So he delivered an understandably frustrated testimony, explaining that he had been scandalized by the failure of the public to react to the tattoo and had therefore felt obligated to at least document it and inform the staff. It took three tries, he explained, and then finally one staff member agreed to take care of it.

The defense attorney entered a statement at this point saying that Zech had left of his own free will and that the witness had committed a punishable offense according to German law by photographing his client without permission and then publishing the photo. The state's attorney nodded and laughed. "I know this law," he responded sarcastically.

"Do you deny that your client displayed his tattoo?" the judge inquired.

"My client confirms that he was present on this day, wearing appropriate swimwear, and that the tattoo in police photographs was visible," Zech's lawyer responded.

The judge wrapped up the introduction by reading from a list of Zech's previous crimes—bodily assault, defamation, driving without a license, and impersonating a police officer. She detailed the list of fines he had received as punishment for those crimes. I knew some of the circumstances connected to those previous convictions, as I had done some research about Zech's activities. I had read about the time he buried a swastika in front of Sachsenhausen concentration camp, and about the time when he tried to illegally obtain the identities of anti-fascist protestors, and about the time he tried to get ahold of addresses where refugees were being housed. Nahrath's defense, when it was finally delivered, did not touch upon any of these details, however. Instead, the attorney seemed to relish the opportunity to promote his own cherished agenda; namely that of attacking the constitutionality of the laws surrounding incitement and Holocaust denial themselves. He essentially used the trial of a petty crime as a showcase for a much larger battle that the extreme right in Germany had been engaged in since the beginning of denazification. By the time he had finished his convoluted lecture, I was very nearly lost.

A recess was then granted so that the prosecution could prepare its address. The burden was on the state's attorney to prove that Zech's tattoo was a punishable offense according to the law forbidding *Volksverhetzung*, or incitement of the people, a subcategory of which was clearly described as actions denoting the approval, denial, or minimization of National Socialism and the crimes that had occurred under its aegis. Although the defense attorney would have liked to imagine those laws themselves were being put on trial, they remained the context for these proceedings.

I looked forward to the state's attorney's summation, but I was sorely disappointed. It was bombastic, it was emotional, it was full of dramatic pauses and theatrical turns of phrase. "You trampled on our constitution," he admonished Zech. "You trampled on the efforts of those who strive to protect it."

The prosecutor continued by issuing an impassioned plea to the German public to condemn such provocations, for the benefit of the rows of press eagerly taking notes. "Not only the law should object, but the public as well. The public must not allow such a provocation to pass without consequence; it must condemn all such objectionable behavior."

When the judge finally handed down a decision after what felt like hours of posturing, it appeared to be a conclusion based on her own legal analysis and not necessarily a response to the arguments that had been heard. Six months' suspended sentence, she announced, based on the charge of expressing approval of National Socialist actions and disturbing the public peace. No mention was made of Zech's position as an elected representative in local parliament. The verdict meant that Zech would go free and continue living exactly as before; the sentence would only have to be served in the event that he should fail to cover up the tattoo in public during a future instance, as generally required of those sporting tattoos of *verfassungswidrige*, or unconstitutional, symbols. Both sides immediately announced their intention to appeal. Zech and his friends left immediately, as if they had been dismissed from the principal's office for cutting class. The whole trial had felt like nothing so much as a hearing for the schoolyard bully.

I watched the state's attorney give preening interviews to a row of cameras and microphones. He surely knew he had delivered the sort of moralizing that makes for good press. Outside, Zech's attorney refused to speak to the German press, having accused them during the trial of judging his client in the public sphere.

"I'm not German," I said to him. "I'm from the States."

"*Sie sind Jüdin?*" he asked.

My heart started to pound again, my mouth went dry, and I felt as if I might accidentally swallow the ends of my words.

"I was raised by an Auschwitz survivor," I answered.

"In the States, from where you come, this wouldn't be punishable at all."

"But there are no Auschwitz tattoos where I come from," I answered, before immediately wondering if that was true.

The law is like a muscle, I thought on the way home. Without exercise, it atrophies, but with too much stress, it strains or tears completely. It needs exactly the right amount of resistance in order to grow strong. The muscle of this particular law had been built in response to trauma, and it had been shielded from exertion for so long that it could only tremble under the weight it was now being called to bear.

I remember happening upon a book during one of my clandestine library visits as a child. At first I thought it was fiction, but close to the end, when the female adolescent protagonist was deported to a concentration camp called Bergen-Belsen, I remember slowly coming to the realization that this was probably a true story. I knew that place, I had heard of it before, because my grandmother had been there, in that mythical time that came "before." Before America, before the Satmars, before me.

On the day that I discovered Anne Frank, I realized that all the horrors and indignities I had just read about were real, and not only that, but that they had happened to someone I knew, someone I loved more than anyone else in the world.

Probably because I was so young, I was unable to deal with this information.

By the time I arrived home from the library, I was gulping down sobs. Naturally my grandmother came quickly from the kitchen to find out what was wrong. She followed me all the way to my room, convinced that she could fix it like she always did, with a hot chocolate and a soothing hand, only this time it was different.

I opened the door to her eventually and confessed the truth. I had read a forbidden book, I had seen it and not been able to resist. The book told the story of the life she had lived before she became the bubby I knew, and now that I had this information I didn't know how to keep on living, because the grief I felt was so huge it was certain to extinguish me. I wanted my grandmother to tell me something so that I could make it right in my head, so I could put the information in its proper place in my brain and continue to function normally, something I was sure she had told herself in order to resume her own life. But this time my grandmother did not offer soothing words. Instead she turned white and seemed to shrink away from me. Her silence was bigger than anything I had ever experienced; it was a ravine that opened in the space between us.

I felt a bubble of pain in my upper chest just beneath my throat. She turned away, with that white, white face, and I knew, without her having said it, that we would never speak of this again. The pain in my throat left a scar that would hurt again and again over the years, for on that day, though I didn't know it at the time, I acquired my grandmother's suffering as my own personal burden. I could not have known that it was a textbook case of transference that an entire generation had already endured; I only knew that because I loved this woman I had to take on the pain that she could not even acknowledge, and bear that burden for her.

I loved my grandmother now more than ever, after I had experienced the physical loss of her presence, and my loyalty to her memory demanded that I keep alive the flame of her suffering in my own heart. How could I ever calm the hysterical child in me if I couldn't convince her that she now lived in a world where Nazis were condemned and punished?

For a long time after that trial, I felt worse. I thought I had betrayed the spirit of my grandmother, which was still in me; it was as if she writhed in agony inside me. At night I would awaken in a panic. I had failed her. I had failed to find her justice; I had failed to make it right. The degradation that she had experienced had been celebrated right in front of me, and I had to live with that fact. This was unbearable.

Nearly a year passed, during which I tried to teach myself to live comfortably in a world I shared with people who celebrated my grandmother's pain. I tried to understand how such a world had come to be. I told myself my suffering wasn't making anything better, that the only way to find an equilibrium was to free myself from the burden I had been carrying so long. I needed to let it go.

So with the help of loving friends and a city that inspires more often than it devastates, I slowly taught myself to still the beating of my heart every time I heard the ugly vocabulary of anti-Semitism. I breathed deeply when I found myself in line with Marcel Zech at the cashier of a Berlin bicycle shop. I told myself that my anguish was not improving the situation. I realized that the wisest reaction was complete and fearless calm; it was my insusceptibility that would serve as the ultimate justice.

Just as I thought I finally had stifled that fire, the case went to the higher courts, and on November 7, 2016, I once again attended the proceedings, fully prepared for a similar outcome. I felt proud of myself for having slept well the night before, for my dry palms and moist mouth, thinking about how far I'd come and wondering if my younger self would have been able to believe it, that I could be in the same room as a neo-Nazi and stay calm and composed.

When the judge came back in to read the verdict, I understood his German perfectly, having become almost fluent by that point. But when the observers around me exhaled happily, I didn't comprehend at first the language that I nevertheless understood. My brain had frozen, unable to process the practical meaning of words I had worked hard to gather into my vocabulary. I leaned over and asked another observer, "Is it a jail sentence?"

She nodded.

"A real one? Not on probation?"

"A real sentence," she answered, and I sat back in shock.

Well, there you go, I thought. Justice for the spirit I thought I had successfully exhumed but that had still been hiding in the recesses of my heart all this time. The old flame flared briefly, then died down, and I walked back out into the crisp autumn air, knowing I was finally free. I had seen justice. Unlike Zech, I had never wanted to hold on to the past. I had wanted to run as fast as I could into the future, and by some great twist of irony, it was he who helped to release me from my compulsion.

Marcel Zech would go on to appeal this verdict yet again,

but six months later, in April 2017, the highest court would confirm it for the third and last time. I would experience this decision as more than just a gesture from a confident state, because the timing of it coincided with a decision in another, more personal story, and would become, at least in retrospect, inextricably tangled with it.

A year into my stay in Berlin, the final letter from the bureau to which my citizenship case had been transferred had arrived, and it was a short, unequivocal rejection. Apparently it had been found that I had not submitted adequate or irrefutable proof of my great-grandfather Gustav Spielmann's German nationality; therefore, they were going to close my case. I was disappointed but felt the matter was out of my hands. Sure, it meant that I would have to line up at the *Auslanderbehörde* every year, that I would have to live with the constant uncertainty and insecurity that comes with conditional and temporary residence permits and their application processes, but countless others were doing it too, and in the end there was always marriage, however unappealing. I knew I would stay, regardless of what that might take; the question was only, at what price?

But everyone I informed of the rejection encouraged me to fight it. I did not know how, though; I did not know what steps to take. The consulate in New York was of no help, advising me to accept the decision. When I informed my German publisher, he immediately got on the phone to one of his many influential friends and explained my situation. "You need a lawyer," the man said, and he promptly connected me with one. His name was Moris Lehner, a jurist who lived in Munich. He had extensive experience with the particular law I was trying to enlist to my advantage, and he agreed to take my case on pro bono, even though, as he informed me, these things could sometimes drag on for years. First it was simply a matter of a power of attorney as well as a letter sent to the bureau to ask for an extension. This would give us time, he explained, for the necessary further research.

Because a book tour in major cities had already been planned following the imminent publication of *Unorthodox* in German, Moris suggested that we meet to go over the details after my reading in Munich, which would be held in the Jewish community center. He was looking forward to attending and learning more about my story; he said it was always nice as a lawyer to have a case that was not just dry technicalities, but a living, breathing one, whose outcome he was personally invested in.

In mid-April I traveled to Munich by train, on a chilly, rainy day, emerging into the old town only a short distance from the community center, where hired Israeli security forces put us through a metal detector. I wondered out loud why they did not simply have policemen outside like the synagogues in Berlin, but Ellen, the center's director, explained to us that the threat level was much higher than most people realized. The problem was, if the constant threats were publicized, Ellen feared that people would be too frightened to come to the center at all. So the solution had been to hire private, well-trained forces from Israel and revamp the entire security system.

The room that evening was full, and after the reading, many joined us at the long table Ellen had set up in the restaurant, including my new lawyer, Moris Lehner. We sat at one end and I told him the little I knew about my mother's side of the family;

Ellen listened attentively. At some point, she jumped up as if she had had an epiphany.

"I'm going to check the archives in my office right now," she said. "If they were living in Munich, there's no way there isn't at least a trace of them in my digitized collection." She scurried off into the darkened office area while the rest of us dug into our main courses.

She returned ten minutes later with a sheaf of freshly printed papers in her hand and placed them on the table between Moris and me.

"I found them!" she announced triumphantly. "I knew I would."

Indeed, she had printed an entry describing Regina Spielmann and her son, Gustav, but the information available was limited in comparison to the entries above and below it. It described her having moved to the Munich area in 1895 and having given birth in 1897 to a son who later migrated to England. It also had a long list of addresses where they had apparently lived together, addresses that Moris explained to me were all located not too far from the building we now found ourselves in, in the former Jewish quarter of the old town. The only additional information available was that Regina had apparently run a dry goods store from her home to support the family.

It was certainly mysterious that no husband, parents, additional children, or any other relatives were listed for Regina. I found it peculiar that she had moved around so much in a small area too, as if settling had come so hard for her. Moris read the confusion on my face and patted my hand.

"Don't worry, Deborah!" he exclaimed. "This is a great start. I have a lot of experience with these things; I know exactly where to go with this information. Pretty soon it will all become clear."

Others at the table who had followed our conversation

chimed in. "Yes, trust me, this community will not let you down," a woman added, winking at me. "We won't rest until we have the answers."

Her friend smiled kindly at me. "You are lucky your ancestors are from Bavaria, because Bavarian Jews are the friendliest and most helpful. We will all help you as if your ancestors are our ancestors."

The next day, on my way back toward Berlin, I felt filled with a kind of mysterious excitement that had become by now somewhat familiar to me, that feeling that something big was on the horizon and fast approaching.

After Moris applied for the extension, the case was transferred to the Senate administration, perhaps as a response to the involvement of legal counsel, although I couldn't be sure, because although my lawyer had many conversations with me over the phone about the process, I often felt confused and overwhelmed by his descriptions of the various statutes and his use of German legalese. In the following weeks I mostly put the matter out of my mind, for deep down I had already reconciled myself to failure in order to avoid disappointment, and having Moris on my side was for a while no more than a due-diligence effort, a way of telling myself that I was still trying, without investing any more emotional energy.

So you can imagine my shock when I received that fateful phone call, the one I warned you about at the very beginning of this story. I remember sitting in a café with another mother from my son's school who lived in the area, chatting about future projects we wanted to work on together, when my phone vibrated with Moris's name on the screen. I excused myself to take the call, assuming he needed a small piece of additional information and that the conversation would be over quickly.

"Deborah," he shouted into the phone as I picked up. "I have goose bumps all over! I can hardly believe it. In all my years as a lawyer, I have never experienced something like this."

I didn't understand what was going on. "What happened?" I asked.

"I've just come out of the Munich archives, where I met with the head of the institution, and you will not believe what he was able to retrieve for me, Deborah. I'm actually still a bit in shock. What an incredible story . . ."

I could hear him yelling through wind and rain into his mobile phone, his voice quivering with excitement.

"I don't understand! What story, Moris?" The sudden high pitch of my voice made my friend look over at me. *Is everything okay?* her raised eyebrows seemed to ask. I made a face back at her, like I had no idea.

Moris got into his car and closed the door, and now his voice was lower and clearer.

"So, Deborah, the reason there is no father listed on your great-grandfather's birth certificate, or a husband listed for Regina, is that she had no husband. Your great-grandfather was an illegitimate child."

I breathed in sharply. This in itself was big news. An illegitimate child, or a bastard, was unheard of in my community, but we had a word for it: *mamzer.* Technically, the term applied solely to children of forbidden unions, which in the general sense this was not (an unmarried Jewish woman, as long as she isn't in an incestuous relationship, cannot issue a *mamzer* according to the strict biblical interpretation), but of course, my community took that interpretation much further. A *mamzer* was the worst thing one could be, for he was permanently cut off from the Jewish nation, as were all his descendants. He could only marry another bastard, but the impurity would be inherited for ten generations to come, so basically until the end of time. In my community, I had been warned that as a woman, if I failed to keep the marital purity laws to the impossibly high standard that was asked of me, my own children could be classified as *mamzerim*, even if I was technically married according to religious law. This threat worked, for it was the worst fate one could imagine for one's children, an eternal brand of impurity. Whether or not it was the case that the fate of one's soul was permanently decided, it was surely the case that the stigma associated with even the smallest hint of doubt cast upon the purity of one's birth would linger for not only a lifetime but many lifetimes. In the world I was raised in, such scandals were indelible regardless of what biblical texts had to say on the matter; they were proof of the unacceptable influence of contamination, an attack on the spiritual integrity of our world.

"So Gustav was born out of wedlock," Moris explained, but he had more to say. "And his father was, believe it or not, a Catholic! From the Austrian Empire. His name was Gustav Kollarz, so your great-grandfather was actually named after him. Deborah, I've made copies of all the documents Dr. Heusler was able to retrieve from the archives, and I'm going to scan and send them to you. Not everything can be easily understood, because it's mostly handwritten in Old German script, but you will see, even just understanding ten percent will tell you a crazy story. We've uncovered the big family secret. Someone wanted to keep this information hidden. I think you are the first person to discover the truth."

. . .

Apologizing profusely and stumbling over my own confused explanations, I broke off the meeting with my friend and hurried home to print the files that Moris was emailing me. I spent the next hour poring over them. I learned that Regina Spielmann and Gustav Kollarz were born in the same small town in the part of the Austrian Empire that would later become southeastern Poland (Galicia). Gustav's father, Josef, had studied and practiced veterinary medicine with Regina's father, and as a consequence they must have known each other from birth. However, she was a young woman and he a middle-aged man of independent means, fifteen years her senior, when they ran away to Munich together to escape the judgment and condemnation of both their families. She and her illicit, upper-class, Austrian Catholic lover would move from apartment to apartment in the Jewish quarter of Munich (I counted a total of twenty addresses in the official records!), living as outcasts on the fringes of their respective societies. Gustav was nearing fifty when their son was born. He died twenty years later, and she continued to support herself and her son through her small dry goods business. She would die a few months before the Nuremburg Laws went into effect. A little more than a year later, her son would dedicate his doctoral thesis to her *unvergessliche* memory. Unforgettable, indeed, I thought, for I could never have imagined a woman with such bravery in my family tree. A woman who had fled her family, her religious fealties, her home country, to raise a son largely by herself, in difficult and lonely circumstances, in a time when single parenthood and illegitimacy were taboos in every society? Well, after all, I had to admit it did sound a bit familiar. We never really know what we inherit, I realized.

So my great-grandfather was only half Jewish, I repeated to myself, and now this revelation catapulted me back into that past, when I had tortured myself with the question of my ethnic purity. What did this mean? It was all too much to process so quickly, and yet I felt my skin prickling, my hairs standing on end, for it was the discovery I had yearned for and waited for since childhood, confirmation of all my fears and hopes. I looked at the photo of my great-grandfather as a young man and wondered how much of him I carried within me. With one non-Jewish great-great-grandfather (and who knew, really, how many similar ancestral stories had managed to stay effectively hidden), I was at the very least one-sixteenth not Jewish as well. Not that it was something to be either proud or ashamed of. No, it was more like the comfort of not being one hundred percent of anything. It was as if this incompletion was a confirmation of humanness, of a personhood that superseded ethnic denominators. It was as if I had been freed from the prison of identity attribution, as if the impurity itself had rendered me pure.

On the phone, Moris was still encouraging me: "This is good news for your case, Deborah. We can prove that your great-grandfather had German nationality after all, for although his paternity was seen as illegitimate then, it's clear that as an Austrian, he would be considered *Deutschstämmig*—of German descent—"and this will be very helpful for us, I think."

"I still can't believe that I'm the first person to discover this secret," I said. "After all, I'm not the first person to do this kind of research. That uncle of mine, Gustav's youngest son, had all those documents and photos. Surely he must have noticed the inconsistences; surely he must have discovered their cause! But he sent me a photo of his gravestone, and it said 'Ben Avraham'! And he wrote 'Avraham' into the family tree in that spot. Was he knowingly lying? Was he trying to protect the family? Or did he really not know?"

"Oh, that's very interesting that it says 'Ben Avraham' on his gravestone," Moris responded. "Did you know that that's the patronym used by all German Jews who convert? When they are called up to read the Torah in the synagogue, they are always addressed as son of Abraham—you know, the ultimate father, the patriarch of us all."

In the pile of documents Moris had sent, a story did indeed begin to reveal itself, as we studied the pages, trying to make sense of it together. A source for some of the information in his file was listed as "*Gewerbeamt der Arisierungen,*" Office for Aryanizations. My great-grandfather had tried to Aryanize himself; as the society he had grown up in became more and more openly and viciously anti-Semitic, he had struggled to attain Bavarian citizenship on the basis of his illegitimate father. In his application, he had listed his national origins as well as those of his father as "Poland, previously Austria." Moris had explained to me that many Austrian citizens were forced to take Polish citizenship after the fall of the empire, but that if we could prove the original claim was valid, it would work in our favor. Yet, although he was recognized by the authorities as the legal heir of Gustav Kollarz, and his father even undertook responsibility and had gone through the procedures of acknowledgment, it was chilling to read the exchange of correspondence in the protocol to his naturalization file and see that the process had stretched on for a decade.

First I read his own personally handwritten summary and plea for citizenship, which ended with the sentence: "As I was born and raised here and am inextricably enmeshed with local cultural conditions, I am requesting admission to the Bavarian Federal State."

Then I leafed through the various testimonies he had included in his application to speak to his character and worthiness, descriptions he had given of his education, work, and military service histories. The handwriting was cramped and extremely difficult to make sense of. I came across one of the rare typed documents, dated 1928, toward the end of the struggle:

> Gustav Spielmann, a graduate economist in Munich, joined the Turner–Landsturm–Regiment, of which I was the founder, in August 1914 as a high school student and has distinguished himself through diligence and zeal, as well as his patriotic attitude towards Germany. I have come to know him as a thoroughly reliable and respectable character. I consider him a worthy and suitable candidate for Bavarian citizenship.
>
> [illegible signature] by [illegible]
> Reichsbahnoberamtmann u. Major d.R.a.D

In the early twenties, the notes in his file, typed in by various officials, had still been somewhat neutral: "*No detriment is apparent in the character of the applicant.*" "*There are no indications that he is of anti-German sentiment.*"

But a few years later, the situation looked very different. His case had made the rounds three times by now, and in each round Gustav had striven to meet the ever-increasing requirements and standards, adding additional references and proofs, filling in small résumé gaps, giving new testimonies. But in the

last round I read new language typed in the space designated
for the argument's conclusion:

> *Any liabilities are unknown at this time. Apart from the*
> *question of race, there are no indications that speak for or*
> *against. Anti-German sentiments are not presumed.*

And later, in the final document, titled *"Beschluß des*
Hauptausschusses als Senat," issued in 1929:

> *The applicant is of Galician origin and a Polish national. The*
> *Munich City Council General Assembly has decided to refuse*
> *naturalization applications from Polish citizens until further*
> *notice, considering that cultural interests call for restraint*
> *towards naturalization applications from states whose citizens*
> *may be said to originate from cultures which are of lesser*
> *value. Furthermore, a gradual penetration of German culture*
> *with elements alien to its nature and harmful to the*
> *maintenance of its individuality should continue to be*
> *prevented.*
>
> *In economic terms, too, naturalization is quite undesirable;*
> *The applicant is currently studying economics and has no*
> *income of his own; In addition to his mother's aid, he lives on*
> *grants from the city youth welfare office, in whose files he is*
> *now described as a "benefitsswindler," as a result of the*
> *support granted by the University of Munich and the*
> *"Studentenhaus" association while posing as an out-of-work*
> *traveler to the welfare office and receiving the unemployment*
> *benefit. The District Welfare Office does not grant the*
> *citizenship request.*

With this spew of vitriol, the file comes to an end. There are some private comments scribbled by relevant officials, but the case is officially closed in April 1929.

Reading this was physically painful for me, perhaps because I imagined how it would feel to get an answer like this right now, in relation to my own case, and how it would speak to something in me that I already believed, namely, that there was something in me that was poisonous, that was inferior, that deserved to be marginalized. And I wondered how he must have felt then, he who had grown up with one acceptable parent and one alienated one, with a foot in each world but no real standing in either one, with a yearning to be part of something, before the ultimate rejection had crushed those dreams. Ultimately he must have struggled with shame, grief, and unworthiness many times greater than my own.

I thought of how I had struggled as a child to prove worthy of acceptance in our community, and while it wasn't an equal comparison, I still felt lucky to have escaped that framework. I had essentially freed myself from the affliction of having to perceive myself through the alienating lens of others. He had not been able to do the same. In his NS-victim file it said he had been arrested on October 28, 1938, imprisoned in Stadelheim Jail, and then deported via *Sonderzug*, "special train," to the Polish border. He had made his way back to his family on foot and immediately left for England. Yes, he had escaped successfully, at the age of forty-two, with his wife and two children, and had started a new life there, completely reinventing his past in order to be accepted by the Jewish community. He had even expanded his family, but I had heard enough stories about him from my mother to know that he had never fully recovered from this blow. His decade-long struggle to assimilate himself and see this effort legitimized by the state in which he had been born, raised, and educated had failed. This was a shot of pure poison, designed to debilitate and degrade. Just reading the words, I could feel them degrade me. They were printed on an official-looking piece of paper, issued by an office of a state, and this gave them a kind of weight that seemed to hold even now, even though the paper was yellowed with age and more than eighty-five years had passed.

But Moris comforted me and said that all this information was very useful; in fact, he had changed his mind about how to file the case. Before, we would have simply gone the routine route by requesting the return of ostensibly confiscated citizenship. Now he was going to move for an *Ermessenseinbürgerung*, a discretionary naturalization, for which he explained to me there were many different preconditions. One of them was a *Verfolgungsbedingtefamilienschicksal*, an inexplicably long German word denoting a "familial fate marked by persecution." He could present it as a *Wiedergutmachung* case with unique conditions, by which he meant we would present reasoning for the acquisition of the citizenship that had been withheld from my great-grandfather for reasons that were now seen as unconstitutional. And these letters were all the proof we needed for that, clear as day.

"In the end, Deborah," he said to me, "it will be a great triumph, to gain from the state something your grandfather was unable to do. It will close the chapter for him. *Der kreis wird sich schliessen*, the circle will close."

Would it bring peace to his soul, I wondered, to see this

great injustice rectified almost a century later? Would it bring peace to mine?

———

When I made the decision to abandon the community that Holocaust survivors had founded in order to separate themselves from the rest of the world and the evil in it, I unconsciously took with me the teachings I had been raised with, and I began to practice hiding my Jewishness until it felt safe to reveal it. I learned a very American thing: how to pass.

In the dreams I had then, I often found myself attempting to convince the faceless man to let me out of the line completely. I tried to explain to him that it was a mistake that I was there at all. I desired nothing more than for him to acknowledge that I was not like the others standing with me. I no longer yearned to be selected to accompany my grandmother; I now yearned to be pulled out of the ranks completely, to be told I was exempt.

My first visit to Germany when I was twenty-five was in many ways a confirmation of all the fears I had nursed as a child. I returned to America convinced it was the scorched earth my elders had always warned me about. Only something else had happened too: I had met a real person. And this person was German, and through this man I met other Germans, and while not all of my encounters were pleasant, there were many individuals with whom I came to form friendships and who impressed me deeply with their political convictions and ideals. And since I had always felt that my Jewishness was an accident of birth, I began to ask myself why Germanness was not the same. And thus I formed the question that had never occurred to me before, namely, what if I had been German during that time?

Recently I began to have a new version of that old Auschwitz dream. Now I am not in line at all anymore. Now I am sometimes in uniform myself. Each time I slip into that familiar scene, I inhabit a different role. I am no longer able to identify with that singular position I inhabited as a child. My brain seems to keep insisting on that question: What if?

I understand now that while being in the victim position is painful and frightening, it is also relatively easier to process emotionally. But when I try to imagine myself as a German in that scenario, I immediately lose the comfort of having the moral high ground. There is no clarity in the answer to that question. It does not compute, to picture myself going through the motions that would have been assigned to me. After all, I had doubted my ability to survive as a child, so how could I not doubt that I would have had the moral courage to risk my life if the situation were reversed? Was it really a matter of certainty that I would have had the mettle to disobey orders as an oppressor? I want to believe it, of course. I want to be able to categorically claim that I know myself well enough to be sure that becoming a perpetrator was not a possibility, but in that tiny one percent sliver of uncertainty lies enough doubt to dismantle my entire thesis about good and evil.

As I watch myself switch roles in my dream, I finally learn to understand the world in new terms, not as bad and good, but as constantly in flux. The world could change at any moment, and the only heroism lies in understanding this as it is happening, instead of looking back in hindsight with regrets.

EPILOGUE

In regard to my application for discretionary naturalization, the Ministry of the Interior sent notice of their decision in the affirmative on April 18, 2017. It can be deduced that a case like this reaches a positive conclusion most probably as a result of what is euphemistically termed "cultural interest."

I have lived in Germany now for six years, and in that time, even as I have borne personal witness to hate, I have beheld the courage of individuals in the face of it, individuals who have utilized their knowledge of history to react sensitively and bravely in situations where it is far easier to simply sit back. It is the sum total of these individual actions that served to reassure me.

I feel that the memory of Auschwitz is neither solely a Jewish nor solely a German responsibility. For me, the act of remembering the Holocaust is a therapeutic opportunity to meditate on a shared vulnerability and to reinforce our common bond in the battle to protect it. Hate will never disappear, not here, not anywhere else, but the citizens of this country will not remain passive in the face of it. I am surrounded by those who have shown themselves willing to take a stand against the momentum of hatred building in our society, and should they need me to do the same, I can truly say that I have learned to find that courage within myself. Because it is here, where ordinary citizens have learned the act of moral fortitude in the most painful way, that I finally was able to go back to that child within myself, the one who doubted that she had the strength to withstand the tests that life threw at her, and teach her that to prevail is a decision, one that we make as individuals, but also one we make together.

My instinctual and primal rejection of the country I would also one day designate as my home was and remains an integral and indistinguishable part of the process of reclaiming it. As my grandmother had once told me, the world was created in opposites; without darkness there could be no light, without the force of my own repulsion there would be no propulsion.

I have always sensed a struggle in me similar to that of an automatic lens seeking focus, torn between a wide-angle, far-away setting, which reduces everything to a "big picture" with few details, a setting that was programmed into me from a young age, and the desire to "zoom in" and examine the details, to see the trees instead of the forest, which somehow managed to flourish within me despite the attempts to repress it. During my first trips to Germany as well as the first few years spent living here, I often felt as if the lens in my mind was stuck on the setting programmed into me, and no matter how much I wanted to "zoom," all that happened when I attempted to do so was that strange choking and stuttering that anyone familiar with an automatic camera incapable of focusing will understand.

Later, as I managed to free myself from this stuttering panic,

I fell into a state that I already thought of then in German as *Schwanken* (the state of a pendulum that has already seen its most extreme swing and is now swaying back and forth as the reverberating force of that climax ripples onward). And while the *Schwanken* may be a phenomenon that will last a long time, maybe even a lifetime, I believe that it will steadily diminish, that these plunges will become less frequent and, when they do occur, less extreme. The pendulum may never come to perfect stillness, but it is questionable whether I would still be the same person if it could.

There are still moments right now when I fail to see what is in front of me and instead project onto it the past that once haunted my childhood dreams: I see something threatening in an angular, pale face; I interpret someone's rudeness as reflective of a greater evil, for example. But I have learned to focus on the individual instead of the whole, to think in new terms instead of the ones drilled into me, and in that process I have been freed from many fears and limitations. I believe I was enabled in this process largely by literature. There are various authors who not only inspired me but guided me through specific phases in my life, who first taught me to ask the right questions and then pushed me to learn their answers. And even after I left my community and for a brief moment pushed away the books because it was painful to realize that I was still stuck in their pages instead of living my own story, it was from them that I eventually learned to mold my new narrative. From Jean Améry I learned intellectual courage; from Salomon Maimon I learned to trust in myself; from Primo Levi I learned compassion and forgiveness, not only for humanity in general but also for myself, in all our flaws; from Czesław Miłosz I learned that identity is where we come from, but that it must not dictate where we are going; from Adrienne Rich I learned that even two halves that have been "split" can still come together as a whole; from Baudrillard I learned the importance of a relationship with one's surroundings and how to develop that; and yes, from Gregor von Rezzori I learned that racism is a part of human nature, that it is a parasite waiting to pounce in all of us, even myself.

Rezzori artfully not only describes the prejudices against Jews and the inescapability of their social rank, but also quite cleverly illustrates the deep and age-old desire of a people who yearn to supersede their imposed limitations, who wish to be free of the identity they were born with, who, like their enemies, have no special desire to sacrifice their humanity for the reward of being counted among an ethnic minority. When one changes one's name, one wants to be counted among those for whom the name is recognizable. I abandoned both my Hebrew first name and my conspicuous maiden surname to blend in more easily; I wanted not just to be back in Europe—no, I also wanted to be a European, and I would discover, like many have before me, that only the first is a simple and practical matter. The second goal requires more of a struggle. But if it's so difficult, if all I can do is complain, then why am I here? Why have I accepted German citizenship and dedicated my life to this new language, to this culture, to these people? Even for native Germans, Germanness is something they view with ambivalence at best and *Ressentiments* at worst, and yet here I am, product of a society for whom *Deutsch-sein*, being German, was the ultimate evil, embracing that dreaded state.

Primo Levi recalls in his last work, *The Drowned and the Saved*, being often asked if Auschwitz will return. He points to a "concurrence of a number of factors" that would be a prerequisite for a repeat performance. He says, "These factors can occur again and are already recurring in various parts of the world." And yet he states, where the "*Lagers* of World War II are still part of the memory of many, on both the popular and governmental levels, and a sort of immunizational defense is at work which amply coincides with the shame of which I have spoken," such a recurrence is more unlikely than anywhere else. This is a theory that coincides with one I developed prior to reading this work. I surmised that if Rezzori was right, and racism was a disease infecting us all, the only hope was a strong immune defense to keep it in check. And if there is anything I've learned in my time here, it's that the immune system is stronger where there is memory, where it is kept alive through careful, painstaking care, and that perhaps by becoming a part of this collective act of remembering, I could contribute to its continued strength.

I did not come to Germany because I was running away from my past, although it is true that the physical distance has had an enormous impact on my feeling of safety and peace. I did not come here seeking some utopia either. I do not want or need to hide from evil, or rather, the tragedy of mortal fallibility, the way that my community would like to do. If the combination of social action, political constructs, and a system of law acts like a network of muscles in the body of the state, then I came to a place where I could see that muscle tested enough to build its strength, to witness it flexing in response to stress, to support it so that it can withstand exertion without tearing. I came to be a small fiber in that muscle.

I am not yet this. Even though I am in possession of the

passport, I suspect it will take some time before I "become" German. But it is the beginning of my new story, the story I finally discovered within myself, one of various disparate threads woven together to create a new cloth, and like the stories that came before, it is becoming one I may well tell you someday.

ACKNOWLEDGMENTS

Thank you to Penguin Random House for giving me another chance at this endeavor! It just goes to show that it's never too late to find a kindred spirit in publishing, by which I mean my editor, Maya Ziv, at Dutton and Plume. Thank you so much for your open mind, contagious enthusiasm, and unflagging willingness to slog through all the hard work. I'm also grateful to my German agent, Matthias Landwehr, and his American partner, Markus Hoffmann, for assisting me with this transition. It is such a tremendous relief to be able to reconnect with my English-language readers; they were my first audience, after all, and it is because of their warm engagement that all this began, and their continued interest and support is a big part of what sustains me.

I feel so lucky to have fellow travelers in my wanderings and am especially thankful to Richard T. Scott, Milena Kartowski-Aiach, and Esther Munkacsi for the guidance they shared along the way. Zoltán Janosi, Gabi Losonczi, and Farkas Bacsi—those few days I spent with you all in Nyíregyháza were some of the most poignant and transformative of my life. I will never be able to repay your immense generosity and kindness. Per, thank you for helping me translate that file, even though it was written in old Swedish. Gina, those few days that you hosted us in Murnau were transcendent. Thank you for opening up your home and your heart to total strangers. I have been so fortunate to find anonymous yet heartfelt kindness in unexpected corners and will try to pay that kindness forward to the next traveler I meet.

In addition, in regards to the lengthy process of acquiring German citizenship so integral to this story, I must pay tribute to the incredible kindness of Ernst Mannheimer, Moris Lehner, and Dr. Andreas Heusler. A heartfelt thanks goes out as well to Ellen Presser and the Jewish community of Munich, whose warm welcome in the spring of 2016 will remain forever engraved into my memory.

In regards to the terrible but ultimately triumphant story of "The Man with the Auschwitz Tattoo," I would like to use this opportunity to express my bottomless admiration for the journalists whose integrity and tireless devotion to their work helped make a satisfying ending to the tale possible, among whom I will name Alexander Fröhlich of *Der Tagesspiegel/PNN*, who personally assisted with fact-checking some of the text in this book; and Alexander Margiuer of *Cicero* magazine, whose civil courage and moral indignation shone for me like a beacon in darkness. Thank you to all of the journalists in Germany who dedicate themselves with a singular passion to the fight for truth and accountability.

Thank you to all of my beloved friends who bestow upon me the gift of their love, support, and acceptance: Arno Papenheim, Sophia Fenger, Linda Rachel Sabiers, Benyamin Reich,

Emmanuel Bornstein, Anja Bröker, Anna Winger, and Alexa Karolinski. All of you are like family to me.

Lastly, I thank my son for supporting me during the writing of this book, as I often find myself juggling motherhood and writing in a manner that sometimes tips into imbalance, and his understanding has always been remarkable. I hope I can one day do the same for him, when he finds his passion.

ABOUT THE AUTHOR

Deborah Feldman was raised in the Satmar Hasidic community in Williamsburg, Brooklyn. Her first memoir, *Unorthodox*, was a *New York Times* bestseller and the inspiration for the Emmy Award–winning Netflix series. She lives in Berlin with her son.